the Modern Bride

survival guide

the Modern Bride

survival guide

ANTONIA VAN DER MEER, EDITOR-IN-CHIEF

WITH LISA MILBRAND AND THE EDITORS OF *MODERN BRIDE*

BICENTENNIAL
1807
WILEY
2007
BICENTENNIAL

JOHN WILEY & SONS, INC.

Published by John Wiley & Sons, Inc., Hoboken, New Jersey
Published simultaneously in Canada

For general information on our other products and services or for technical support, please
contact our Customer Care Department within the United States at (800) 762-2974, outside the
United States at (317) 572-3993 or fax (317) 572-4002.

Wiley also publishes its books in a variety of electronic formats. Some content that
appears in print may not be available in electronic books. For more information about Wiley
products, visit our web site at www.wiley.com.

Library of Congress Cataloging-in-Publication Data:

The Modern Bride Survival Guide / Antonia van der Meer, editor-in-chief with Lisa Milbrand
and the editors of Modern Bride.
        p. cm.
    Includes index.
    ISBN 978-0-470-17055-7 (cloth)
    1. Weddings–Planning. 2. Wedding etiquette.   I. van der Meer, Antonia. II. Milbrand, Lisa. III.
Modern Bride.
    HQ745.M658 2007
    395.2'2–dc22

                                        2007012092

Printed in the United States of America

10 9 8 7 6 5 4 3 2 1

*To my husband, Peter, with whom I just
celebrated a 25th anniversary. Because of you,
I know that the wedding reception is just
the beginning of the party!*

. . . .

To all the readers of Modern Bride.
*I am constantly in awe of all the exciting things you do
at your weddings and the great care you take
in creating events that embrace your families, your
friends, your personalities and your style.*

contents

introduction

Whenever someone finds out that I am the editor-in-chief of *Modern Bride,* they invariably ask me what the new trends are in weddings, and what about weddings has changed since I began in this position. I hardly know where to begin, as weddings change constantly to incorporate new ideas and new traditions. The fun of my job, in truth, lies in the fact that weddings are always evolving. One minute we're registering mainly for housewares, the next minute we're adding kayaks to the list. We used to be comfortable only with same-sex attendants. Now we see best women and bridesmen. Once upon a time, there was chicken or beef. Now there are sushi stations and s'mores bars. As the rules surrounding weddings have grown looser, our creativity in throwing weddings has grown exponentially. And this inevitably leads to more questions and concerns. What's okay? What's not okay? When should I do this? What if I don't want to do that? And so I came up with the idea for this book, *The* Modern Bride *Survival Guide,* to help you navigate the wedding-planning months. Sure, this time is fun and filled with a wonderful sense of anticipation as you are about to embark on a new life as a married couple.

But these days are also filled with worry and with wondering and with plain old hard work. This book is laid out as simply as possible so that everything you need to know is clear and easy to find. We start, appropriately enough, with a chapter called "Get Started." In it, you'll take the first steps toward getting organized, choosing a date and determining your wedding style. Then you're off and running. I hope you'll use this book to tackle all your planning chores in a logical, stress-free way. You don't have to read this book in any particular order; feel free to dive right into the chapter that means the most to you right now, whether that's dress shopping or choosing a ceremony site. With *The* Modern Bride *Survival Guide,* you can zero in on what you need, when you need it. I want you to be able to create a wedding that's uniquely your own and one that reflects your relationship and sense of style. To help you, I've included lots of inspirational photos, practical information and the answers to a bride's most common questions. This book is just the beginning of a wonderful process during which you will be exploring your wedding vision and strengthening your bonds with fiancé and family. I wish you well.

Antonia van der Meer

CHAPTER 1

Get Started

**BEGIN YOUR WEDDING PLANNING
ON THE RIGHT FOOT**

Who would have thought that one simple *yes* could lead to so many questions? But after the proposal comes the planning, and you'll have big decisions to make early on: What kind of wedding should we have? When—and where—should we tie the knot? How much can we afford? And where do we start? Just follow these steps.

Set your style

With so many cool ways to wed, how do you narrow down your options and choose the right style for you?

Consider your personalities. Envision your dream wedding: Odds are it'll incorporate the things that make you happy and what you like to do for fun. So if you and your fiancé are total beach bums, skip the Cinderella fantasy and say your vows along the shore. If you both love to throw together gourmet dinners for your friends, maybe a food-focused reception at a top-notch restaurant is a must for you.

Think of your history. Look back over the course of your courtship: If your fiancé proposed in a park, an outdoor garden may serve as an equally romantic backdrop for your celebration. A couple who met through their college theater group could weave a dramatic motif throughout their event, from *Playbill*-like programs to a show-tune-heavy playlist.

Factor in your guests. Your wedding is your day—we firmly believe that—but you should still consider your guests' enjoyment. You and your fiancé may be gung-ho about hosting a black-tie event, but if your family and friends consider a collared shirt and khakis "dressed up," an ultraswanky wedding may make them uncomfortable.

Find a happy medium. If you and your groom have different wedding visions—you're thinking ballroom, he's thinking outdoor bash—figure out how to combine the best of both worlds. Maybe you'll wed and take photos on the beach, but move the party indoors to a restaurant or yacht club with ocean views. Or maybe you can add a few grand details—crystal chandeliers, parquet floor, silk tablecloths—to a shoreside tent. Either way, you can create a celebration that's a perfect marriage of your tastes.

Home or Away?

Once upon a time, weddings always took place in the bride's hometown (which was, more often than not, the groom's hometown as well). But these days, there may be no clear-cut spot to hold your wedding if you and your fiancé are from different parts of the country—or world—and you've moved away from where you grew up. Nearly 15 percent of all couples opt for destination weddings, inviting their guests to celebrate with them in a unique vacation spot (see Chapter 18 for more on that). So how do you decide where to wed? Here are a few pointers.

Figure out the logistics. Getting married in your hometown can be sweet and sentimental—and a challenge, if you live thousands of miles away. You'll need to determine whether you'll be able to make enough trips home—and get enough help from friends and family members who still live there—to handle the long-distance details.

Consider your guests. Will your starving-artist buddies be able to fork over the cash for airline tickets to the Caribbean? Can Grandma Josie handle a climb to a mountaintop ceremony spot? Look for a location that's convenient for most, if not all, of your guests.

Think about your budget. It will cost you considerably more to wed in a big city like Los Angeles or Chicago than it will in Burlingame or Batavia, so you may be able to afford a larger guest list or a much grander event if you opt to tie the knot in a smaller town.

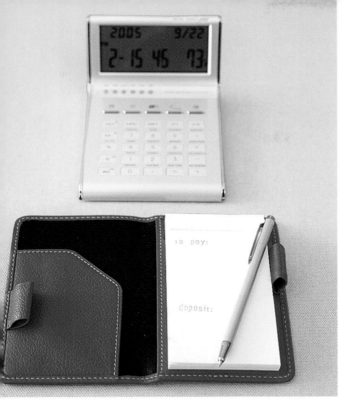

Figure out your finances

Back in the day, the bride's parents footed the bill for the bulk of the wedding celebration. But with prices skyrocketing (the average wedding now costs nearly $30,000) and most to-be-weds living on their own before the big day, many couples pay for at least part of their own nuptials, often with contributions from both sets of parents. But figuring out who's chipping in—and what strings are attached to contributions—can be tougher to determine in this anything-goes scenario.

First, figure out how much you and your fiancé can reasonably put into the wedding pot. If your bank account is bare, take a closer look at your spending habits to see if there's anything you'd be willing to give up for some additional money toward your wedding. (After all, a year's worth of mocha lattes could equal a wedding dress!)

Next, sit down with each set of parents individually to talk about your wedding plans and find out what, if anything, they plan to contribute. Ask them how much input they expect to have regarding how the money is spent and how the wedding is planned, then determine whether you can live with their requests: Maybe you don't mind allowing them to invite a few business colleagues if they're willing to spring for the catering.

Finally, make sure your wedding dreams will fit your budget reality. As you start pricing out the details, you may need to prioritize and fund the key ones, while scaling back on others.

Bride to Bride

My fiancé and I feel that our wedding should reflect who we are, not who our parents are. So we told them that their monetary gifts are very much appreciated, but their money does not "buy" them more room on the guest list or the right to choose the menu. Fortunately our families have been fine with this, and I think we've prevented a lot of problems by being honest up front. —Melanie

{expert tip} Set up a separate checking account to keep track of funds—this way you'll know where all the money is at all times and if you're running low.

—*JoAnn Gregoli, wedding planner, New York City*

Pick the date

Once you have the concept and the funding squared away, it's time to pull out your schedules and figure out which date works best.

Check your calendars. Look for any potential conflicts: planned vacations, holidays, even hectic times at work. One sports-addicted groom we talked to wanted his wedding planned around the college football schedule. And don't forget to ask your must-have VIPs what they have planned: You'll need to rethink your plans if your fiancé's parents will be cruising in Polynesia then, or your pregnant sister's due date is within a few weeks of your intended wedding date.

Consider the climate. This involves more than whether you want blooming flowers or crisp autumn leaves framing your photos: If your wedding falls during hurricane season or midwinter, when storms could leave guests stranded or damage your site, you may need to make peace with the possibility that nature could wreak havoc on your plans.

Debate the holidays. While a long weekend may be enticing if you're planning a host of activities around your wedding, some guests may already have plans for those dates that they can't change and out-of-towners may find travel a challenge.

Discuss switching from the standard Saturday. There are only 52 of them each year, and hundreds of thousands of brides vying for them. A Friday or Sunday could work for you, or you could move beyond the weekend into weeknights, where you'll likely have your pick of vendors.

Keep special dates in mind. Some couples like to choose sentimental anniversaries for their weddings: You might wed on the day you first met or on your parents' anniversary.

Find out what's available. If you have your heart set on marrying in your house of worship or using a particular caterer, put in a quick phone call to make sure that your potential date is still open before you start booking your other vendors.

Give yourselves enough time. Be realistic about how long it will take you to pull together these details while still having a life—and whether you and your other wedding contributors need some time to save up for your big event.

Getting Your Groom Involved

Planning a wedding is a great test of your teamwork skills, as you and your groom negotiate big financial agreements with your pros and little details with each other, like whether the wedding colors will be blush pink or navy blue. Here's some advice from recent brides.

Make a list of all your decisions and plans—then hand it to him. For instance, write down the names of the bridal party and who is paired with whom or a list of songs for the reception. After reading the list, he will most likely have comments and changes. In my experience, men need to be able to read things to get a better idea of what's involved.
—*Christine*

Start referring to the wedding as "his" wedding. I asked my fiancé, "What do you think of this song or that dinner menu for your wedding?" Soon after that, he began to view the wedding as something that was not only "mine" or "ours" but also "his"—and that got him more involved. —*Dana*

Let him make some of the decisions on his own. Since I picked out my dress and my bridesmaids' dresses, I thought it was only fair that my fiancé got to choose the tuxes for himself and his friends. They weren't exactly what I would have picked out for him, but he was happy, and that's what mattered. —*Lisa*

Think about the things he enjoys. If he likes to cook, have him pick out the pots and pans for the registry. Let him help pick out the DJ or band, and ask him to make a list of his favorite songs. Keep him busy with things you know he likes (music), and avoid harassing him about the decisions he may not care about (flowers). —*Peggy*

Lunch-Hour Planner

How do you cram wedding tasks into your already overbooked life? Here are a few things you can cross off your list during your next lunch hour (from your desk, no less!).

1 **Prepare your song list.** Ask your band or DJ to fax you a list of tunes. Check off the ones you definitely want played, and cross out the ones you don't.

2 **Update your registry.** Go online and see which gifts have already been purchased. Add or delete items at will.

3 **Create a spreadsheet.** Be sure to make enough columns so that you can easily keep track of all your wedding guests' addresses, acceptances and gifts.

4 **Fire off some thank-you notes.** It's fine to keep them short— just get those letters of gratitude in the mail!

5 **Get a gift.** Start searching online for meaningful items to give your parents or attendants. If you're really pressed for time, you can pay the few extra dollars to have them gift-wrapped.

6 **Work on a wedding Web site.** Upload a recent snapshot of the two of you, update the travel information for your out-of-town guests, or put together a list of local restaurants and attractions you recommend.

Dedicate a tidy
corner of your home
to wedding-planning
activities. Lessen
the chances of lost
papers with a good
filing system.

TO CALL: TO PAY: TO DO:

scrapbook

photographs

Get organized

All those wedding details come with baggage: a huge pile of swatches, samples, contracts and clippings. So how do you keep track of the paper and paraphernalia?

Most brides start with a binder or organizer of some sort, whether it's one that's made specifically for planning a wedding, or a portable accordion file or three-ring binder with pockets where you can store the contracts, brochures, lists, magazine clippings and receipts. All you need is something that'll help you keep the essentials in one spot. Include the checklist on page 249, which will help ensure you don't miss a single detail.

Of course, there are high-tech ways of staying organized. You can take digital pictures of sites or centerpiece options to store on your computer, construct spreadsheets to help you manage your guest list and use a PDA or computer to keep track of your to-do list.

The key is to find a system that works for you—even if it's just a few manila envelopes you stuff with contracts and clippings. As long as you can find what you need, it'll work.

{expert tip}

Envision the wedding as if you were attending it. Forget you're the bride and make sure you would enjoy every bit of the event as a guest.

—*Marcy Blum, wedding consultant, New York City*

Cutting Your Guest List

As you devise your plans, try to figure out the magic number of guests you can invite, whether your budget, your preferences or your site size sets the limit—then split that number as evenly as possible between you and your parents. But if you're way beyond the max, it's time to trim out a few invitees. Here's how to make cuts as painlessly as possible.

1 Lose the "and guest"s. Your single pals can come solo unless they have serious beaus or fiancés.

2 Avoid "chain" invitees. If you can't have your best book-club pal there without the rest of the girls, you may need to skip her.

3 Keep it personal. Colleagues and clients will understand if you say, "We're keeping it to family and close friends only." That'll still allow you to invite the work buddies you regularly hang out with on the weekends, without having to include the entire accounting department.

4 Reconsider the kids. Set a limit for your party—no one 12 or under, or just first cousins or immediate family members. If you do decide to make exceptions for your nieces and nephews or cousins, let the other parents on your guest list know ahead of time where you've made the cutoff, so they don't wonder why their kids are at home while others are hokey-pokeying on the dance floor.

{modern bride wisdom}

If you still can't get your guest list under control, ask your parents and future in-laws to help you prioritize. After allotting each set an equal number of people to invite, have them rank their desired invitees in order of importance, with non-negotiables at the top. (You and your fiancé should do the same.) Then compare all the lists to eliminate potential repeats, and start trimming an equal number from the lowest names on each list until you reach a workable number of guests.

Do You Need a *Consultant?*

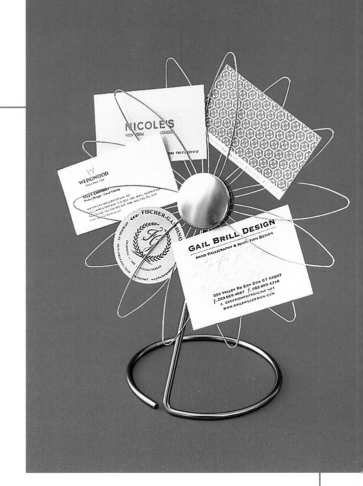

Wedding consultants and planners can be a real asset to your planning: They can brainstorm ideas and fix sticky situations, and they'll help you stay on schedule and on budget. You can hire a consultant to stay with you through the whole process, from choosing the site until after the final guest leaves, or just to help at key moments: an advice session or two before you begin the planning or someone to come in only on the wedding day to make sure everything runs smoothly.

But all this extra help can come at a price: Most consultants charge about 10 percent of the total wedding budget or a flat fee. Will it be worth it for you? Here's what to consider.

PROS

- They've built relationships with the best vendors around, and they may be able to work out great deals for you.
- If you're planning long distance, they can handle the details to help you minimize trips to the location.
- On the wedding day, they can deal with any hiccups so you can simply enjoy the day.
- Consultants are organized and can help you keep track of your to-dos and payment schedules.
- If you have tricky family issues—divorced parents, overbearing mothers—consultants can run interference.

CONS

- Their fees can take another bite out of your overall wedding budget.
- If you like to be really hands-on with every detail, you might have trouble giving up control.
- If you find yourself at odds with their style or their personality, working with your wedding planner may end up being frustrating at times.
- Many consultants have long-standing relationships with certain vendors, and they may not be as open to trying out new talent.

Keep the Peace

AVOIDING CONFLICTS WITH YOUR RELATIVES—AND HIS

You've heard the old saying: A marriage combines more than two people—it combines two families. And for many to-be-weds, that means managing the requests and wishes of various family members while still having the wedding that they want. Here's how to keep everyone as happy as possible.

Lay the ground rules ahead of time. It's important to discuss your wedding vision with both sets of parents before you make a single plan—or take a single cent of financial help. If your parents don't like your big-day plans or want more of a say in the details, you'll need to decide what's more important to you: the extra funding or the planning freedom.

Keep everyone in the loop. Share the details of your big event as they are made, and consider inviting your parents (and his) along on some key excursions: the cake tasting, the final dress decision and other fun events.

Put Mom to work. If you're worried that your mom might be overbearing and try to choose everything from your reception site to your bouquet, give her something else to keep her occupied—the more time-consuming and the less important to you, the better. If the two of you see eye to eye and work well together as a team, then approach tasks jointly.

Pick your battles. It's hard not to get emotionally invested in every single detail of the wedding, but try to keep your perspective, and save the heated arguments for the things that really matter to you. If your dad wants to wear his gray suit instead of a tux, it's probably less important than if he insists on having a church wedding and you want to have something more secular.

Handle your own family. Don't butt in if your in-laws start insisting on extra guests above the limit—let your fiancé do the talking. (And you can handle your own mother's gripes about the band you and your groom chose.) Taking on your in-laws now will only start your relationship off on the wrong foot, and it's much more difficult to recover from that than it will be for your mate to make up with his own family.

Q&A

Q My fiancé and I want a short engagement period, but I'm worried we won't have enough time to plan our wedding. How should we handle this?

A If you want to get married within a few months, consider bringing in a wedding consultant to get things moving. As long as you're willing to compromise (on short notice, your first choices might not be available), she can make it happen. If a consultant isn't in your budget, here's how to do it yourselves: Start by picking the date and securing the ceremony and reception sites. Opt for a locale that offers everything (catering, floral decorations, cake bakers on premises, tables,chairs, tents, etc.). Next, line up the rest of your vendors (officiant, photographer, band or DJ and stationer). Ask for recommendations from recently married friends or from your site manager to cut down on the legwork. Once the vendors are secured, decide which other elements are most important to you and your guy. Devise your condensed "wedding to-do list," plan weekly goals and, before you know it, your fabulous wedding will be here. Still not fast enough for the two of you? Then there's always Vegas, baby!

Q My fiancé's family is much bigger than mine, and our guest list is really lopsided. How can we handle this?

A Problems with an uneven guest list often revolve around costs, specifically how much each family decides to kick in. Sometimes the family with the bigger guest list will offer to make a larger contribution to the celebration, but that's not always the case. Avoid problems by making sure both sets of parents know in advance that the guest list will lean heavily toward one family. If your family is footing the entire bill, it might also help to point out that your fiancé can't do anything about the size of his family. The larger family shouldn't be penalized with a smaller guest list. If both families are contributing, sit down with everyone involved (not necessarily at the same time) and come up with your total budget. This will guide you toward deciding how many people you can actually accommodate. At this point, you may find that you simply cannot invite everyone in both families and it's time to make the dreaded guest-list cuts. When you decide who's out (such as the "and guest" or children), make cuts across the board, not only to the larger family.

Q Should we send out a wedding newsletter to our guests?

A Sure. A newsletter is a great way to keep everyone up-to-date on your wedding details. If you haven't already tucked this information in with your invites, you can include directions to the ceremony and reception, along with attire suggestions. If you are planning some cool weekend activities like a pre-wedding pool party or a next-day brunch, explain this in your newsletter. It's also a great place to say, "This is how we met," with an abridged version of your love story. And consider adding a few spotlight bios and pictures of special guests (the friend who introduced you to your fiancé, for example, or the guest who will be traveling the farthest distance). To distribute your newsletter, consider e-mailing it to avoid the expense of stamps, or creating a Web page for guests to visit, which you can update regularly.

Q **Should we base our reception budget on the number of people we think will actually attend our wedding or the number of people we are inviting?**

A Trying to predict your RSVPs is difficult. People you're certain wouldn't miss your big day for anything might have a scheduling conflict, and folks you'd throw in the not-a-chance pile might surprise you and show up. If you base your budget on perfect attendance, you risk allocating too much money for your reception (which is often calculated by a per-person cost). The safest bet is to assume 20 percent of your total guest count will have to decline. This means that any per-person costs should be calculated at 80 percent of your original guest count.

However, if more than 80 percent of your invited guests end up RSVPing "yes," make sure you're prepared to pare down other wedding costs to cover it. For example, a rehearsal dinner at a fancy restaurant could be changed to a less-expensive venue or the string quartet for your ceremony could be switched to the church organist.

Q **I'm not very close to my aunts, uncles and first cousins. Do I have to invite them to my wedding?**

A Many of us have relatives we couldn't pick out of a lineup. However, before you scratch them off the list, talk to your parents. It might not matter to you that your aunts, uncles and cousins aren't there to watch you tie the knot, but it might matter to your folks. When divvying up the guest list, both sets of parents should get the same number of invites. If your parents want to use theirs to include these relatives, by all means let them—but if they start requesting additional invites to fit these folks, it's time to switch to the "A-list/B-list" plan. Here's the plan in a nutshell: Your A-list should contain the people everyone agrees must be invited. Send invitations to them at least eight weeks before the big day. You will also have a B-list of guests (which can include relatives you're not close to) who will be invited only if an

A-lister declines. Once you get an A-lister's "no," drop a B-lister's invite in the mail. This ensures you stick to your guest count. But remember, no B-list invite should go out any later than four weeks before your wedding day—you don't want anyone feeling like an afterthought. In the end, if you just don't have room for these not-so-close relatives, consider ordering some wedding announcements along with your invitations. This way, people who didn't make the final cut still get to hear the news straight from you.

Q **My mother lives in another state. What can she do to help me out?**

A For starters, she can help you search online for wedding vendors in your area. Once the invitations come in, ask her to assemble, address and mail them to the guests she invited (of course, this won't work if you're having your invitations calligraphed). Also, if the RSVPs are being returned to her address, she can relay the final guest count and meal choices to the caterer. If she's crafty, put her in charge of the favors and out-of-town welcome baskets. Knowing that Mom is handling these time-consuming projects can put your mind at ease. Finally, if you spot a must-have for your wedding day, ask her to look around in her area to do a little comparison shopping. We all know that moms always find the best deals.

CHAPTER 2

Create Your *Ceremony*

**TIPS FOR PLANNING A
MEANINGFUL SERVICE**

The ceremony is perhaps the most important part of the whole day. This is the moment that makes it official and transforms you into a married couple. You'll want to give a lot of thought to where and how the vow exchange will be made and who will officiate. Here's everything you need to know for a meaningful ceremony.

Setting Your Site

HOW TO FIND THE RIGHT PLACE TO TIE THE KNOT

If you're marrying in your house of worship, it's merely a matter of calling your church or temple before you book your reception site to make sure it's available. But if you don't have a church or temple you regularly attend, you'll need to scout a great ceremony locale. **Consider your reception site.** Holding the ceremony and reception at the same location can help simplify your planning, as you'll have only one site to negotiate—and one destination once the wedding day arrives. Ask where the site manager recommends setting up the ceremony. Ideally, it should be in a separate area from the reception room, so your florists and other vendors have more time to set up the party, and your ceremony feels more special.

Research local houses of worship. If you and your fiancé want to wed in a church or temple, take a look around at nearby sites. Make sure you attend services there a few times as well so you can get a sense of how the rabbi or pastor leads his congregation.

Scout out the great outdoors. Many couples opt to have an outdoor ceremony, followed by a reception indoors or under a tent. Look around for great parks, beaches or gardens that make a pretty backdrop for your ceremony. You'll need to have a backup location in case of rain.

Search for other locations. You might find your perfect ceremony setting in the lobby of a grand building, atop a lighthouse or inside a rustic barn—whatever fits your wedding style.

Who Should Perform Your Ceremony?

DECIDE WHICH TYPE OF OFFICIANT SUITS YOU

Religious officiant: A rabbi, minister or priest can preside over your ceremony, so you're legally wed in the eyes of the state and your religion. If you're equally devout but practice different faiths, you might ask your religious leaders if they can create an interfaith ceremony.

Nondenominational minister: This is an appropriate choice for a couple who wants to combine both of their faiths into the ceremony without having two officiants or for a couple who wants a wedding with a spiritual component without making one particular religion a central focus of the ceremony.

Civil officiant: For a secular ceremony, turn to a justice of the peace, mayor, county clerk, judge, magistrate or clerk of the superior court. (Find out from your county clerk's office who can legally marry you in your jurisdiction.)

Loved one: In many states, friends and family members need only fill out a few forms online to get the legal authority to pronounce you husband and wife. If someone you know would be perfect for the role—he or she is comfortable with public speaking and knows you both well—call your county clerk's office to see what needs to be done to make him or her official.

1
What types of readings and songs can we include?
Religious ceremonies may have requirements for the types of secular readings and songs used in your ceremony; a civil ceremony generally has fewer rules.

2
Do we need to have any prenuptial counseling?
Some religions require prenuptial classes and counseling before the ceremony—and some states, like Florida, even offer discounts on the marriage license if you complete a basic "Marriage 101" class.

3
Who files the license?
Some officiants ask you to file it, while others take care of that detail for you.

4
How long will the ceremony last?
Some civil ceremonies last mere minutes, and there are religious ceremonies that go on for an hour or more. It's good to know approximately when you'll be officially named husband and wife so you can schedule the celebration accordingly.

QUESTIONS TO ASK

TALK TO YOUR OFFICIANT ABOUT THESE TOPICS

5
Can we write our own vows?
Most religious faiths have their own vows and may not let you stray from their texts (although adding personal vows to these during your ceremony may be permitted).

6
Will you give a sermon— and what will you discuss?
Many officiants have a standard speech, while others tailor their words to the couple. Share a bit of your history with the officiant so he can try to work it into the ceremony, then discuss what he'll cover in his speech so you can choose related readings.

7
What's not allowed during the ceremony?
The site or the officiant may have rules about flash photography, runners, tossing birdseed or petals or the volume of the music—now's the time to ask.

8
Will you be available for the wedding rehearsal?
Your officiant can help direct the rehearsal, showing members of your wedding party where to stand, giving cues to your readers, and helping everyone become more comfortable with the ceremony's timeline. If he isn't available, ask him who will take his place to lead the way.

Writing *Your Vows*

Having a tough time finding the right words? Try one of these quick fixes.

Go on a vow-making date. Spend an evening or a romantic meal together talking about the things that make your relationship special.

Ask your friends. Check around with people who know both you and your fiancé to get their perspectives on why your relationship is unique. Their thoughts will help you get started.

Do some research. Lots of books and Web sites contain ideas for vows. Reread some favorite poems or even children's books. Check out famous quotations about love and marriage. You may get inspired.

Loosen up. If you're having trouble getting started, try writing a letter to your fiancé. Some of the thoughts or ideas that come up may be perfect for your vows.

Get a little more inspiration. Think about the first time you realized you loved him, the reasons you know he's The One, the kind of marriage you hope to have and the promises you want to make. These are all excellent starting points for your wedding vows.

Bride to Bride

My fiancé is a DJ, and we both love music. I have taken lines from our favorite love songs— by artists as varied as Faith Hill and Led Zeppelin—and put them together to create unique vows for our wedding. —Mary

{modern bride wisdom}

Write your vows on little "cheat sheets" (pretty paper or index cards) and carry them with you for insurance— even the most rehearsed couples can find themselves getting flustered and forgetting their lines.

Choosing the Readings

Finding the most meaningful words for your wedding can take a little research and a lot of thought. Here's how to sort through the stacks of contenders to find the perfect ones for you.

DO talk it over with your officiant. He may ask that you draw from certain texts (Biblical passages only, for example) or offer some suggestions of readings that worked well for other weddings.

DON'T limit yourself to the usual suspects. Classical poems and religious texts may be the gold standard, but there are plenty of great options beyond them. Look at the lyrics of your favorite songs and the screenplays of your favorite movies. You might find the optimal reading right there.

DO consider your reader. Your 11-year-old niece may have a hard time with Shakespeare's iambic pentameter and Elizabethan styling, and your hubby's macho brother may feel uncomfortable reading something mushy like Elizabeth Barrett Browning's "How Do I Love Thee?"

DON'T try to be something you're not. Find a text that meshes with your personalities. If you and your groom are planning an offbeat wedding to match your fun-loving style, the lyrics to the Partridge Family classic "I Think I Love You" may be more your speed than a Byronic ode.

DO keep the length in mind. A few paragraphs is all you need—going longer than a page could drag down the pace of your ceremony.

Group Participation

These are some cool ways to get the guests involved in your ceremony.

Say it with flowers. During the ceremony. recognize the special people in your lives by handing them small bouquets.

Open the floor. Encourage guests to step forward during the ceremony to share their best-wishes, advice or special thoughts about you and your groom.

Give them a say. Have the officiant ask guests to affirm your union. They can respond by applauding or shouting, "We do!"

Foster a friendly vibe. Ask your officiant to encourage guests to take a moment to greet their neighbors.

Create a ritual that includes them. At a beach-side wedding, have your guests make wishes and throw seashells into the sea at the end of your ceremony.

A Show of Unity

UNIQUE RITUALS TO SYMBOLIZE YOUR NEW BOND

Breaking a glass: The groom steps on a glass to shatter it in this traditional finale to a Jewish wedding. There are several different interpretations of this ritual; the most modern is that it symbolizes a break with the past and a new life for the couple.

Exchanging flowers: In Hindu and Hawaiian ceremonies, the bride and groom often drape flower garlands over each other to signify their union.

Jumping the broom: In the African-American culture, the newlyweds jump over a broom to symbolize a clean start in life.

Lighting a unity candle: Usually included in Christian ceremonies, the bride and groom take separate tapers to light a single candle to show that two separate people have become joined together as one. Variations on this include pouring from two separate bottles of wine into one glass (which the couple can later drink from) or two separate vessels of sand into one vase.

Tying the knot: Ribbons or rope are used to bind the couple's clasped hands; it's a component of Celtic and pagan wedding ceremonies. In many Latino ceremonies, a length of rope, called a lasso, is placed over the couple in a figure eight to demonstrate their eternal bond.

Wearing joined crowns: A Greek Orthodox couple wears two crowns joined together with ribbon to symbolize their union.

Remembering Loved Ones

Many couples would like to honor deceased family members and friends at some point during the ceremony—the trick is to make it special without putting a damper on the joy of the occasion. Here's how to strike that balance.

Put it in the program. Include a short paragraph or two that sums up how special the person was and perhaps your thoughts on how she'll be there in spirit.

Incorporate what they loved. Have someone read one of Shakespeare's sonnets in honor of your late English-teacher aunt, use peonies in the floral arrangements if those were your grandmother's favorite, or wear your father's wedding band on your necklace. It may be on the subtle side, but that makes it a little more personal.

Write him into a prayer. If you're having a religious service, ask your officiant if he could include a brief mention of your loved one.

HONOR ROLES

GREAT WAYS TO INCLUDE YOUR FAVORITE PEOPLE

Reader: A loved one can read a meaningful passage to add depth to your ceremony.

Candle lighter: While the mothers of the bride and groom usually light the two flames of the tapers used by the bride and groom to light the unity candle, other loved ones can light candles along the aisle just before your arrival.

Musician: Friends and family members with musical talents can be asked to perform at the ceremony.

Guest-book coordinator: An outgoing friend is the perfect choice to greet guests and make sure they leave a note for you.

Honorary attendant: Give corsages or boutonnieres to special people who aren't in the bridal party to make them unofficial bridesmaids and groomsmen.

Program/send-off distributor: Passing out programs and bubbles, birdseed or other tosses is a perfect job for a younger VIP.

Other special roles: Some religious and cultural traditions have unique rituals that require participants. In Jewish ceremonies, loved ones can hold the poles of the chuppah to shelter the couple; Catholic ceremonies may need eucharistic ministers to serve communion. Latino couples often ask special guests to serve as *padrinos,* or patrons of their marriage; the *padrinos* participate in aspects of the wedding (like helping with the lasso that joins the couple together).

MODERN BRIDE 5

Including Your Children

Ask them to serve as attendants. Have your son walk you down the aisle, or have a daughter and son serve as maid of honor and best man.

Exchange family vows. Share promises with your children to show them that they'll be an integral part of your new marriage.

Give them a gift. Present your children with necklaces, bracelets or watches after the vow exchange.

Create a unique ritual. Some families tie a set of balloons together and release them to show that their lives are now intertwined.

Walk out of the ceremony as a family. Join hands with your children for your grand exit.

PARTY GIRLS AND BOYS

If you're asking your youngest relatives and friends to serve in your bridal party, you have to be prepared to go with the flow. Follow these tips to encourage a flawless performance.

Know what they can handle. Don't expect a 2-year-old to walk the aisle unaided—she may need to be carted in a wagon or have an adult escort. Children over the age of 3 may be able to walk alone, though a shy child may have difficulty with stage fright.

Give them sturdy accessories. A dainty sweet-pea bouquet is darling—until your flower girl repeatedly drops it on the floor and makes it a bruised mess. Brainstorm an appropriate accessory for your flower girl, and use hardy blooms or silk flowers to minimize bruising and breakage. (You can view a few sweet options on page 129.)

Hold on to the rings. Even the sturdiest tying job may be no match for a 4-year-old ring bearer. Put fakes on his pillow, and give the real deal to the best man or groom.

Let them practice. Have them walk up and down the aisle several times during the rehearsal so they understand where they're supposed to go.

Involve their parents. Make sure the kids' parents are seated up front, and have your flower girl or ring bearer sit by their side, instead of with the rest of the party.

Expect the unexpected. Your vivacious 3-year-old niece may suddenly get stage fright on the big day, or your ring bearer may decide to turn around and wave frantically to his cousins halfway down the aisle. Rest assured, these less-than-perfect performances will only make your wedding more memorable.

Pet Project

If you can't imagine getting married without your furriest family member by your side, you're not alone—today, many couples have their pets participate in the ceremony. This is the right way to do it.

Consider your pet's personality.
If your dog is particularly shy or on the wild side, you may have a tough time coaxing him down the aisle. In this case, the pet could attend under the watchful eye of a friend or trainer but should not be forced to participate in any other way.

Work on it ahead of time. If you think your pet can handle it, start training your pooch to walk down the aisle effortlessly. You can stage an aisle and enlist a few friends to sit along it so you can see how he'll react to performing in front of a crowd.

Test out his duds. If you're planning to have your dog don a tux or a collar of flowers, try this on him well in advance of the big day so he can get used to it. Otherwise your dog may spend more time scratching himself than looking dignified. If you find an outfit too fussy, dress him up with a fancy collar—maybe one with rhinestones.

Get him a date. If you have a regular dog walker or sitter, ask her to attend the wedding and take the leash after his part in the ceremony is through. She can stay to take charge of him while the wedding continues. That way, you won't have to worry about your dog snatching a chunk of your wedding cake while you're mingling.

Get him festive food. Be sure you've planned ahead for your dog's meal as well as your guests'. Have water available throughout the ceremony and reception and find a quiet corner where he can eat without interruption.

Getting in Order

Somehow, you've got to get a dozen or more people organized and ordered so they can glide down the aisle before your processional song has ended. To avoid last-minute chaos, try one of these organizational options.

TRADITIONAL CHRISTIAN PROCESSIONAL
- mother or parents of the groom
- mother of the bride
- bridesmaids (with or without groomsmen)
- ring bearer and/or flower girl
- maid or matron of honor
- bride with father

TRADITIONAL JEWISH PROCESSIONAL
- rabbi and/or cantor
- grandparents of the bride
- grandparents of the groom
- groomsmen (in pairs)
- best man
- groom and his parents
- bridesmaids (in pairs)
- maid or matron of honor
- ring bearer and/or flower girl
- bride and her parents

Bride to Bride

My fiancé escorted his mother down the aisle. It made them both feel so good to have their own special thing at the wedding.

—Amanda

Divorce Dilemmas

In the case of divorced parents and stepparents, you'll need to decide what will make everyone comfortable.

For the aisle walk, some brides opt to have Mom and Dad walk them down the aisle, while others split the walk, letting the biological father start out (because he started her out in life), then having her stepfather take her the rest of the way. If the situation becomes too contentious, walking alone is a peacekeeping option.

Seating can also be an issue: Some opt to have all their parents and stepparents in the front row, while others put their mother and stepfather in the first row with a few key relatives and their father and stepmother in the second. If that's still too close for comfort, place a buffer row of relatives—siblings, grandparents—between the two.

Setting the Scene

CREATE THE CEREMONY'S LOOK

Whether you're setting up your ceremony site from scratch or working with built-in benches or fixtures, there are ways to create a more personal, intimate space.

Start by thinking beyond the traditional theater-style seating. You can set up the seats either "in the round," so guests completely surround you as you say your vows, or in a semicircle, which gives everyone a great view of the special moment.

If you're working with a set space, consider dressing up the standard seating. Work with your florist to create special pew markers to line the aisle—even something as simple as a cone of rose petals or a special photo of you and your mate hung from a piece of ribbon will add a personal touch. Ask your florist to come up with more elaborate arrangements to designate the rows where your VIPs—parents, bridal party members, and yourselves—will sit, to make it easier for your groomsmen to seat everyone properly.

Calming the Jitters

If you start to feel nervous before you walk down the aisle, follow these tips to help you squelch your stage fright.

Breathe. Take a few deep, calming breaths to settle down and clear your mind.

Focus. If the 200 pairs of eyes looking at you start making you nervous, focus on a single pair—your groom's.

Practice beforehand. Rehearse your vows, walk the aisle and go over the ceremony order yet again. All that practice will make you feel more confident and in control.

Accentuate the positive. Think happy thoughts—how excited you are to be marrying your fiancé, how much fun you'll have on your honeymoon—to bring you to a joyful place.

Eat something. You may not feel like you have much of an appetite, but skipping breakfast before your wedding will only make you lightheaded. Choose a combination of protein and carbs (such as a peanut butter sandwich or eggs and toast), which will keep you satiated through even the longest ceremony.

Bride to Bride

We celebrated our wedding on a yacht. As my husband and I departed, guests tossed bundles of goldfish—Pepperidge Farm, that is—instead of rice. —Charlise

Plan a Rehearsal

MAKE SURE YOUR WEDDING GOES OFF WITHOUT A HITCH

A wedding ceremony may not seem worthy of a full-blown rehearsal—after all, you simply walk down the aisle, repeat after the officiant or read from your notes, then kiss and leave as husband and wife. But there are unique nuances to every ceremony, and you'll want your wedding party, readers and other ceremony participants to know how to perform their roles.

Most houses of worship schedule a rehearsal for you, usually the evening before the ceremony. Even if you won't have access to your site or your officiant for a run-through, it pays to have a brief meeting with your bridal party in the days leading up to the ceremony. Here's what to cover.

1 **Processional/recessional order:** If you're pairing up attendants, let them know who'll be escorting them down the aisle—and which pairs go first. Decide when you'll want your attendants to hit the aisle: Should they wait until the people ahead of them are halfway down the aisle or all the way to the front? (Unless you have a really large wedding party or a really long aisle, you can let each set of attendants walk the whole way before the next starts down.)

2 **Ceremony order:** Walk your VIPs through your ceremony timeline, noting any spots where they may need to do something—for instance, you'll want to let your maid of honor know when the vow exchange will happen so she can step forward to take your bouquet just before you begin.

3 **Readings:** If you're having your rehearsal at your site, see if you can give your readers a few minutes to practice with the sound system so they'll be more confident as they step up to the podium.

Ceremony Sendoffs

CLEVER IDEAS FOR A FOND FAREWELL

- flower petals
- ribbon streamers
- bubbles
- jingle bells to ring
- birdseed
- sparklers
- candy
- confetti
- origami cranes
- butterfly or dove release

Q & A

Q **We are composing our own vows. Should we try to memorize the words or write them down?**

A Write 'em down. Think of how many times Hollywood stars have pulled out prewritten speeches at the Oscars—and these folks memorize lines for a living! They know that when someone is caught in the moment and emotions are running high, it's sometimes difficult to think straight. Reciting your vows during your ceremony is probably one of the most personal things you'll do on your wedding day. Although you can certainly memorize your vows as opposed to reading them, it's best to have a hard copy available in case you get flustered. However, this doesn't mean you have to pull out a crumpled piece of paper from your pocket. Pen your vows on pretty stationery or, if you are having a calligrapher address your invitations, consider asking her to do your vows, too. They make perfect keepsakes to frame later. Then, give your vows to your maid of honor and best man or officiant to hold in case either of you needs to refer to them. You may not end up using the written versions, but the peace of mind you'll have knowing they're nearby is well worth it.

Q **We have a huge wedding party. What are some options for the processional that won't take as much time as the standard two-by-two march?**

A Send more than two folks down the aisle at a time. For example, one groomsman can escort two bridesmaids, followed by one bridesmaid with two groomsmen and so on. If you have an uneven number of guys and gals, not to worry. Send as many as possible down in groups of three, and the rest can walk in groups of two or solo if necessary. Another way to speed things up a bit is to instruct your marchers to follow a little more closely behind one another instead of putting the requisite "half an aisle length" between them. Bonus tip: The tempo of the processional song can influence how quickly people walk down the aisle. Consider keeping things a little livelier for your wedding party and then slowing things down when it's your turn to hit the road.

Q **What are some special ideas for including my mom in the wedding?**

A There are many unique ways to include her. Rather than just ushering her to her seat at the ceremony, lock arms with Dad *and* Mom and march up the aisle together. (This is already a wonderful tradition at Jewish weddings.) If you really want her to take center stage, you can ask her to be your maid of honor and stand with you at the ceremony. After all, she's stood by your side your entire life. Also, perhaps she'd like a turn at the mike during the reception so she can speak about what you and your wedding day mean to her. If your mom's not comfortable with these front-and-center ideas, another great way to make her feel extra special on your big day is to pamper her. If you are planning any beauty treatments for you or your 'maids, plan the same for Mom. You'll show her she's a VIP and deserves special treatment. If you hadn't planned on a big day of beauty for you and your crew, book manicures or hair and makeup appointments for just you and your mom. This way, she gets you all to herself for a couple of hours.

Q **We'd like our close friend to perform our wedding ceremony. How can we make that happen?**

A There are numerous Web sites now that offer instant ordainment. One of the most reputable ones is The Universal Life Church Monastery (ulc.org), a nondenominational institution that only asks its members to promote "freedom of religion" and "doing what's right." About six months prior to the big day, have your friend log onto the site, click on "Free Online Ordination" and start plugging in his information (full legal name, mailing address and e-mail address). A few more clicks and that's it—he's legally an ordained minister (for life!) able to perform wedding ceremonies in the

United States. The site will create online credentials for him that can be printed out and used as proof of ministry. (We recommend also ordering a hard copy, just to be safe.) This site also offers marriage certificates, basic minister how-to packets and wedding ceremony handbooks. (Allow about four weeks for items to be delivered.) Here's a crucial step: You must call the county clerk's office where you plan to marry and ask about your state's specific requirements. Some require only that a signed marriage certificate be sent to the county clerk's office post-ceremony. Others ask ministers to register their names and addresses or present copies of their credentials to the county or state before they perform the wedding. This can be done in about an hour, for a small fee. (Although your friend could register in the morning before the wedding, provided the office is open, we recommend he visit the office a few days in advance.) Still other states require ministers to obtain specific licenses to marry; this can take up to three months.

Q **Can we have a denominational ceremony at a nondenominational location?**

A In most cases, yes, but it depends largely on the religion. For example, if you're planning to have a traditional Catholic ceremony anywhere

other than a church, you have to speak with a priest to get a "dispensation of place," a document that will allow a ceremony in an alternative location (outdoor weddings are discouraged). Secular locations are usually allowed for most Jewish and Protestant ceremonies, though this may vary from synagogue to synagogue and parish to parish. If you have your heart set on your childhood rabbi or priest overseeing your nuptials, the best thing to do is ask. If he can't perform the ceremony or if you don't have a particular person in mind, search online and ask friends—there are lots of officiants available for any style of service you may want. You might want to consider why you've chosen a secular location. If you're religious, but your (or his) family isn't, consider having two ceremonies: a small gathering at the church or synagogue, and a larger, nonreligious affair at the reception site. Or, you could have your minister co-officiate with a secular leader, such as a justice of the peace, to make everyone happy. Remember that by choosing a secular space, you'll sacrifice the sacred feel of a synagogue or church. To recreate the atmosphere, set up an altar or candles like you would find in your family church, play your favorite hymns as guests enter, or bring in family heirlooms, such as your grandmother's Bible or grandfather's Kiddish cup, to incorporate into the service.

Plan a Great Reception

HOW TO DESIGN A BETTER CELEBRATION

A carriage gives a touch of
authenticity to a historic wedding.

The key to a great reception is making it unique. Be sure the day reflects who you are as a couple—from favorite colors to special sites and captivating themes.

Dream Themes

The term "wedding theme" may conjure up images of men in tights at a Renaissance wedding, but modern themes are more about subtlety and style than costumes and kitsch. To do a theme without overdoing it, follow these steps.

Make it personal. Choose a theme that resonates with you and your fiancé; something that represents your history or reflects a passion. For instance, you may decide to do a picnic menu if your first date was a picnic, or you might incorporate elements from your favorite movies throughout the day if you and your fiancé are both major film buffs.

Keep it subtle. In-your-face details like *Star Wars* figures atop the wedding cake and an officiant in a Darth Vader costume may overpower your celebration and take the focus off you. For a sophisticated take, be subtle—an autumnal wedding might call for a gilded-leaf decoration atop the invitation, sugar leaves and mini pumpkins adorning the cake, and soup served in hollowed-out pumpkins.

Weave it throughout the wedding. A theme can be expressed so that guests can experience it with each of their senses. For instance, a beach wedding can feature reggae or calypso music for the cocktail hour and a tropically inspired signature cocktail.

Bride to Bride

Music played a role in how we met, so we gave our wedding a musical theme. The flower girls carried maracas, the invitations were printed on custom paper made from a music score, a cake tier was decorated with musical notes—and I even gave my fiancé, Kevin, music-note cufflinks on our wedding day. —Wendy

{expert tip} We "mine the territory" of the couple to come up with special details: the rituals you've created as a couple or hope to foster as a family. For example, one groom we met gives his bride a white rose every Friday, so we attached their escort cards to roses.

—David Stark, event designer, New York City

Selecting Your Site

WHICH PARTY SPOT SUITS YOUR ENTERTAINING STYLE? FIND OUT HERE.

Restaurant

What's Cool: You're guaranteed top-notch cuisine and a well-trained waitstaff, making this option the ideal choice for a foodie couple. Restaurants often tailor their decor to their menu, so you may find that the room is well appointed to suit your decorating style.

What's Not: If the restaurant doesn't have a dedicated event space, it may not be ideally set up for a wedding with a dance floor or a spot for the band—or for privacy, if your guest list isn't large enough to require you to rent out the whole place for the evening.

Home

What's Cool: You can totally customize your party in this sentimental spot, since you have complete control over the decor. You can even plant flowers around the area where you'll marry.

What's Not: It may be cost prohibitive, once you factor in rentals—you'll need to bring in everything from tents to toilets. Noise ordinances in your town may mean you'll need to end the party earlier than you'd like.

Outdoors

What's Cool: It's hard to beat the beauty of nature—a manicured garden, a rugged mountainside or a scenic beach—as a backdrop for your celebration.

What's Not: You may spend the weeks leading up to the wedding constantly checking the weather forecast, creating additional stress during one of the most hectic times of your life. You'll need a Plan B in case the weather doesn't cooperate, and that may even involve booking a secondary site (requiring a deposit) just in case. Many municipalities have noise rules, so you may need to wrap things up earlier than you'd want.

Historic Home/Museum

What's Cool: These are spots with lots of character. With antique furnishings and detailing or grand works of art in the background, you're destined to have a memorable affair.

What's Not: The party facilities may be relatively limited, so you may be holding your celebration in a tent on the lawn, or your caterer may have a very small kitchen space that limits your menu options. In order to protect the artwork and artifacts, the site may impose restrictions on your party—you may not be able to grill food because the smoke could damage the art, or red wine may be banned because it could stain the marble floors or antique rugs.

Country Club

What's Cool: A gorgeous pastoral setting (with an equally gorgeous interior) can give your event a luxe feel. You'll likely

have the services of a catering or events manager to help you plan every detail of your wedding.

What's Not: There may be limitations on what you can do outdoors—most clubs don't want your guests traipsing around on the greens, leaving stiletto holes in their well-groomed turf. And you may need to actually join the club (for a pricey fee) in order to host your wedding there or at least find a member to agree to sponsor you.

Yacht

What's Cool: Guests can enjoy an ever-changing, scenic backdrop as you whisk them away on a three-hour (or more) tour.

What's Not: Some yachts have only ladders connecting different decks, so guests with disabilities (or even those wearing big, poufy dresses) may have a hard time getting from place

to place. Galley kitchens are notoriously small, so the caterer may be limited in what he can prepare.

Loft/Raw Space

What's Cool: Consider it your opportunity to create the party of your dreams. You can bring tables, decorations and furniture to create a completely customized atmosphere. Many lofts offer banks of windows with glorious views of city skylines or harbors, adding extra beauty to the space. **What's Not:** A blank canvas needs plenty of finessing to achieve party perfection—and all those party rentals and decorations could cost you a serious sum.

Hotel

What's Cool: If you have out-of-towners on your guest list, this is the easiest option: Guests can stay at the hotel and simply head downstairs to the festivities. Hotels often offer event rooms of various sizes, so they can accommodate small or large weddings, have dedicated staff to help you plan your

affair—and they may even throw in a wedding-night suite for you and your groom to sweeten the deal. **What's Not:** Hotels' event spaces are usually pretty neutral, to make them versatile enough to host different types of events— corporate conferences, class reunions, etc.—so they may need to be spiffed up to be wedding-worthy. If the hotel has several party spaces, yours may not be the only wedding taking place, which could make your celebration feel a little less special.

What's in the contract?

- ☐ Wedding date and time
- ☐ Hours booked
- ☐ Additional fees (such as for overtime)
- ☐ Exactly what's included (the site only or furnishings and catering)
- ☐ Deposit and payment schedule
- ☐ Head count due date
- ☐ Cancellation policy
- ☐ Details selected (linen colors, menu items, glassware)

Package Deal or à la Carte?

Many sites will lump together several aspects of the wedding into one big package, while others provide just a single service, leaving you to book the rest of the details yourself. Which scenario is right for you?

YOU MIGHT WANT A PACKAGE DEAL IF...

Your overbooked schedule leaves you little time to attend to details. With a package deal, you have only one pro to look into and check references on, instead of a whole slew.

You're not familiar with what's available in the locale you've chosen. If you're planning a wedding far from home, this can help you avoid trying to suss out the best caterer or baker in the area—and making frequent trips home to meet with them.

You want to save money. Often, pros offer savings within a package that you won't get by booking services separately.

YOU MIGHT WANT AN À LA CARTE OPTION IF...

You're hoping to create a truly unique event. While there's some customization allowed in any package, there are limits— you'll find more flexibility if you hire each pro separately.

You are free to find other professionals in the area than the ones the site will provide. The site's baker may be excellent, but if you have your heart set on a couture cake from a star baker, you won't want a package that includes someone else.

You want to be in command. Hiring à la carte will give you greater freedom and control over your wedding details.

QUESTIONS TO ASK

WHEN EXPLORING POTENTIAL SITES, POSE THESE QUERIES

Do you offer any packages, and if so, what's included?

Some bare-bones sites offer only the space—it's up to you to find a caterer and party rentals like china and tables on your own. Others offer deluxe packages, which can include the cost of the catering, bar service, and even the cake or a wedding-night suite for you and your groom.

What other fees are involved?

Some sites charge a cake-cutting fee if you bring in an outside confection, or a corkage fee for serving your own champagne. You'll also want to ask if they charge for the time your musicians and other vendors will need to set up before the reception, and what it'll cost to keep the party going strong after the agreed-upon time.

Can we use any vendors we want?

Some sites have exclusive contracts with certain caterers, florists and other pros. You may consider this a plus if you're still searching for most of these vendors. But if you planned to use a vendor that isn't on the site's list, you'll need to decide what's more important—using that florist or having this site.

Are there any rules or restrictions we need to follow?

If you're looking to set up extensive decorations or elaborate food stations, it pays to ask this in advance. Many sites won't allow you to drape fabric on the walls or use twinkle lights or lit candles due to fire regulations; historic homes or museums may even limit the types of food and beverages that can be served, in order to protect their furniture and floors.

How many people can fit into the space for this type of reception?

A room that seats 100 for dinner may be able to squeeze in twice that number for a cocktail or dessert reception, where people will be mixing and mingling. You may not want to choose a room that's on either extreme of the space issue: If you're hosting the bare minimum guests in that space, the room may look and feel empty, and maxing it out may make it seem too cramped.

Will we have access to any other spaces?

You may want a separate bridal suite where you and your attendants can get ready or take a quick breather during the festivities, or you might want to host your cocktail hour or after-party on a veranda or in a separate lounge area.

Will ours be the only event taking place that day?

If the site has more than one reception space, other events may be going on simultaneously. Ask how the event managers juggle multiple parties. Find out what else is booked in your space that day: A brunch right before your evening wedding could give your florist less time to set up; an evening affair after your brunch could limit your ability to go into overtime.

How much parking is available?

Make sure that there's ample space for your guests to park. You may also want to ask about the availability of valet parking, especially if you have a lot of elderly guests or are hosting a wedding at a time of year when bad weather could be a problem.

Seasonal Celebrations

The time of year you wed can influence your wedding details, from the color scheme to the menu. Each season has a distinct feel, so we asked some of the country's best wedding planners to choose one and then share their most inspired ideas. Here's how to carry your wedding's season through all aspects of your celebration.

Spring

Invites: Spring calls for light touches and whimsy. Incorporate your monogram into a colorful pattern and have it printed on the back of your invitations for a fun and unexpected twist.

Decor: Pair spring pastels with unexpected earthy hues, such as pink with brown, lavender with chartreuse or yellow with burgundy for linens and arrangements.

Menu: Serve premium rack of lamb marinated with lemon, fresh rosemary, garlic, olive oil and cracked peppercorns—and have it grilled at the site.

Dessert: Along with the wedding cake, offer your guests fun, fruity dessert martinis such as Lemon Meringue (light rum, limoncello, orange liqueur, lemon juice) or Cherry Pie martinis (vodka, brandy, cherry brandy).

Favors: Send guests home with cupcakes topped with candied violets or peach blossoms (available only in the spring).

—Sasha Souza, event planner, Los Angeles and Napa, CA

Summer

Invites: For a lighthearted but festive look, use white handmade paper in a modern square shape and adorn it with a gerbera-daisy insignia.

Decor: Deck tables in gingham linens and top with galvanized tins filled with fresh grass and colorful gerbera daisies.

Menu: Try updates on the barbecue for the cocktail hour: mini hamburgers (with blue cheese, sautéed onions and other toppings), mini sandwiches, grilled chicken, ribs and assorted salads.

Dessert: Have waiters serve guests miniature snow cones in summery flavors like lemon, peach, blueberry or watermelon. (And champagne granitas are great any time of year!)

Favors: Give everyone Chinese paper parasols with cute name tags stamped with your wedding date.

—Yifat Oren, event planner, Sherman Oaks, CA

Fall

Invites: Package the wedding information and travel details for out-of-town guests in a save-the-date journal designed with an autumnal leaf motif.

Decor: Mix flowers made of sparkling beads (also called French beaded flowers, which can be purchased online or at craft stores) in fall hues with fresh blooms in crimsons, yellows and oranges.

Menu: Offer your guests this autumnal dish: honey vol-au-vent (a puff-pastry shell) filled with curried Dungeness crab, butternut squash and fall pear velouté (a white sauce) and garnished with spiced pecans.

Dessert: In keeping with a fall harvest feel, give guests a bounty of dessert options. Arrange a station serving cookies, pudding cups and chocolate-covered espresso beans.

Favors: Offer guests a beverage to savor later: a bottle of cider or a hot-toddy mix tucked into a glass mug. Add customized labels for a personal touch.

—*JoAnn Gregoli, event planner, New York City*

Winter

Invites: Choose garnet card stock with pearlized ink. Wrap invites in snowflake-pattern vellum with silver snowflake seals; use the same vellum to line envelopes.

Decor: Top tables with garnet taffeta cloths, then drape with an overlay of rich, black-burgundy velvet accented with garnet satin piping.

Menu: Instead of placing a bread basket on each table, serve guests warm, doughy popovers with an herbed butter—it's an elegant wintry comfort food.

Dessert: Treat your guests to an extra-rich and decadent wedding cake: Black Forest torte decorated with dark-chocolate icing, chocolate shavings and sugared fruit.

Favors: Fill an oversized, monogrammed ceramic mug with a bag of gourmet hot chocolate and wrap in a box with garnet satin ribbon.

—*Elizabeth K. Allen, event planner, New York City*

Table Tips

It's easy to get caught up in decisions on center-pieces and menus. But the table settings play a big role in creating the overall mood of the event, so you may decide to move beyond white linens and round tables. Here are some of your options.

THE FURNISHINGS: While 60-inch round tables have long been the standard choice for weddings, there are other possibilities: 48-inch squares, which can seat eight guests; six-foot or longer rectangular tables that give the meal a more communal, dinner-party feel; and even curvy serpentine tables, a fresh twist on the rectangle. And if the site's chairs don't work with your color scheme, consider trading them for rentals—you can find anything from casu-al bamboo folding chairs to formal Chiavari chairs—or using slipcovers to mask them.

LINENS: The tablecloths are important to your over-all decorating scheme, as that sea of reception tables takes up a lot of real estate. Choose something that reflects your wedding style: Shimmering organza will give your party an ethereal, summery vibe, while rich velvet is perfect for a winter wedding. If the linens you love are too costly, save money by using that decadent fabric you love as an overlay or table runner instead of a full tablecloth. (You can lay a single runner down the length of a rectangular table or use two crisscrossed to cover a round table.)

{expert tip} When you're creating a theme, start with the color first. Use only one or two colors to make the theme more dramatic.

—*Preston Bailey, event designer, New York City*

DISHES: Most sites offer basic white plates, but you can change up the shape, style or material of the dishes to create a more elegant table. A square shape gives a table a more modern vibe (and perfectly complements a square or rectangular table), while a thick terra-cotta pottery plate lends the wedding a more earthy, down-home feeling.

GLASSES: There are more options in glasses than ever before—even something as simple as a wineglass can come in elaborate cut crystal or plain glass, clear or colored, and stemmed or stemless to fit in with the rest of the table. Consider using a colored water goblet to liven up each place setting.

FLATWARE: Your eating utensils should complement the other elements of the place setting. Choose a sleek, modern set to go with square dishes, or an antique, intricately patterned set to make simple china seem more elaborate.

Color Code
FIND THE RIGHT SHADES FOR YOUR PARTY

THE HUE	THE MOOD	COMBINE IT WITH
RED	passionate and wild	pink, purple, pale green
PINK	fun and feminine	brown, green, red
ORANGE	happy and warm	green, purple, yellow
YELLOW	cheerful and vibrant	pale purple, navy blue
GREEN	relaxed and inviting	pale purple, brown
BLUE	soothing and sophisticated	pink, yellow, pale green
VIOLET	luxurious and sexy	pale green, pink

TABLE MARKERS: You don't have to use numbers. Instead, name your tables after places you love or flowers or favorite movies, and find a unique way to use these elements to mark the table. Perhaps each centerpiece can feature the chosen bloom, or postcard-sized movie posters can lead guests to the *Casablanca* or *Gone With the Wind* tables.

{expert tip} Spend the money on a charger plate because that's what everyone will notice most. You can serve dinner on a plain white dish because at that point, people are focused on the food presentation. And to really get more bang for your buck, reuse the charger for dessert. You're getting two for the price of one.

—*Errin Verdesca, TriServe Party Rentals, New York City*

Q & A

Q Should we hire a lighting specialist for our reception?

A First, consider the current lighting situation at your venue and the atmosphere it will create. Does it feel like the kind of place in which you'd have an intimate dinner reception or a party-till-dawn dancefest? Chances are it won't feel like both, and this is where a lighting specialist can come in. He can transform a romantic restaurant into a high-energy discotheque with some unique lighting effects that will signal to the guests that it's time to stop savoring their meals and to get up and shake their booties. (However, keep in mind that if you're having a daytime wedding and your site is filled with natural light, a lighting specialist might not be worth the expense.) You can also use lighting to enhance your decor by focusing it on specific elements in the room. Pinspotting the cake and center-pieces and placing lights under the dinner tables are popular strategies for this. Basic lighting packages start at about $500, but it's helpful to note that the use of lighting can, in some cases, cut decor costs; you won't need as many flowers or decorative items if you use lighting effectively.

Q I want my ceremony and reception to be held in a public park near my family's home. What do I need to do?

A You should start by calling your local parks and recreation department to see if you have to secure a permit to hold your celebration in the park. (Some public parks do not require a permit, and you may hold your event there without notification, but we don't recommend it: If no on needs to be notified, then you have no way of knowing how many other events are taking place, and how crowded and noisy the area will be.) Be sure to mention how many guests will attend and how many people will be working at your wedding. Don't forget to ask about alcohol permits, restroom access and potential party pitfalls like off-limit areas, restricted hours and parking or other scheduled events. You can expect to pay a fee for any permit you obtain, and you may have to add a security deposit just in case one of your guests, for example, accidentally steps on a bunch of delicate flowers.

Q Do we need to have a seating chart, or can guests seat themselves?

A You really should have a seating chart, though it can be modified depending on the size of your wedding. If you're expecting 50 guests or fewer, suggest table numbers for each guest, but don't specify a certain seat. But before you decide to abandon the traditional chart, consider whether you have any special circumstances to take into account. For example, divorced parents might be more at ease knowing ahead of time that they can sit at tables far apart from each other. Larger receptions are a different story: Here, a seating chart will help avoid unnecessary confusion and keep your celebration running smoothly. If guests are wandering from table to table trying to find an open seat when dinner is announced, the only thing that will be eaten up quickly is valuable reception time.

Q **My fiancé and I want to make a grand exit. What are some fun ideas?**

A Most brides think about making that all-important dramatic entrance, but your departure can also be an exciting moment at your wedding. For a grand good-bye at the end of your ceremony, be creative with your getaway vehicle; rather than jumping into a standard car, like a limo, you could take off in a hot-air balloon or a helicopter. Feel the need for speed? Whiz away in a motorboat or take off in a seaplane if your locale is near the water. For a wintry affair, consider departing by horse and sleigh, or in warmer weather, if you're experienced drivers, hop on a motorcycle and ride off into the wind. However you decide to leave your ceremony, note that some of these vehicles probably won't be able to take you directly to your reception; distance and logis-

tics might call for a car to be waiting somewhere to take you the rest of the way. Creative modes of transportation aren't the only way to make an exciting exit. You could arrange for a choir to be waiting outside your ceremony site. (There's nothing like a good love song to mark the moment.) Or, have a bagpiper or flutist escort you and your crew to the reception if it's within walking distance. Want to give a little nod to nature? Consider having doves or butterflies released as you and your new husband make your escape. And after an evening ceremony, a round of fireworks accompanied by a band makes for a grand finale guests aren't likely to forget.

Q **My fiancé has his heart set on a formal reception, but I would really prefer to have an outdoor celebration. Can we have the best of both?**

A Of course. If your fiancé thinks *outdoors* means beach party with volleyball and Frisbees, assure him that you can hold the party outside and still have it be quite formal. Choosing a later time of day to start the wedding, specifying a formal or semiformal attire for guests and having your food beautifully presented can all up the elegance factor. Additionally, country-club terraces, hotel courtyards, vineyards and botanical gardens are all gorgeous outdoor

backdrops for a formal celebration. And don't discount a seaside celebration, even if you decide to forgo the beach party—a park by a river or a dinner cruise featuring a jazz band are both ideal settings for a reception overflowing with ambience and style.

Q **We are having several courses served at our reception. How can we encourage our guests to get up and dance between bites?**

A Careful scheduling is very important here. Guests are unlikely to hit the dance floor if they think the next course is coming out right on the heels of the last, so tell your caterer that you'd like some built-in breaks between each course. Allowing 20 to 30 minutes in between courses will give guests enough time to eat and take a couple of turns around the dance floor. To clue everyone in, have your DJ or bandleader announce after each course that the next won't be served for a while and that the dance floor is officially open. Also, nothing gets people on their feet faster than some fun, high-energy tunes. Bonus tip: If your guests still seem reluctant to get up, grab your new hubby and hit the dance floor. Once the DJ announces that the bride and groom want to share a dance with their guests, you can be certain that the floor will fill up in no time.

CHAPTER 4

Dress Your *Best*

**FASHION ADVICE TO
HELP YOU FIND
THE PERFECT STYLE**

The wedding dress is the stuff of dreams. It is the only dress choice that will likely make you (or someone you love) cry. For such an important purchase you need to be armed with the right information. To help you find the very best look for your day, we have compiled a guide to silhouettes, necklines, trains and veils that will help you navigate the world of bridal-dress shopping.

Be a Savvy Shopper

THE DO'S AND DONT'S OF BUYING A DRESS

DO give yourself time. Most experts recommend starting the shopping as soon as you have your wedding date set, at least six months before the wedding. That should give you enough time to go on a few shopping expeditions, order your dress and have it made, then have it fitted. Some designers, however, require even more time than that.

DON'T show up without an appointment. Most salons request that you reserve a time, so you can have the undivided attention of a salon consultant.

DO bring your ideas. Consultants love to see images of what you like—and what you don't—culled from bridal magazines, so they'll get a sense of your taste and they're better able to focus your hunt. Tell your consultant about your sense of style—both the details of your wedding and your general fashion sense. (If you live in khakis and T-shirts, you'll probably opt for a different dress than a woman who has multiple beaded dresses lining her closet.)

DON'T be afraid to try on something that falls outside your vision, especially if the consultant suggests it. You may not envision yourself in a slinky mermaid silhouette, but your consultant may find one that's perfectly you.

DO remember to share how much you have to spend, so your consultant brings you only dresses in your price range. That way, you won't be tempted to blow your budget.

DON'T bring a huge entourage. Invite just a couple of trusted friends and your mother to try on dresses. Cramming a dozen people into a boutique—and fielding 12 different opinions on which gown to choose—can be an overwhelming experience. (Once you've settled on the perfect gown, you can bring other VIPs to let them ooh and ahh over it.)

DO dress the part. We're not saying you need to head to your stylist for an updo before you embark on the dress hunt, but you'll get a better sense of how you'll really look in the gown if your hair and makeup look good. (If you're leaning toward an updo for the big day, at least put your hair in a ponytail or bun so you can see how the dress will look with your hair up.) Bring along control-top pantyhose, a strapless bra, and shoes with the same heel height you plan to wear that day, so you can better judge which dress will work on you.

Bride to Bride

When my fiancé proposed, he gave me the ring in a big box tied with about a yard of beautiful silver satin ribbon. I saved the ribbon and used it as the trim around the waist of my wedding gown. —Chadlee

You really can't tell if a gown is right for you unless you try it on—so go ahead, give it a shot.

SILHOUETTES

One of the first questions you are likely to be asked upon entering a bridal salon: "What kind of silhouette are you looking for?" Never having worn a dress like this before, you may not know how to answer. Take a look at this guide to silhouettes and try to imagine yourself in each one. You'll still want to experiment with many looks, but this will give you a jump-start on selecting the most likely shapes for you.

A-line/Princess: There's no defined waist; the dress flows along the bodice and waist, then out into a full skirt.

Ball gown: The classic Cinderella silhouette— a body-hugging bodice, which flares out at the waist into a big, billowing skirt.

Basque: This waistline drops to a point in the front, creating a V along the waist. This makes your middle appear thinner.

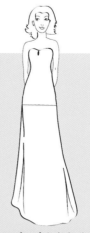

Dropped waist: It looks just the way it sounds: The waistline sits below your natural waist, lengthening your torso.

Empire: The skirt flows out from beneath a tightly gathered bust. It's a very forgiving dress line, skimming over the waist and hips.

Mermaid: This silhouette hugs every curve from the bust to the knees, then fans out to create a trumpet skirt.

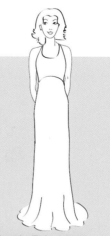

Sheath: This dress is slim all over, skimming your body from top to bottom.

Error

 46   The *Modern Bride* Survival Guide

NECKLINES

Bateau: The top of the dress is cut straight across your collarbone.

Halter: This arm- and shoulder-baring style features two straps that meet behind the neck.

Portrait: Named for the way it "frames" the face, this neckline curves gently from shoulder to shoulder in a slight scoop.

Choose the most flattering neckline for your figure from among the ones pictured here. You can assume that the necklines that work for you in everyday clothes will also work for you in a formal gown. Then you can search Web sites by neckline type to find designers with dresses that fit the bill. It's also helpful to let the consultant in the bridal salon know if you are leaning toward a halter or V-neck, for example.

Tip of the shoulder: The neckline of this style curves slightly as it heads from the very edge of one shoulder to the edge of the other.

Sweetheart: This neckline mimics a heart shape, curving up on each side, then down into a small V in the center of the bust.

V-neck: As the name implies, the neckline dips down into a point in the center of the torso.

The moment your whole look comes together? When you put on your veil.

TRAINS

The train of a dress dictates how dramatic it is. If you want a formal look for your ceremony but also want to hit the dance floor unencumbered, look for a style with a detachable train. Or have your gown bustled, which will secure the lower half higher up.

Sweep: This is a simple wisp of a train, which barely grazes the floor.

Chapel: This "midsized" train trails about a foot behind you.

Cathedral: If you want a dramatic look for your aisle walk, try this long, grand train, which stretches two or more feet behind you.

The Right Style for Your Shape

BODY TYPE: PETITE

Best Bet: A dress that has long, uninterrupted lines. This will help create the illusion of height. Think princess line, where the vertical seams flow gently into a full skirt.

Look For: Gowns with delicate details—a hint of beading, a touch of lace—as really busy dresses might overwhelm your small build.

BODY TYPE: THICK WAIST

Best Bet: An empire silhouette. Material flows loosely past the waist, camouflaging a wider middle.

Look For: Pleated detailing at the waistline, which can help create a more hourglass shape.

BODY TYPE: BIG BUST

Best Bet: A ball gown. The big, dramatic skirt can help balance your silhouette.

Look For: Dresses with open necklines and minimal detailing at the bust, which can help minimize your upper body by drawing attention to your face.

BODY TYPE: PLUS-SIZE

Best Bet: An empire waist will lengthen your body and make you look taller and slimmer—or consider a basque waist, which will flatten your tummy.

Look For: Dresses with open necklines to help draw attention to your face and lighten the look of the dress; illusion sleeves will give you coverage without bulking you up.

Bride to Bride

Consider shopping by yourself. There's a lot less pressure, and you don't end up trying on dresses you know you'll hate. Once you've found your dress, you can ask everyone to see it to "make sure it's perfect." —Whitney

Make sure you can move easily in your dress. You want to feel comfortable.

Get a Perfect Fit

Having a formal gown custom made for you is quite different from buying a dress off the rack. Numerous fittings may be required to make sure the fit is exactly right. Be sure you bring your bra and other undergarments to the fittings. Make sure that they don't peek out from the edges of the dress, or create unsightly bumps beneath it. Also, have your shoes with you so your seamstress can hem the dress to the appropriate length. How can you tell if your gown is tailored well? You should be able to:

- Raise your arms above your head
- Do a little dance
- Sit down and cross your legs on both a cushioned couch and a straight-back chair
- Bend at the waist
- Walk easily around the store

{expert tip} Don't worry too much about the rules. You don't want to wear a ball gown to a beach wedding, of course, but you can wear a dress that's not technically "appropriate" for your site. If you love it, there's magic, and you'll look beautiful.

—*Monique Lhuillier, bridal designer, Los Angeles*

{modern bride wisdom}

Don't freak out if your salon consultant orders you a size 12 or 14 dress when you normally wear a 10. She's not trying to earn extra alterations fees—most bridal designers use a different size chart than their ready-to-wear counterparts, so their sizes run a bit smaller. She'll choose the one that best matches your measurements.

A Guide to Fabrics

Alençon: It's a Chantilly-style lace that's been re-embroidered to accentuate certain details.

Brocade: This heavy fabric is woven with a rich, raised design, creating a highly textured effect.

Chantilly: This is a fine mesh lace with a delicate floral pattern.

Chiffon: If you're looking for a dress that feels light and airy, try one made of this soft, sheer silk or rayon material.

Doupioni: This is a coarser, yet still shiny, weave of silk.

Duchesse satin: Silk and polyester are combined to create a material that feels crisp and lustrous.

Guipure: This type of lace is usually bold with large patterns.

Illusion: It's another soft, sheer fabric. Illusion is often used for sleeves.

Organza: This lightweight fabric is made of silk, nylon, rayon or polyester.

Satin: Woven of polyester or silk, satin is a shiny, smooth fabric.

Schiffli: This lace is delicate and embroidered and machine made.

Shantung: Cotton or silk is woven to give this fabric a rougher texture.

Silk: Spun from the cocoons of silkworms, silk has a soft, smooth feel—and it also has a hefty price tag. Heavier silk fabric is called silk mikado.

Taffeta: This crinkly, crisp fabric has a touch of shimmer.

Tulle: This sheer netting can be soft when made of silk or stiff when made of nylon.

Venise: This is a heavy lace with a floral or geometric pattern.

Chantilly lace

Embroidered lace

Fashionable Alternatives

These days, you can wear anything from black sequins to blue denim when you say your wedding vows. Try one of these options:

Mini dress: Short can be chic, especially for a beach or outdoor wedding.

Pantsuit: For a modern twist on elegance, pair slinky heels with a sleek and fitted pantsuit—you may even be able to wear it again.

Colorful ensemble: Choose an evening dress in any hue you love, from sage green to lipstick red.

Dual dresses: If you want the big "white-gown moment" but don't want to boogie down in a ball gown, pick a more traditional style for the ceremony, then slip into a more comfortable dress for the party.

Foreign fashion: Skip the western-style white gown and opt for another culture's bridal wear: a sleek red cheongsam from China, or a beautifully embroidered sari from India.

Old, New, Borrowed and Blue

IDEAS FOR INCORPORATING THE TRADITION

OLD
- ticket stub from your first date, tucked into your bouquet
- lace from your grandmother's dress sewn into the hem of yours
- antique ribbons to adorn your garter

NEW
- your dress
- a gift from your groom (earrings, a necklace)
- a brooch you plan to pass down to your future children as a keepsake

BORROWED
- a bracelet from your best friend
- a handkerchief from your dad (used as a bouquet wrap)
- your mother's pearl or diamond studs

BLUE
- satin slippers to dance in
- your married initials embroidered inside the gown
- forget-me-nots tucked into your bouquet

Adding a fur wrap (real or faux) can give your dress a whole new look of glamour.

Finishing Touches

HOW TO FIND THE RIGHT ACCESSORIES FOR YOUR DRESS

Let your gown be your guide. Your dress will help determine what the headpiece and other accessories should be: You'll be better off pairing a crystal-encrusted dress with diamonds (or cubic zirconia) than pearls. A very simple dress can take either sleek accessories that mirror its understated style or more elaborate ones. What you want to avoid is too much visual "noise"—an elaborate tiara and lacy veil with a billowing, heavily embroidered dress has too many competing details that overshadow you.

Do a trial run. Bring your jewelry and accessories to a dress fitting to make sure you like how the whole ensemble goes together.

Mix and match. Trying to exactly match your shoe color to your dress can be nearly impossible. Look for similar finishes to the fabric—you don't want ultra-shiny satin shoes with a more matte-finished satin dress—or opt for a different type of fabric altogether, like a brocade wrap with a satin gown, so a hue clash won't be as noticeable. If you are planning on a shawl or jacket, ask your salon consultant if she can order a few extra yards of fabric when they place your dress order, so you can have the wrap custom made to match.

Consider your comfort. You'll be wearing your wedding ensemble for many hours of mixing, mingling and merrymaking, so you'll want every piece to be comfortable. Choose shoes in a height that you're comfortable wearing; if you're a flats girl, three-inch stilettos will make you very unhappy. If your veil is attached to your headpiece with Velcro or another fastener, you can remove just the veil after the ceremony and party all night without being hindered.

Dress Up Your Hair

CHOOSE THE IDEAL HEADPIECE FOR YOU

Combs: Simple combs often hold a veil into the hair, though jeweled combs can be used to adorn a French twist or pull back a simpler style. Combs work best with fine hair. Look for teeth that are set close together to ensure against slippage.

Jeweled pins & sticks: Add a little sparkle to a simple updo by scattering a few pins or sticks throughout. Pins can also be used to dress up a very short hairstyle and make it wedding perfect.

Tiara: The reigning queen of wedding headpieces, the tiara comes in shapes and sizes that will work with every style and cut. Try a big tiara to balance out a tall updo; headband styles will stay put in shorter hair.

Vines: This ultra-flexible headpiece—basically, a bejeweled adornment strung on wire that will bend easily—can be used in many different ways: It can be worked along the head for hair that's worn down, for example, or wrapped around an updo.

VEILS

Ballet: The veil ends between your knees and your ankles.

Blusher: A small piece of veiling that's worn over the face for the walk down the aisle—and the romantic reveal when you reach your groom.

Elbow: A simple veil that ends at your elbows.

Some designers create veils that specifically match the wedding dress. The veil may contain a bit of the lace or beading from the dress, which really completes the whole look. Ask your consultant at the dress shop if this is the case with your dress, or if the designer would be willing to make a matching veil for you. You can also purchase beautiful veils separately.

Fingertip: A mid-length veil—the end reaches your fingertips when your hands are at your sides.

Fountain: A style that poufs a bit at the top of the head, then cascades down to the elbows or shoulders.

Flyaway: A dramatic veil made of multiple layers of tulle, which ends at the shoulders.

Mantilla: A lacy veil that frames the face— a simple comb is all that's used to hold it in place.

BRIDESMAID STYLE

HOW TO PICK DRESSES THAT PLEASE YOUR ENTIRE PARTY

Unless your wedding party is made up of a set of identical twins (with identical taste), odds are your bridesmaids will have different body shapes, different complexions and very different senses of style. So, how do you make your whole crowd happy? Take our advice:

Choose a dress that'll be easy for them to find. If your bridesmaids are scattered around the country, try to find a dress at a national chain so all of your attendants can try the dress on before they buy.

Don't feel like you're limited to one dress style. These days, it's common for members of the wedding party to sport different looks—and many fashion designers offer separates within a color scheme, so bridesmaids can mix and match skirts and tops to create looks that suit their styles and their bodies. But even if you don't go the separates route, you could simply

pick a hue or a fabric and have your bridesmaids shop for their own dress or have one designed for them.

Consider different colors. Some dress their maids and matrons of honor in one shade, and the rest of the bridal party in another. Others pick two coordinating shades (pink and chocolate brown, for example), and let their bridesmaids decide which hue suits them best.

Keep the price down. Your friends may be just as financially strapped as you are these days, so an ensemble that costs as much as their monthly rent is obviously not going to be a crowd pleaser.

Consider contributing toward their look. Some brides chip in toward the bridesmaids' dresses as part of their thank-you gift, while others opt to give their friends chic accessories—necklaces, handbags, wraps—to finish off the ensemble.

Dressing Mom

Sometimes, finding perfect dresses for the mothers in the wedding party can be tougher than outfitting the bridesmaids. Mothers want to look special, without overshadowing the rest of the wedding party—or stepping on each other's toes by wearing a similar color or style.

● Give the mothers a heads-up on the color scheme for the bridal party before they hit the stores. That way, they can choose a color that'll complement what the rest of the VIPs are wearing. If there are certain hues you don't want them to wear (no ivory or white, for instance), let them know before they order their dresses.

● Make sure they know how formal you're going. Are you envisioning them in long, beaded gowns or stylish sundresses? Help them know what sort of fashion statement to make.

● Suggest separates. These have become really popular, especially dresses with a wrap or jacket, which can be worn for the ceremony then ditched for dancing. Another bonus? Your mom may be able to rewear the skirt or jacket with more casual pieces after the big day.

● Be sure the moms discuss their dress selections. They may want to choose complementary colors. They will also want to avoid looking too similar.

From Here to Maternity

TIPS ON BEING STYLISHLY PREGNANT AT THE WEDDING

If you're still deciding on a dress when you discover you're pregnant (or a bridesmaid finds out her own happy news), you'll need to factor the pregnancy into your choice. Empire-waist gowns tend to be a comfortable option for expectant moms, and their looser fit over the waist make them easier to alter for an expanding belly. You could also look for more forgiving fabrics, like chiffon, instead of stiff, not-so-stretchy satin. For your attendants, you might opt for separates, so your expectant bridesmaid can choose a pregnancy-friendly silhouette and your other friends can opt for something slinkier, or let her wear a different dress than the rest of the party.

If you or your 'maid learn of the pregnancy after the dress has already been ordered, call the salon to see what can be done. They may be able to order extra fabric for alterations, or change the dress to a larger size.

When the dress arrives, ask the salon to schedule fittings as close to the wedding date as possible to ensure that the gown fits nicely on the big day.

Bride to Bride

I was seven months pregnant when I got married and my size-11 feet had grown noticeably larger. I spent weeks looking for shoes that didn't hurt and actually managed to find two pretty, inexpensive pairs. But on my wedding day my feet were so swollen, I had to go barefoot for the service. And then I wore Pumas for the after-dinner dancing. —Molly

Q & A

Q **I've put on some weight since my first dress fitting. When I went in for my second, the dress was too tight. Can I plan on losing the weight before my final fitting, or should I have the dress let out?**

A Depending on how much time you have before the final fitting, which is usually somewhere between 3 and 10 days before the wedding, you should be able to calculate if you have the time to trim. It's safe to lose about a pound per week. To help the process along, scale down your portion sizes; limit your intake of fatty foods; and sneak in lots of exercise (take the stairs, park in the farthest spot from the store, etc). If you fall short of your weight-loss goal, fret not. Most dresses will accommodate a five-pound weight gain. If you end up having to let the dress out, go back to your fitter or find a reputable seamstress. And in the days leading up to the wedding, avoid eating foods that'll make you feel bloated—which is basically anything with a high salt content, such as pretzels, chips, hearts of palm, soy sauce and sandwich meats.

Q **Is it okay to go strapless in the dead of winter?**

A Although a winter wedding might have some bearing on your ceremony site and reception locale, you don't have to let it affect your dress choice. If you love the look of a strapless dress, then go for it. Just make sure that you're prepared for the elements. If you'll be exposed to the frosty temperatures while darting from your limo to the ceremony and reception, you should be okay with only a shawl or shrug. However, if you suspect that you'll be outside for a longer period of time (perhaps a receiving line will take place on the church steps), think about a cozy stole or a matching satin overcoat to keep you a bit warmer. Do you have your heart set on a photo shoot outside in a magical winter wonderland? Okay, now you might want to rethink the dress. Photographs always take longer than you expect and if you're shivering and miserable, your pictures will certainly show it. So before you finalize your dress choice, remember that you'll be in this getup for most of the day. As long as you're sure you'll be comfortable, anything goes.

Q **I've always wanted a wedding dress with a full, flowing skirt and a long train, but I also want to be able to dance. I'm worried that the dress will be too heavy. Should I change into something else for the reception?**

A Lots of designers are making voluminous dresses out of lightweight material such as tulle and chiffon, which are easy to move in. But assuming that your budget allows, changing into a second dress is definitely an option, and one that's become increasingly popular. You might also want to consider a two-piece ensemble comprised of a top and a skirt. This is another big trend among designers, and could give you a little more freedom when you hit the dance floor.

Q **I want my wedding dress to be a color other than white. My mother, a traditionalist, is having a fit about this. She's the one footing the bill, so how can I make her understand that times have changed?**

A Start by arming yourself with the facts. Tell your mom that colorful dresses are a truly hot trend in bridalwear. In addition to being quite fashionable, colorful dresses can also be very meaningful. Yes, white represents purity, but so does blue. All the other colors of the rainbow have their own significance, too. For example, purple symbolizes spirituality, and yellow represents joy and happiness. You may even be drawn to a color because it makes you feel great, or it has something special to do with your relationship with your fiancé (it's the color of the blouse you wore when you first met or the exact shade of pink of the first roses he sent you). After you explain your desire for color, offer to take your mom out dress-shopping

with you. She may need to see for herself just how beautiful colorful wedding dresses are.

Q **I just ordered my wedding dress and the salesclerk said it would take six months to arrive. Why so long?**

A Every bridal salon's time frame for dress delivery is different. In fact, some places can take as long as eight to 12 months to deliver a dress. But for the most part, four to six months is the average waiting period you should expect. The time it takes for your dress to arrive depends on several factors. In some cases, you can walk into a bridal store and buy a dress right off the rack. It's more common, however, that the bridal salons you visit will carry only samples of dresses (solely for try-on purposes) and the manufacturer will ship your gown to the store. As long as the manufacturer has your size in stock, your order should take no more than a month to arrive. But if a manufacturer has a backlog of orders, you might be looking at roughly two months. When a bridal salon quotes an even longer period of time for your dress to arrive (say, four to six months), it could be because the gown might have to be custom-made. If that's the case, your measurements will be taken at the time that you place your order and then the manufacturer will make your

dress according to your specific size and shape. Another cause for delay: if the dress you have chosen has intricate details that need to be done by hand, such as beading or embroidery. And finally, if your dress manufacturer is not based in the United States, your gorgeous gown might need to cross an ocean before it gets to you.

Q **What are some things I might do with my wedding dress if I decide not to preserve it?**

A If you hate to think of your dress gathering dust in the back of your closet, gather up your courage and do something radical: Give your dress a second life with the help of a seamstress. Depending on the style, you might have it dyed and cropped into a short party dress. Some brides use their dresses to make christening gowns for their first baby. Others have turned some of the material into a quilt or made decorative pillows with the fabric. You could even create a table runner. Less sentimental brides might choose to sell their gown. There are many online shops that allow you to do this. Would you prefer to donate your dress? An organization in New York City called The Bridal Garden accepts gown donations and resells the dresses; the proceeds benefit disadvantaged children.

CHAPTER 5

Get Gorgeous

**HOW TO GET FIT
AND FABULOUS
FOR THE BIG DAY**

Perfect, glowing skin is the obvious goal for brides. To achieve this, start pampering and prepping well before the big day.

Beauty *Countdown*

YOUR 9-MONTH PLAN TO GET GLOWING

6 TO 9 MONTHS BEFORE

Keep your hair in shape. Book a series of monthly haircuts and conditioning treatments.

Start your research. Ask friends and family members—and your hairstylist—for suggestions for wedding-day makeup artists.

Keep your skin flawless. Schedule monthly facials, microdermabrasion treatments or glycolic peels at a spa or with a dermatologist.

Flaunt that ring hand. Start getting weekly manicures, with a pedicure every third treatment.

Get in shape. Consult your doctor for the go-ahead to begin your diet and exercise regimen.

4 TO 6 MONTHS BEFORE

Book 'em. Schedule your big-day hair appointment, plus a trial run two months before.

Try it out. Once you've narrowed the field to two makeup experts, have them each do your makeup on a day when you'll be particularly busy afterward, so you can see how their makeup stands up when you're active.

Get motivated. If your workouts are starting to wane, schedule some time with a personal trainer. (Three sessions a week should guarantee results.)

Stay sleek. Start getting monthly waxings or more permanent (and costly) laser hair removal.

Tame your brows. Have them shaped by a pro once a month.

2 TO 4 MONTHS BEFORE

Do a dry run. Bring your headpiece to the salon for a trial run with your stylist. Also bring a photo of your dress and wear a similar neckline so you can get the best sense of whether that style works for you.

4 TO 5 DAYS BEFORE

Show your glow. Get your final facial and treatment.

Care for your hair. Apply a deep-conditioning treatment.

1 DAY BEFORE

Stay polished. Get your last manicure and pedicure.

WEDDING DAY

Get gorgeous. Your only task? Have your hair and makeup done.

Great Styles

How should you wear your hair? Up, down or in between? Here are some guidelines that may help you choose.

● When hair is up, it can give an instant lift to your features: Your cheekbones look higher, your neck seems longer and your eyes look more open.

● Brides with oval faces are the best candidates for an updo that sweeps hair completely off the face. If your face is round, you, too, can pull off this classic look, as long as you add some height at the crown.

● The perfect accent for a tall updo? A simple, sweet tiara. Or try wearing a headband tucked into the base of your updo at the crown.

● Half-up, half-down is the perfect solution if you don't want to call attention to a jawline that's less than well defined. This alternative gives you the illusion—and glamour—of putting your hair up and the softer, face-framing flattery of longer hair.

● You can't go wrong with the classic French twist. It's great for all hair types. The one exception: very layered hair. The short layers won't blend into the twist.

MODERN 5 BRIDE

Unique Hair Adornments

Tiaras and veils are always stylish, but if you're looking for a twist on the traditional, consider one of these options.

Flowers: Whether you opt for silk or real blooms, a whole wreath or single bold flower, it's a romantic choice.

A necklace: Give a favorite heirloom or dramatic jewelry a new assignment—a necklace can be pinned into an updo or used as a headband if you wear your hair down.

Natural adornments: Shells, feathers or even seed pods can dress up your tresses.

A hat: A staple at English weddings, hats are a fun alternative to a veil and look great with a sleeker wedding dress.

Ribbons: A beautiful piece of ribbon can be braided into your hair or used as a headband.

{expert tip} With a strapless dress, a low chignon is gorgeous, and years from now it won't look dated in photos. —*Frédéric Fekkai, hairstylist, New York City*

All it takes is a small crystal hairpin to turn an updo from simple to special.

BUN

Hair is gathered and pinned on the back of the head, either at the nape of your neck or at the crown.

CHIGNON

Hair is woven into a knot, worn low on your head.

FINGER CURLS

Gentle, rippling waves are set when the hair is damp, then dried to hold the style.

Wedding Words

LEARN TO SPEAK YOUR STYLIST'S LANGUAGE

FALL

A fall is a hairpiece that's pinned in to help you create extra fullness for a particular style.

EXTENSIONS

You can get long tresses in a flash with this process, which weaves human or faux hair into your existing hair.

HIGHLIGHTS

Small sections of hair are chemically lightened to mimic the brightening effects of sunlight. If you're going for an updo, be sure your stylist gives you highlights underneath as well.

FLAT IRON

You can straighten the waves and get rid of frizz with this appliance—two hot metal plates that you run your hair between.

FRENCH TWIST

Hair is rolled into a twist along the back of your head, then pinned into place.

LOWLIGHTS

The opposite of highlights: Small strips of hair are darkened chemically to add richness and depth to the hair.

The Art of the Run-Through

THESE TIPS WILL GET YOU THE LOOK YOU'RE GOING FOR

1 FIND A STYLIST AT LEAST SIX MONTHS BEFORE YOUR BIG DAY. You'll want time to go for a few complimentary consultations until you find the right person. Then stick with her as you get your hair in shape with regular trims and color.

2 SHOW THE STYLIST HOW YOU NORMALLY STYLE YOURSELF. At your wedding, you likely want to look like the best version of you, not a completely different person altogether. If you're an all-natural, no-makeup kind of girl, for example, tell your stylist so she doesn't go overboard.

3 BRING ALONG SWATCHES AND PHOTOS. Your wedding ensemble will factor into your styling—if you're carrying a bold-hued bouquet, you may want your makeup artist to make the hues a little stronger; if you're wearing a ball gown, your hairstyle may need to be more dramatic to balance it out.

4 DECIDE WHERE THE SERVICES WILL BE DONE. Some brides like the idea of heading out to the salon on their big day, while others consider at-home or on-site styling more relaxing. Make sure the stylist you choose will work where you want.

5 TAKE A TEST DRIVE. Do it on a particularly busy day, so you can see how the hair and makeup stand up to a lot of activity—after all, this hairdo will need to last through a long day of mixing and mingling.

6 DON'T FORGET THE PROPS. When scheduling a visit to your stylist for a hair trial, remember to bring any accessories you plan to incorporate into your hairstyle. It'll be much easier to envision your wedding-day looks if you're able to see how your tiara, veil or hair combs can be worked into your style.

Skincare Essentials

Be good to your body. Work from the inside out for glowing skin: A healthy diet, a good night's sleep and regular exercise can keep your skin in shape.
Slather on sunscreen. Don't leave home without layering on a little sun protection to prevent premature aging and lower your risk of skin cancer. SPF 15 is perfect for everyday wear, but you'll want to go for the bigger guns—at least an SPF 30—for a day at the beach.
Visit the doctor. A dermatologist can help with any skin problems you're facing: acne, dark spots, wrinkles or spider veins.
Keep it clean. Get rid of daily dirt and grime before you hit the sack—use a gentle cleanser on your face, as harsh scrubs could irritate your skin.
Attack acne. A low-cut dress might put the spotlight on below-the-neck breakouts. To keep skin clear, use a body wash with antibacterial agents like salicylic acid or benzoyl peroxide.
Perk up pale skin. A sunless tanner can provide the perfect contrast to a white dress—and make ripples and dimples less obvious.

{expert tip}

Spa facials are adequate for those with problem-free skin. But if you're breakout-prone, it's better to get a facial from a dermatologist, since we can do so much more, such as deeper peels using glycolic acids or topical antibiotics to clear up acne.

—Debra Jaliman, M.D.,
dermatologist, New York City

Makeup 101

YOUR GUIDE TO LOOKING GREAT ON THE WEDDING DAY

1. **Start with a primer or moisturizer.** Foundation on bare skin will start to settle into the creases and look splotchy before the day is through.

2. **Mask any imperfections.** Apply concealer to camouflage dark circles and blemishes. The concealer should be a shade lighter than your foundation color to help it mask the darker skin beneath.

3. **Find the right hue.** Foundation should match the skin between your cheekbone and jaw—when you're testing them, look for a shade that seems to disappear into your skin. Apply foundation with a light hand, only where you need it to even out your coloring—otherwise, it'll start to look like a mask.

4. **Focus on one feature.** Don't do strong eyes with bold lips—choose one to highlight, and go for the drama there.

5. **Give your lipcolor staying power.** Start by filling in your lip with pencil in the same hue as your lipstick, then apply the lipstick, blot, and reapply.

6. **Smearproof your eye makeup.** Waterproof mascara is a must, in case you tear up during your vows. Powder shadows and liners will last for hours.

7. **Be a blushing bride.** Apply a rosy or bronzy hue to the apples of the cheeks to enhance your bridal glow. Apply a cream blush first to give the powder something to adhere to.

8. **Wear long-lasting formulas.** Lipsticks and glosses with a bit of shimmer tend to last longer than matte products. Choose a shade with a subtle shimmer for the most flattering look.

9. **Don't forget to exfoliate.** Help minimize fine lines and even out skin tone by getting a professional micro-dermabrasion treatment. For the best

results, schedule a series of four to six biweekly treatments.

10. **Get eyes that pop.** Use a sky blue or white eyeliner to line the inner rim of your lower eyelid. This evens out any redness and helps the whites of your eyes look even brighter.

11. **Camoflauge a blemish.** Reduce swelling by holding an ice cube on the spot. Minimize redness by dabbing the area with eye drops.

12. **Refuse to shine.** Carry a package of facial blotting tissues in your wedding-day kit, to absorb oil throughout the day.

13. **Blend, please.** Your décolletage is usually a shade or two lighter than of your face, so even out your color by dusting bronzing powder over your neck and chest. (Take care to avoid your dress.)

14. **Get camera-ready.** If you're planning to take black-and-white photos, wear a lipstick or gloss in a flattering pink or neutral shade. Too-dark hues can look black in your pictures.

15. **Keep your brows in check.** Have them professionally shaped, and on your wedding day, apply a swipe of eyebrow mascara for a flawless finish.

{modern bride wisdom}

For supersoft lips, gently exfoliate with a facial scrub to remove dry cells, and then apply a moisturizing lip-care treatment.

Wedding-Day Beauty Bag

PACK THESE ESSENTIALS TO HELP YOU STAY GORGEOUS ALL DAY LONG

- lipgloss (to reapply for color and shine)
- concealer (to hide any blemishes or undereye circles)
- powder (to ensure a matte finish)
- fragrance (to freshen up)
- blotting papers (to remove excess oil and eliminate shine)
- travel-sized hair spray or antifrizz spray (to reapply as needed)
- bobby pins, clips or elastics (to help a sagging updo)

- hem tape and safety pins (to shore up any snags in wedding attire)
- stain remover wipes (to remove any smudges from your attire)
- dental floss
- clear nail polish (to fix chips; also stops panty-hose runs)
- nail file and clippers, tweezers
- tampons and panty-liners
- breath mints

—*Danna Weiss, celebrity stylist, New York City*

{expert tips}

To retouch lipstick, wipe off the first layer completely and start over, rather than just adding another layer— that never really works.

—*Charlie Green, makeup artist, New York City*

For dense, dramatic eyelashes, wiggle the mascara brush at the base of your lashes, then sweep it upward. This deposits more color at the base, which in turn helps make eyelashes look thicker.

—*Alison Raffaele, makeup artist, New York City*

When it comes to shimmer, follow the "rule of two" to avoid overload: Add shine to face and eyes, face and lips or eyes and lips; never face, eyes and lips.

—*Bobbi Brown, makeup artist, New York City*

The Nail Files

GET YOUR TIPS IN TOP SHAPE

For your wedding-day manicure, choose a classic shade that complements the rest of your wedding details and ensemble—a soft pink if you're carrying a pastel bouquet, for example, or a deep red for a wedding with a bolder color palette. To start getting your nails in their best form, begin to schedule regular manicures at least six months before your wedding. During this time, you can also start to test different shades, so you have an idea of what will and won't work on your wedding day. If you plan to marry in the spring or summer, a neutral shade looks great on long nails and will last longer, since chips won't be as visible. If you're having a fall or winter wedding, a dark, sultry red or brown is perfect on shorter, square-shaped tips. For a fun take on the classic French manicure, choose a reverse French (the darker hue goes on the tip, while the base of the nail is neutral).

Remember to protect your hands by wearing gloves while outside in cold weather, and use rubber gloves while you're cleaning or washing dishes, to prevent your nails from chipping and your skin from the chapping that detergents can cause. Keeping your hands well moisturized is also a must, so stash hand lotion in your desk at work, near your kitchen sink and in your purse, and apply it periodically to keep your hands feeling soft. And the last piece of advice: Apply a fortifying, clear top coat a few times a week to help your nails stay strong and your manicure look fresh.

Some brides like to choose their wedding-day nail color to complement their bouquet.

10 Ways to Burn 100 Calories

PICK YOUR FAVORITE ACTIVITY AND GO!

Walk 1.25 miles in 20 minutes

Bicycle 2.5 miles in 15 minutes

Perform low-impact aerobics for 20 minutes

Dance for 15 minutes

Run 1 mile in 10 minutes

Jump rope for 15 minutes

Bowl for 30 minutes

Do yoga for 30 minutes

Clean the house for 30 minutes

Swim freestyle 25 yards per minute for 25 minutes

Note: *Calculations are based on a 140-pound woman*

The Wedding Workout Plan

Your wedding day will be here before you know it, and you're ready to jump headfirst into your new diet and workout routine. Here are some smart tips to help you stay on track and in charge of your fitness progress.

Recruit a buddy. Sharing your workout goals and plans with a friend will keep you motivated and excited to get to the gym. Meet your sister for a yoga class, or go on an hour-long hike with your fiancé. You'll be able to fit in quality time while sticking to your new plan.

Put it in your calendar. Schedule gym sessions the same way you would schedule a meeting or a lunch with friends. You've heard it before, but it works: By carving out a specific time frame to devote to exercise and getting another person involved, you'll be less likely to cancel a workout.

Stay hydrated. Have at least eight glasses of water every day. This will really help you fight candy-bar cravings by keeping you feeling full, and will also help reduce bloating.

Energize at snack time. On the days you work out, eat a healthy combo of protein and carbohydrates (such as half a banana) before you exercise. This will sustain your energy level throughout your pre-wedding training.

Vary your workouts. To continue to see results, add more strengthening moves, complete an extra set of biceps curls or hike a new trail. You'll also keep it fun and challenging.

Look out for diet traps. There is a significant amount of calories in the places you least expect them, such as vitamin-fortified waters, condiments and some "diet" snacks. Opt for sparkling water and low-cal spreads like mustard and salsa, and munch on fruits and veggies instead.

Always ask for a doggie bag. Most restaurant portions are huge, so don't scarf down the entire entrée—save half to enjoy for lunch the next day.

Keep a healthy balance. While at the gym, spend time on weight lifting as well as your cardio routine. Incorporating strength training will build muscle that burns fat fast.

Guilt-free Snacks

ENJOY—EACH IS 100 CALORIES OR FEWER

1 small banana

4 Hershey's kisses

2 breadsticks

10 regular potato chips (or 20 soy chips)

33 grapes

3 graham-cracker squares

2 oz. low-fat cheese

3 cups air-popped popcorn

1 small cappuccino made with fat-free milk

1 Jell-O fat-free pudding snack

1 medium apple

2 clementines

12 reduced-fat Wheat Thins

15 mini pretzels

24 baby carrots

10 dried apricot halves

9 animal crackers

25 pistachio nuts

{expert tip} You've got to fit workouts into your schedule, even if they're abbreviated. Doing something is always better than doing nothing. —*David Kirsch, wellness trainer, New York City*

Q & A

Q **Are there any special rules I should follow when I do my makeup for photographs?**

A Yes. Remember that moderation is a must. Your goal should be to look, as the saying goes, like you, only better. Use a lightweight foundation or tinted moisturizer for coverage that leaves skin looking healthy. Also, applying a bit of highlighter under your brows will make your eyes pop. Although shimmer can be pretty, as it adds another dimension to makeup, be careful to avoid harsh, frosty colors or bright glitter. When it comes to lip gloss, natural shades of pink and beige are flattering to all complexions, but beware of extra-shiny formulas that may reflect way too much on film. Finish off your camera-ready look with a light dusting of loose powder down the center of your face, which will keep shine at bay. And, to avoid the pale-face/dark-neck contrast that often occurs with flash photography, remember to apply the same loose powder onto your neck and chest as well.

Q **I'm madly trying to grow out my hair for an updo. How fast will it grow?**

A Unfortunately, our locks don't grow as fast as we'd like them to: The average growth rate is one-half inch per month. Although certain hair lessons have been ingrained in us since we were teenagers—like getting regular trims every month to avoid split ends—it's okay to break the rules just a bit when your wedding date is rapidly approaching. Instead of frequently getting a complete cut, cheat a little by keeping the front of your hair, like your bangs and side sections, looking good with regular trims, while letting the rest of your hair grow out as much as possible. Be sure that you're also getting enough vitamins and nutrients in your diet, since a vitamin deficiency can easily stunt the growth of your hair. Also, asking your stylist for a hot-oil treatment or deep-conditioning mask will help to protect the hair's shaft against damage while leaving it looking fuller and healthier.

Q **How can I prevent a breakout before the wedding?**

A Keeping your pores clear is the key to staying blemish-free for your wedding. To do so, try exfoliating at home with a scrub or use a moisturizer with alpha hydroxy acid (AHA) after washing your face. Be sure to look for a lotion that contains 12 percent AHA. A deep-cleaning, pore-refining mask will also help keep breakouts under control. If you'd like to take your pre-wedding exfoliation to the next level, you can try professional microdermabrasion, which can be done by a doctor or spa aesthetician. During your treatment, ultrafine crystals (made of either aluminum or salt) are sprayed over the face, then sucked away along with any pore-clogging debris your skin may have been harboring. You'll see the best results by scheduling weekly treatments two or three months before the big day. Don't be surprised if your skin is a little more prone to breakouts during the wedding-planning process. Stress causes the body to produce androgens—male hormones that increase sebum production, which in turn clogs pores. Visit your dermatologist, and if androgens are to blame for your recent flare-ups, your doctor can prescribe an orally administered antiandrogen, which will cut down on oily-skin woes.

Q **I'm having my hair blown out the day before the wedding. How can I maintain the sleekness?**

A For starters, take a small umbrella with you to the salon and stick a loose-fitting baseball cap in your tote in case you get caught in the rain. It's easy to forget about hair care once you're back home, but be vigilant about indoor humidity: Turn on the air conditioner, clip your hair back when washing your face and be sure to use a hair tie that's soft so that your freshly styled tresses will stay dent-free. Take a bath—a quick one—instead of standing under a shower, then leave the humid area quickly to towel off. At bedtime, use a smooth pillowcase

made of satin or cotton sateen instead of one that's flannel or cotton. On the morning of your wedding, running a flat iron over sections of your hair can restore some sleekness if necessary. Also, make sure you're prepared to create a Plan B style in case the weather doesn't cooperate, such as an easy updo fastened with a couple of bejeweled hairpins.

Q **My fiancé and I want to lose weight before the big day. Is there a diet and exercise plan we can do together?**

A Teaming up is smart—not only will your workouts be fun, but you'll stay motivated to maintain a long-term fitness regimen. Don't worry about finding a special couples' fitness program; you two can do the same workout but lift different amounts of weight. Also, if you're not at the same fitness level—you're a sprinter, he's a walker—it's a good idea to hit up your local gym. This way you're able to go at a pace that's comfortable for you, while still getting in quality time together. For your diet, you should both aim to eat low-fat, healthy foods, such as fresh fruits and veggies, chicken, fish and whole-grain carbs like brown rice. Although you'll be working out at the same time and eating the same foods, you probably shouldn't eat the same amounts. If you're smaller than your fiancé, you won't need as

big a portion as he does to stay full. Pencil in your workout "dates" on your calendar, and challenge each other to meet your fitness goals. Make it interesting by placing a bet on who can reach their goal weight fastest—the loser has to cook (healthy) meals for the winner for a week!

Q **When I get home from the gym, I'm so hungry that I wind up blowing my diet. What can I eat before and after working out that's filling and energizing?**

A Make sure that your body is properly fueled for your cardio and weight-lifting sessions, which should be done on alternate days to avoid fatigue. When doing cardio—regardless of the activity—be sure to drink a glass of water an hour before your workout so that you stay properly hydrated. On the days you also strength-train, munch on a healthy snack (such as a handful of almonds) between your cardio and weight-training sessions to help sustain your energy level through your workout. After you're finished training, eat a small meal with a balance of protein and complex carbohydrates, such as oatmeal and egg whites in the morning, or roast turkey with brown rice at night. Doing this will help your body rebuild itself after an invigorating workout and keep you energized so you won't be tempted to reach for a candy bar.

CHAPTER 6

Select Your Registry

**EVERYTHING YOU NEED TO KNOW ABOUT
THE GIFTS YOU'LL WANT TO RECEIVE**

When it comes to registry, the more you know, the more successful you'll be with your choices. Here you'll discover the difference between fine china and everyday dishes, between cookware and ovenware. You'll learn how to choose the best linens, kitchen electrics, and more. When you've finished this chapter, you'll have an ideal list of gifts.

All About Registering

HOW TO HAVE FUN SETTING UP YOUR GIFT LIST

Registering can be a really cool thing: You and your fiancé get to wander around your favorite stores, choosing the items you'll want your loved ones to buy for you to use in your new home. What's less cool is the confusion that often accompanies the process. It's easy to get overwhelmed, especially if you focus on the idea that every item you choose will likely be with you for years to come. So do your research about what you really need, and what the differences are between any given products.

Before you register, you and your fiancé should take stock of what you already own. If you don't live together yet, you could have a lot of doubles. Once you see what you have, what's staying and what needs an upgrade, take our Registry Checklist (see page 250) and start crossing off items you don't need.

Now it's time to make a preliminary sweep through the stores you've targeted. We recommend registering at three places. Start with a large, general department store that has everything—and several nationwide locations to give guests the option of going to the store rather than shopping online. Next, consider a store that has cool stuff for decorating your home so you can get some unique pieces that reflect your and your fiancé's personalities. You could also try a specialty store that caters to a hobby or passion you two share.

During your run-through, you'll have a chance to eyeball some options and hammer out any differences in opinion (gold- or platinum-rimmed china, floral sheets or solids, etc.). After you scout out the goods, sign up for them online or make appointments, spacing them days apart (registering is fun, but not if you do it all at once). As you and your fiancé finish at each store, get a printout of your completed registry and look it over at home, in case he snuck in a Lawn Boy or home-theater package without discussing it with you first.

Fine Dinnerware

Most brides are interested in registering for fine china—it's perfect for holidays and formal meals as well as everyday use. Fine china, which has been treasured over the years for its elegance and beauty, can be used on special occasions, but what many people don't know is that it is strong and durable enough for everyday use.

Porcelain (aka fine china) has been produced in the Orient since the earliest periods of civilization and wasn't made in Europe until slightly more than 200 years ago. It's called *china* in honor of those who first made it. The ultimate in dinnerware, china is made from a combination of elements—kaolin, quartz and feldspar—which produces a fine quality clay. It is very hard and extremely durable. Fine china becomes fully vitrified—which means glasslike—because it is fired in a kiln at very high temperatures so that it becomes nonporous, hard and smooth. Truly fine china is translucent: If you hold a dinner plate up to the light and pass your hand behind it, you will see your hand's shadow. This translucency is treasured.

Bone china is porcelain made even harder by the addition of animal ash, mostly ox bone, which has been ground into a fine powder. This also gives the clay a greater whiteness, its most important quality.

Fine dinnerware prices are quoted in five-piece place settings that include one of each of the following: dinner, salad and bread-and-butter plates, and a cup and saucer. This is usually the easiest and most economical way to purchase your china. "Open stock" refers to individual pieces, so you can customize what you decide to buy, or add pieces to your set later.

Everyday Dinnerware

Everyday dinnerware is made from the same clay as fine china, but three things set it apart: the clays used to make earthenware are less fine (so it's always opaque); the ware is fired at lower temperatures, which makes it more porous (and therefore less strong); and the final product is heavier than porcelain. Casual dinnerware is sturdy and always dishwasher-safe, a real plus for newlyweds.

It falls into two categories: ceramics and nonceramics. With ceramics, there's stoneware, the connecting link between earthenware and china. It looks like the former, but because of the high firing temperature and composition of the clays, its

{expert tip} Use your registry to acquire practical objects. Ask for things you will use seven days a week, not just fancy crystal you'll store away. —*Nate Berkus, decorator, Chicago*

strength and durability are much closer to that of china. There's also earthenware, the general term used for casual dinnerware made from less refined clays. It's fired at much lower temperatures than other casual ceramics, which makes it possible to get strong, rich colors. It is not as durable as stoneware or porcelain. Ironstone is a stronger, finer kind of earthenware, made with purer clays and fired at a higher temperature.

Finally, there's terra-cotta, which means "baked earth." It has a low-fired red-clay body when unglazed (picture a flower pot), although a top glaze is usually added to make it nonabsorbent, durable and resistant to wear and breakage.

Nonceramic dishes are made of glass (which is usually inexpensive, not generally purchased in place settings, and often heat-resistant) or finer cut crystal or art glass. These are typically much more expensive.

Everyday dinnerware is sold in either a four-piece or five-piece place setting, depending on what pieces have been made—sometimes a mug is substituted for a cup and saucer, for example. Sets of 16 and 20 pieces are also very common. Don't forget to register for other pieces, such as serving bowls, platters, salt and pepper shakers, a sugar bowl and more.

Stemware

Stemware is most often used for entertaining, though you'll certainly get more use out of it if you and your fiancé regularly enjoy wine with dinner. All glass is made from humble materials—sand, lead, lime, soda, potash and manganese—which are heated together in a furnace, with bits of broken glass added to help the melting process. It's what's done with the molten materials next that affects the finished product's quality and price.

Crystal, strictly speaking, is no different from glass. The term is usually used to refer to all fine glassware. Lead is added to some glass, which gives it more weight, increases its resilience and adds brilliant sparkle. (Full-lead crystal contains at least 24 percent lead oxide.) The cost of fine glassware can be attributed to the materials and the extensive handwork that go into each glass.

Wineware has a specific glass for every category of wine, and the shapes really do bring out the special properties

(or the body) and bouquet (the fragrance) of each type.

A red wineglass has a large, generously shaped bowl to project the wine's bouquet. A balloon wineglass is a full-bodied, all-purpose wineglass that is larger than a standard red wineglass. A white wineglass is smaller in both height and capacity size because chilled whites don't need as much breathing room. A hock wineglass, for white Rhine wines, is usually taller than a regular wineglass, with a squat bowl. A champagne glass has a flute- or saucer-shape bowl made to keep the bubbles effervescing for a much longer period than other shapes.

Barware

Unless you've taken a mixology course, chances are you're not entirely sure which glass is used with which type of drink. Highballs/tumblers, the biggest of the barware glasses, come in assorted shapes and sizes with a

capacity that ranges from 10 to 16 ounces. They can be used for everything from a glass of soda or iced tea to a tall vodka tonic. Double old-fashioneds, shorter and squatter than the highball, have about a 10- to 14-ounce capacity. They are usually used for on-the-rocks beverages. Pilsners are the perfect glass from which to drink a fresh, foamy beer. This footed, V-shaped glass usually holds 10 to 12 ounces. Martini glasses are stemmed with a flared bowl, and can also be used for other cocktails, like cosmopolitans, gimlets and more. Brandy glasses traditionally have a distinctive short-stemmed, chubby shape so the drinker can warm the brandy with his hand and savor its aroma. Sherry and port glasses are basically smaller versions of wineglasses. The average capacity is 1 to 2 ounces, and they can also be used for liqueurs and cordials. Pitchers can serve water or even hold enough martinis for a dinner party. Decanters are used for serving wine, aperitifs, cordials or other after-dinner drinks.

Most fine barware is sold by the glass, although you

will occasionally see sets of two or four. Because they're often fragile, and it's not unheard of for a pattern to be discontinued, it's best to register for eight of each type of glass.

In addition to glasses, you'll want to check out bar accessories. Consider a strainer, which is available in many shapes and sizes to fit different glasses. It's used to separate the ice from the drink when pouring, as you would when making a martini. Double-ended jiggers are used to measure alcohol. The large end holds 1½ ounces; the small end, 1 ounce. Then you've got cocktail shakers, used for martinis, cosmopolitans and other retro cocktails, which are so popular today. When serving guests, up the style quotient with pretty cocktail napkins and stirrers made of glass, silver or stainless steel. Finally, ice buckets are must-haves for parties; look for one that's insulated and big enough to get through an entire evening of cocktails without a refill. (And don't forget a set of tongs, to keep your hands out of the ice bucket.)

Flatware

Ask any couple who's registered and they'll tell you that choosing flatware is a surprisingly big deal. Odds are good that you'll use it more regularly than any other item on your list.

People frequently apply the term *silverware* to any utensil used for eating and serving. But actually there are three major materials to consider.

Sterling silver flatware is made of 92.5 percent pure silver and 7.5 percent base metals (pure silver is too soft to use on its own). Usually copper is added to give strength and hardness. The use of the word *sterling* is governed by law, so only silver articles containing the required amount of this metal are marked sterling.

You can think of silverplate as silver that is only skin deep. Under the surface is a base metal (usually an alloy of nickel, copper and zinc, or sometimes just nickel or copper). The quality, and therefore the cost, of silverplate depends on the amount of silver that's actually used (measured in microns of weight); the type and the thickness of the base metal; and the size, design and decoration of the piece.

Stainless is an alloy of iron, chromium and nickel, and comes in several grades. The term 18/8 means 18 percent chromium and 8 percent nickel have been added to the basic alloy. The indication 18/10 means that 2 percent more nickel was added to give the steel an even richer luster. Although stainless is generally the least-expensive flatware choice, there are also a variety of high-design and high-style stainless patterns available, which can cost more than some silverplate.

Prices for sterling flatware are usually quoted for a five-piece place setting, which generally includes a teaspoon, place spoon, salad fork, knife and fork. Sterling and most silverplate can also be purchased as individual pieces, which is called "open stock." Stainless, from the finest to the least expensive, is generally purchased in 20-piece-or-larger sets. Many mass-market brands offer 45-piece sets, too, which often include extras, such as serving pieces. Finer stainless steel, which is usually more expensive because it is highly designed, is most commonly sold in five-piece table settings.

Once you've picked a pattern, think about the serving pieces, of which there are many types. Serving spoons are extremely useful pieces, so you may want to register for two. Use them for vegetables, salads, desserts—even sauces. Pierced spoons are also handy; they're perfect for any fruit or vegetable served with liquid. A gravy ladle is used for gravies or dressings. The sauce ladle is a smaller version and is great for fruit sauces and vinaigrettes. Fish servers come in pairs: a fork and knife with broad, flat surfaces used for deboning and serving. Cake/pie servers have a flat surface that can handily dispatch desserts.

The list goes on: Cheese knives are used for cheeses both hard and soft; the pointed end is meant to pick up slices of harder cheese. Cold-meat forks serve sliced meats and chops, and lettuce and tomato slices, as well as a variety of salads when paired with a serving spoon. Butter knives come in two varieties: serving, which is for the table, and individual, which is for each guest. They can be used for pâté, too. Sugar shell spoons are generally placed in or beside a sugar bowl.

Popular Patterns

Scandinavian designs are typically sculptural and simple.

American patterns hearken back to Colonial times and often reference architectural details, like the leg of a Queen Anne chair.

Contemporary flatware is easily recognized by its sleek lines and graphic shapes.

French patterns range from simple architectural details to romantic, rococo styles, with shells, vines, leaves or swags.

Renaissance designs are often the most ornate and heavily detailed, exhibiting great depth in the pattern.

COOKWARE

Depending on how often you cook, you may want to start with a small, good-quality set (four to five pieces), and then add other pieces for specific cooking needs.

Your best bet is to get a large (10- or 12-inch) sauté pan with lid; a 1½, 2- and 3- or 4-quart covered saucepan; a 10- to 12-inch covered skillet; a deep 8-quart stockpot with lid for soups and pasta; and a 5- to 6-quart covered casserole. A well-made piece will have a heavy base for even heat distribution, top-grade finishes for easy cleanup, and strong, stay-cool handles that are reinforced for extra durability.

As for cookware materials, cast aluminum is a great conductor of heat, although it is a softer metal that can dent, get surface scratches and darken. Hard-anodized aluminum has a tough surface with superior heat conductivity; some have nonstick interiors. Stainless steel resists dents and scratches and is also the easiest to clean, but it's the least heat conductive. Now, high-end stainless comes with glass bottoms that have copper and aluminum discs.

Stainless steel-clad and copper-clad cookware has multiple layers of metals permanently bonded to an aluminum-core base. These are used for superior heat conductivity. Copper is the most responsive heat conductor (it heats up and cools down quickly, meaning you can really control your cooking). It is beautiful, heavy, expensive and high maintenance (to keep it gleaming). For the best of all worlds, consider a copper exterior with a stainless interior and an aluminum core. Cast iron conducts heat very well and is nonstick when the pan is prepared correctly. It's good for slow cooking as well as high-heat preparations, such as searing and browning meats, so it's the perfect material for skillets and stovetop grills. Enamel over cast iron keeps acidic foods like tomatoes from reacting with the iron surface, and comes in vibrant colors, unlike all the metal you'll have in your kitchen. On the down side, enamel can sometimes chip. Porcelain enamel over aluminum keeps the cookware looking new longer, and nonstick interiors are a plus.

{modern bride wisdom}

Nonstick surfaces have revolutionized cooking—and simplified cleanup. Be sure to use plastic or wooden utensils to prevent scratching and extend the life of your nonstick pans.

Ovenware

This is an especially fun category because it covers all of the extras—the items you'll need to make all of your specialties and favorite side dishes.

Casseroles are the workhorses of oven cooking. They're great for oven-to-table meals. A roaster and rack do double duty. Register for the strongest nonstick rack and pan you can find (you'll be happy when you host your first Thanksgiving). Au gratin pans are great for roasted vegetables, mac and cheese and potatoes au gratin because you can put them right up under the broiler. These shallow pans come in a variety of materials. Lasagna pans are a popular registry item. The pan can be of glass, ceramic, stainless steel, cast aluminum and other materials. Loaf pans are great for baking everything from meatloaf to banana bread. Cookie sheets are best when insulated and nonstick, as it lessens the chance of burned bottoms. Pie pans are most common in 9- and 10-inch diameters. Cake pans and Bundt pans are still major staples of registries. Springform pans come in two pieces. A clip release allows you to remove the outer ring, so you don't damage your quiche, tart or cheesecake. Muffin tins are most commonly made from aluminum or stainless steel.

Kitchen Electrics

Small kitchen appliances go way beyond the toaster. This is what's showing up on couples' registries these days.

Hand mixers are perfect if your baking involves mainly beating eggs, whipping cream or blending cake batter; they're also excellent for mashing potatoes. Stand mixers are best if you'll be working with heavy bread or cookie doughs, since they have a stronger motor. Food processors can be used for almost any prep task: They purée, chop, slice and dice. A pulse speed mixes batters and doughs, too. You may also want a food processor and stand mixer combined. Some models have a special blade for making whipped creams and sauces.

Blenders can whip up a perfect fruit smoothie, crush ice to make a frozen margarita or purée a soup. Juicers are a hot item on registries; consider whether you'll need a citrus juicer for simple drinks, or a larger machine to manage hard fruits and vegetables, like apples, beets or carrots.

Coffeemakers have gone high tech: You can choose from drip coffeemakers, percolators, combination grinding and brewing machines and single-serve (or "pod") coffeemakers. Espresso machines come in two varieties: Pump machines heat an espresso-cup-sized measure of water, then force (or "express") the heated water through densely packed, powdery, ground coffee at high pressure. This creates a rich, less-bitter coffee with a thick caramel-colored foam topping called "crema." Simpler, less expensive steam machines heat many cups of water through the grinds at a slower speed, producing a lighter flavor and a thinner crema.

The toaster, that classic wedding gift, has gotten a major update in the past few years. Toasters now feature preprogrammed functions for defrosting and reheating; touch-pad controls; deeper and wider slots to accommodate breads of all sizes, including bagels; and warming trays for Danishes and croissants.

Cutlery

You'll be very happy when you stock your kitchen with high-quality knives: They make all your tasks go faster.

A paring knife (with either a 3- or 4-inch blade) is for basic prep work. It's perfect for peeling fruits and vegetables. Slicers are versatile knives that come in three sizes: 6-inch and 8-inch knives are excellent for slicing tomatoes, chicken and small roasts; the 10-inch size is perfect for hams and turkeys. A utility knife is ideal for fruit, cheese and small vegetables. A chef's knife is a kitchen necessity because it makes quick work of chopping, dicing and mincing vegetables or meat, and comes in 6-, 8-, and 10-inch lengths. A serrated knife (one with teeth) is designed to cut through crusty breads and delicate cakes without crushing their interiors. A Santoku knife is a cleaver and chef's knife combined. It's used for mincing and slicing, especially for meat and fish. The dimples on the blade create air pockets so that food won't stick to it. Kitchen shears are must-haves. They make chores like cutting artichoke leaves, snipping herbs and cutting up chicken much simpler.

{modern bride wisdom}

Frequently sharpen your knives with a sharpening steel. This will keep the blades honed to a fine edge.

Our best advice for choosing your sheets is to simply feel them. If they're soft and not too starchy or scratchy, then you ought to feel comfortable (in every way) with your selection.

Pillows are available in down, feather-and-down combinations, polydacron or in viscoelastic foam, which molds to the shape of your head. What you buy is purely a personal choice (although you should take allergies into consideration when choosing guest pillows), as well as the level of fill (soft to firm). You may want to have at least five on hand, more if you're a multiple-pillow sleeper.

Comforters may be filled with either down, feathers or down alternatives—usually polyester. As with pillows, consider possible allergies. (Tip: To remove dust, aerate down-feather comforters and pillows in a cool dryer with a sneaker tossed in.) Comforter covers (also called duvet covers) come in a variety of fabrics and patterns. It's nice to have at least two on hand.

As for towels, register for at least four complete sets of matching towels, choosing everyday sets as well as a luxury brand to use for guest towels—or for yourselves. The most luxurious towels available are made from Egyptian cotton. Towels woven with loops of this cotton have incredible durability, a brilliant luster and a silky feel. The number of loops in a towel determines its drying ability—the more loops, the greater the absorbency. And when you're choosing, remember that good towels will often last for more than 10 years.

LINENS

Sheets, blankets and towels may feel like some of your most crucial picks, since you'll be using them so frequently and because they tend to add to the decor of your bedroom and bathroom.

Sheets generally have a thread count that ranges from 100 to more than 1000. But a high count doesn't necessarily equal softness or a long-lasting quality. For instance, jersey knits, flannel and linen can all have a lower thread count than certain kinds of expensive sheets, but also feel softer. Register for at least three sets of sheets—one for the bed, one for the closet and one for the laundry.

Blankets come in many fabrics, of course, from machine-washable acrylic to super-luxurious cashmere and silk, but most couples will want to have at least one summer-weight wool, like 100-percent merino.

Cleaning Tools

Motivate yourselves to keep a clean house by registering for top-of-the-line equipment.

Vacuums seem to improve every year. Decide whether you want one where the dirt is collected in a bag, or one where it's all captured in a vessel. And consider tapping into the craze that's literally sweeping the nation: robotic vacuums, which slowly make their way around your home—on both carpets and hard floors—sucking up dust and debris. Regardless of which type you select, consider also getting a hand vac for quick cleanups of small spills (some even pick up liquid).

Bride to Bride

When you're registering, once your guy decides he doesn't like something, move on. It's not worth making him give in. Because every time you bring out the item in question, he'll tell you how much he hates it. —Christy

Home Electronics

In the past few years, more and more couples have added high-tech gadgets and electronics to their wish lists, including high-definition televisions, MP3 players, speakers, cell phones and digital cameras.

Even if you own these items already, new features may make an upgrade seem like a good idea. Be sure to ask what warranty is included with purchase—and don't forget to shop around for stuff that looks as good as it functions. If you're concerned that home electronics are too expensive, remember that groups of friends or relatives can all chip in for one item.

Bride to Bride

The first time we tried registering was during the holidays. Under no circumstances would I recommend going during the holiday rush, unless you like being hot and ignored by the frenzied sales staff. —Catherine

Q & A

Q My mom is really bugging me to register, but I feel a little funny creating a list of exactly what we want to get. What should we do?

A You need to get over your angst since you're doing a large portion of your family and friends a favor by registering. Most people like being able to buy from registries because they'll know that the time (and, frankly, the money) they spend picking out a gift is going to result in something you and your fiancé really want. Otherwise, your friends and family are left to their own devices, and unless they've had the opportunity to come into your house and take inventory, they won't have a clue that the toaster oven they're buying you will only end up serving as a backup for the one you already own. And, on the flip side, a registry is also there to help you. We've all heard the horror stories of couples getting stuck with funky figurines and vases that have no place in their homes besides the attic. A registry will keep these kinds of "unique" gifts (and your time on returns lines after the honeymoon) to a minimum.

Q Is it alright if we tell people where we've registered on our wedding invitations, or would that be rude?

A Including registry information on your invitation makes it seem like buying a gift is a requirement—which, of course, it isn't. Traditionally, to get registry information to your wedding guests you had to rely on word of mouth via family, bridesmaids and friends. This method has worked for decades and is still a great way to get the word out. Trust us, if someone wants to know where you are registered, they'll pick up the phone and start calling until they find out. But now that online registries have emerged, tradition is changing a bit. It now seems acceptable to include registry info in your save-the-date letters. But if bucking tradition gives you chills—or if you're sending out very formal invites—stick with good old-fashioned word of mouth.

Q My fiancé and I don't do a lot of formal entertaining. Should we still consider registering for china?

A Absolutely. It's time to throw the "china is only for formal dining" myth out the window. China has come a long way from being the dishes used just for special occasions. In fact, we know of couples who make it a point to serve all of their meals—even if it's just pizza—on their china. China is an incredibly hard material, meaning it's well-suited to everyday life and casual entertaining. Also, patterns have evolved from just formal and elegant styles to more relaxed and casual looks. Even if you decide to not use china for informal dinners, you'll probably want to have it for the special moments that you will celebrate: dinners with the in-laws or the boss, or the first Thanksgiving at your place, for example.

Q **This is a second marriage for both of us. Is it still okay to register?**

A Yes. Just because you've both been hitched before doesn't mean you can't register for the big day. Start by taking inventory of what you both have and what you need. If you discover that you're well stocked with kitchen basics (dishes, flatware, small appliances), consider this: It might be fun to replace the old with the new—after all, it's a new life! Ditch your old blender for the newest and hippest brand on the market or sign up for a high-tech coffeemaker that puts your old one to shame. Still digging your everyday dishes? Then maybe it's time to select that gorgeous china you've always wanted. And it's okay to think beyond household goodies by registering at a sporting-goods store so that you're all geared up for your next vacation together, or at a home center like Home Depot. Of course, if you decide in the end that you don't need or want to register for too many items, consider asking for guests to make a donation to your favorite charity in your name (check out idofoundation.org). This is truly a gift that keeps on giving.

Q **My fiancé and I have expensive taste. Will our guests be upset if we have pricey items on the registry?**

A Not as long as you give them options. You can certainly register for expensive items, and some guests will have no problem splurging a bit since it is, after all, your wedding. Also, it's common for groups of people (like your bridesmaids or coworkers) to band together on a joint gift if they want to give you a big-ticket item that they know you'll have forever (like fine china or sterling flatware). But for those guests who aren't similarly inclined, you should make an effort to register for gifts at all price points—include little things like towels, napkins and kitchen gadgets. As long as you register for a wide range of items, your guests should be happy to hit the shops on your behalf.

Q **A lot of stores seem to have "completion" programs. What are they?**

A It's most common in department stores, and provides great benefits. A completion program is an incentive for you to buy the items your guests haven't purchased from your registry. For example, if you've received only eight of the 12 wine-glasses you'd registered for, a completion program will allow you to buy the other four at a reduced price. The terms vary from store to store, and the program is open to anyone. A completion program can save you money and allow you to pick up those registry items that might have otherwise remained unpurchased.

Q **How long is our registry active?**

A It varies, but often registries are kept open for just over one year past the wedding date. This allows guests who don't come to your wedding armed with a present (it might make more logistical sense to mail it after the fact) to send you something when you return from your honeymoon. Also, stores usually keep registries open to give you the time you need to return duplicate items and replace them with items still left on your registry list. (Duplicates are rare, but they do happen.) With all of the great completion programs out there, it behooves the store to give you the extra time to pick up missing items from your list. And, finally, by keeping the registry open long after the wedding, those guests who have not yet given you a gift shall have time to participate. Friends and family can return to it for any other gift-giving occasions throughout the year, such as birthdays, holidays or your first anniversary.

CHAPTER 7

Choose the *Caterer*

THE DISH ON DECIDING YOUR WEDDING MENU

Even if you choose a buffet, you can have the first course served by the waitstaff.

Buffets/Stations vs. Sit-Down

It's the classic showdown—which is the better option for your dinner party? While each serving style has its own pros and cons, one factor that's hard to gauge is the price. Depending on the types of food served and the size of the waitstaff or amount of extra food required, either option could be the pricer one.

	BUFFETS/STATIONS	SIT-DOWN
WHAT IT IS	Food is presented in large bowls and platters along a big table, and guests help themselves. The station concept, which features lavish, themed food presentations at tables scattered around the room, was born out of buffets.	This is like standard restaurant service: Each course is elegantly plated in the kitchen, then brought out by waiters to your guests.
BENEFITS	Guests get to choose from several entrée and side dish options, so even the pickiest eaters will find something they love. Because the meal isn't served in courses, guests may get on to the dance floor more quickly.	You won't be paying for a lot of unused food, saving on waste. This can be a more sophisticated serving option, perfect for a formal wedding.
POINTS TO CONSIDER	Buffets or stations may be difficult for elderly or physically challenged guests to manage; you may want to have a server assigned to help these guests get their meals. You may end up paying more for the large amount of food that needs to be created to ensure the displays remain full. They can also make your party feel less formal.	If you have a lot of guests who need special meals for health, religious or other reasons, it may be challenging to find entrées that work for all of them. Sit-down meals keep guests in their chairs for a longer period of time, which can make it harder to get everyone on to the dance floor.

{expert tip} If you're doing a sit-down dinner, consider offering plates that have tastes of two or three different entrées. You get the same type of variety that's offered with a buffet but on a smaller scale. If someone doesn't want the scallops, he can leave them.

—*Sasha Souza, event planner, Los Angeles and Napa, CA*

Dining Alternatives

A dinner isn't the only way to celebrate your newlywed status. Some couples host their weddings at other times of day, allowing them greater freedom with their menu choices and the style of the party. Here are a few other options to consider.

Brunch or luncheon Perfect for a pair of early birds, you'll feast on fun fare like omelets, waffles and salads, along with brunch cocktails like Bellinis and Bloody Marys. Lunch, like dinner, can be served in courses but would be lighter with menu choices such as lobster salad or steak and frites.

Tea Go old-school with a sweet afternoon event, featuring dainty sandwiches, elegant petit fours and a selection of exotic brewed teas. Be sure to include lemon slices and pots of honey. (To give your party an extra kick, serve champagne punch in addition to the teas.)

Cocktails Get your guests mixing and mingling as waiters pass around trays of tasteful canapés. This party style is great for couples who want to ensure their guests really get to know one another. Items ranging from cheese puffs to chicken skewers should be carefully chosen to keep guests full and happy.

Dessert Skip the meal and savor everyone's favorite part—dessert. Offer a selection of treats, from a chocolate fondue fountain to an array of fruit tarts, and plenty of dessert wines, champagne and kicked-up coffee confections.

Bride to Bride

We've decided to have an afternoon tea for our reception rather than a sit-down dinner. This way we're still having an elegant event, but our costs are cut dramatically. —Emily

{modern bride wisdom}

If you're doing something unique like a dessert or cocktail reception, mention it on the invitations. That way, guests will know exactly what to expect.

Booking the Cooking

HOW TO FIND A TOP-NOTCH CATERER

For many couples, the search for a caterer is finished as soon as they settle on the site—the in-house caterer will be the one creating their wedding meal. But if your site doesn't come with its own dedicated caterer, it's up to you to search out a culinary master. Here's how to find the person who can build a menu you'll savor.

If you don't have a caterer on speed dial, ask around for some contenders and keep paying close attention to the food at weddings and parties you attend—you may find a caterer that suits your taste at someone else's event.

If you're unfamiliar with the caterer's expertise, ask what types of cuisine he normally prepares. Most chefs specialize in a certain type of cooking—classic French, pan-Asian, Cajun—so you'll want to play to your caterer's strengths. And if you have your heart set on certain dishes—if you want to serve a family recipe, for instance—bring that up with the caterer, too, to ensure you're both on the same page from the get-go.

Ideally, the caterer you want for your wedding will have worked at your party space before. While this isn't a deal-breaker if he hasn't, it's helpful if your caterer is familiar with the kitchen and is aware of any issues, particularly for unique venues like a yacht or a historic home, where kitchen space may be limited or there may be restrictions that affect the menu. (In this case, your caterer might want to look into preparing the food off-premise, if possible.)

Then it's time to get down to the nitty-gritty details. Find out what the caterer's price includes: Is it just the food and service, or does the quote cover dishes, table linens and glassware? Does he offer wedding cakes and bar service? When can you set up a tasting, so you can get a sense of how the menu you've selected will taste and look on your wedding day? And of course, you'll want to ask for references, so you can talk with his former clients about their experiences with the caterer.

WINING AND DINING

Many people are daunted by the prospect of picking wines to go with their meals. But you don't have to be a sommelier to know what you like—and what your guests will appreciate, too.

You shouldn't feel fenced in by those old rules—reds with beef, whites with fish. Simply try several different wines to see which flavors seem right. You may find that a light red, like a pinot noir, will taste better with a tuna entrée than a Riesling or another light white.

Weather may also come into play when you're making your wine-list selections. If you're marrying in winter, be sure your bar is stocked with heartier reds and whites, which will stand up to richer, heavier menus.

You should also consider your guests in your choices. You may want to offer more popular varietals like chardonnays, merlots and syrahs, which even the novice wine drinker will like—though if a less-common varietal works best with your meal, go ahead and offer it.

If there are wineries near your wedding locale, consider choosing a vintage from their stocks: The flavors of the local wine will suit the flavors of the local cuisine very well.

And if you're still stumped after you've sipped at your tasting, ask the chef which one he would recommend—he should be able to steer you to the best flavor combinations.

{expert tip} If you're doing a wine pairing with your meal, be sure to allow more time for dinner. Your servers will need to keep bringing out new wines and new glasses, so you'll need to make sure that you have enough time to do that.

—*Sasha Souza, event planner, Los Angeles and Napa, CA*

Test Drive Your Menu

TIPS TO HELP YOU GET A TASTE OF WHAT'S TO COME

● **Schedule your tasting about two months before your big day.** You want to have it relatively close to the wedding so you may be able to try out some of the chef's seasonal dishes, but not too close, in case you need to do a second tasting to make sure everything's perfect.

● **Utilize all of your senses.** While the flavor of the food is most important, make sure it's also attractively plated and served at the appropriate temperature—and that it smells as great as it tastes.

● **Feel free to make a few suggestions.** We're not talking a major overhaul of your caterer's cooking style, but if you want a little less sauce on the entrée or a dusting of confectioners' sugar on the berry compote, let him know.

● **Try out the wines, too.** If you've chosen specific wines to serve during the meal, try them out with each dish to make sure you like how they taste together.

Contract Essentials

Check your catering contract to be sure it includes these essentials:

☐ Your wedding date, location and reception time—and what time the meal should be served

☐ Serving style selected (sit-down, buffet, etc.)

☐ Length of service and amounts served (for example, a four-hour open bar; a fruit-and-cheese display for 150 people)

☐ Fees for overtime, gratuities and other additional charges

☐ Menu selections (This can be added as a rider after the tasting.)

☐ Deadlines for payments and a final head count

☐ China pattern, linen color and other selections, if the caterer is also providing tableware

☐ Special requests, such as kids' or vegetarian meals

☐ A cancellation policy

{modern bride wisdom}

Ask your caterer to pack up a little gourmet takeout for your wedding night. Most newlyweds barely get a bite of their carefully chosen meals during the reception, so a postnuptial picnic featuring your special menu may be the way to go!

Bride to Bride

My fiancé proposed while we were having a picnic, so we are re-creating the menu from that picnic for our luncheon reception. We'll have ham biscuits, deviled eggs, fresh fruit, guacamole and chips, fine cheeses and a mountain of cupcakes. —Rose

MODERN 5 BRIDE

Cool Menu Ideas

Family recipes: Share your grandmother's secret manicotti recipe, or that beloved twist on s'mores you dreamed up as a kid, with your caterer—and your guests—to add a sentimental touch to your reception menu.

Soup as an hors d'oeuvre: Bring soup into the cocktail hour by serving tiny portions in shot glasses, spoon-shaped breads or hollowed-out tomatoes or cucumbers.

Passed desserts: Instead of calling guests back to their seats for cake and dessert, consider letting the sweets come to them. Waiters can bear trays laden with petite tarts, mini ice-cream cones, decadent cookies and small slices of cake.

Midnight snacks: If your party runs into the wee hours, refuel your dancing guests with a little late-night nosh: pizzas, hot pretzels or cookies and milk.

Comfort food: Wedding fare doesn't have to be pretentious: Many couples opt for menus filled with crowd pleasers like mac and cheese and mashed potatoes, but they give these standards an upscale twist by using gourmet cheeses, letting guests customize them at a bar with fancy toppings or serving tiny portions in ramekins or other clever dishes.

Brides are adding comfort foods, like hamburgers, to their wedding day menus—but with an upscale twist.

FOOD STATIONS

Set up stations so guests can customize their cuisine

Interactive stations are a hot trend in reception dining; couples offer their guests fare from themed tables like raw bars, made-to-order pizzas or Indian cuisine. It's a great way to please a diverse guest list—with so many options, everyone will find something they love. But variety comes at a price: Thanks to the elaborate displays, specially trained chefs, and additional food required, this can be the priciest reception option around.

But even if you opt instead for a traditional buffet or sit-down meal, you can incorporate interactivity into just one aspect of the wedding menu: During the cocktail hour, set up a pommes frites bar where guests can choose their favorite dipping sauces for the tasty fries; or try an ice-cream-sundae, dessert-crepe or gourmet-coffee bar after dinner.

Wedding Words

A MENU OF FOODIE PHRASES

PLATED SERVICE

This is standard sit-down service where waiters deliver plates full of beautifully arranged food to each guest.

BUTLERED SERVICE

This usually refers to the cocktail hour, when waiters work their way around the room, offering guests hors d'oeuvres or glasses of your signature cocktail.

MIXED DRINKS

These require a little finessing from your bartender: Instead of simply pouring the drink (a glass of wine, for example), multiple ingredients and mixing are involved for these choices.

OPEN BAR

Your caterer charges you a flat fee per person for a certain period of time, and guests can drink as much as they like. It's great for a cocktail-loving crowd.

CONSUMPTION BAR

Your caterer keeps tabs on how much your guests drink, then charges you per beverage at the end of the night. This bar style is a great deal if you're inviting a light-drinking crowd or having a brunch or early-afternoon reception, when people are less likely to go overboard.

GRATUITY

Better known as the tip: Most caterers include a 15 to 20 percent gratuity on their bill; if you have truly stellar service, you might decide to add to that amount.

FAMILY STYLE

Consider this a perfect compromise between a buffet and sit-down meal. Waiters bring each table several serving bowls and platters filled with your menu choices, and guests pass them around and take what they want. This will give your reception a more casual, convivial feel—and you'll need fewer servers than a true sit-down meal, and less food than a buffet.

WELL BRANDS

Your bar will be stocked with basic brands of liquor—nothing fancy. If most of your guests drink beer and wine, this could be a good place to save money.

PREMIUM BRANDS

You'll pay extra to stock your bar with name-brand liquor like Grey Goose or Absolut vodka instead of a lesser-known brand. If many of your guests drink their liquor straight, this may be a worthy splurge.

The Cocktail Hour

After the ceremony ends, the celebrating really begins. The cocktail hour can be a highlight of your wedding, allowing you and your guests to meet and mingle over flavorful canapés and drinks. Here's how to do it right.

● Change it up. If you can, host the cocktail hour away from the reception room, in a different lounge or on a veranda off of the main room. That'll preserve the excitement of the reception and allow you to give the cocktail hour a different look, using unique colors and centerpieces. For instance, you could start out with all-white blooms at the ceremony, switch to pink decor for the cocktail hour, then deck your reception hall in rich red.

● Go low. Instead of tall cocktail tables with stools, create little lounge areas with couches, cozy chairs and low tables for placing snacks and drinks.

● Share a little at a time. Instead of having every type of hors d'oeuvre you're serving being passed at once, have waiters start passing a few at the beginning, then move on to other treats later in the hour. This creates anticipation as guests wonder what's coming out of the kitchen next.

● Have fun with the food. The cocktail hour is a great opportunity to offer interactive stations, whether it's custom sushi rolls made by a trained chef or a mashed potato bar where guests can add their favorite toppings, from scallions and bacon bits to wasabi and cheddar cheese. Try serving the hors d'oeuvres in unique ways: bite-sized servings of lobster salad in tiny bread bowls, or shrimp cocktail in a shot glass with a dollop of cocktail sauce.

Consider choosing hors d'oeuvres
with flavors that complement
those in your signature cocktail.

FUN SIGNATURE-DRINK NAMES

Altar-ed State
Blushing Bride
By My Cider
Cloud-Nine Cocktail
Diamond-Ring Sling
Electric-Slide Special
Eternitini
First-Kiss Fizz
Groom's Gimlet
Honeymoon Helper
"I Do" Daiquiri
'Maidarita
Rosy Future
Tie-the-Knot Shot
Tuxedo-politan
True Blue
Veil Ale
Wedding Bell-ini

Creating a *Signature Drink*

Toast to your newlywed status with a favorite beverage, whether it's an appletini like the ones you enjoyed on your first date or a mojito to match your wedding's green color scheme. Your cool cocktail can be sipped with hors d'oeuvres at the start of the reception, or even served before the ceremony to welcome your guests to your celebration.

Find your flavors. Write down your favorite beverages—both alcoholic and nonalcoholic. Whether you're fond of lemonade or dirty martinis, the flavors you favor can be used to inspire your cocktail.

Consider the theme. If your party has an Asian vibe, consider using ingredients from the region: sake as a main ingredient, or lychees as the garnish. If your entire wedding is in shades of green, opt for a cocktail in the same hue.

Ask a bartender for help. The mixologist at your reception site or your favorite bar may be able to suggest drinks that match your theme and your taste.

Try out your contenders. Invite your pals over (or out) to taste a few options and narrow down the field. (Tough research!)

Make it fun. Give the drink a unique name (see some ideas on the opposite page) and create a sign or a tag for it.

Bride to Bride

We have a bunch of party animals in our group, so instead of having a champagne toast, we'll offer shots of tequila—or shots of champagne for our less adventurous guests. —Eva

Bar on a Budget

No matter how limited your budget, don't have a cash bar—no host should expect their guests to pay for their glasses of wine. But even if you can't fund a full bar, you can provide a variety of delicious drinks. Here are a few options.

Limit the liquor to beer and wine. Guests will have fun trying the different vintages and microbrews you're offering, and you'll need only a basic bartending staff, as they simply have to pour the drinks. Be sure you stock a nice variety—crowd pleasers like chardonnays and merlots, plus less popular varietals like chenin blancs and barberas—so guests can try something new.

Serve just your signature cocktail (along with beer and wine). By limiting the bar to one or two drinks, you'll limit the variety required—and the amount of work the bartenders will need to do.

Offer interesting nonalcoholic beverages and add an interactive element to the presentations. Let guests customize iced teas and lemonades by infusing them with fruit juices, or have a smoothie station where guests can order their favorite concoctions.

Q & A

Q **Our crowd has been to a ton of weddings. How can we make our reception menu stand out?**

A One option is to ask your chef to prepare a menu filled with romance by incorporating known aphrodisiacs such as oysters, figs, rosemary, strawberries and chocolate into the dishes. Title your menu "Love Potion #9" and place asterisks next to the aphrodisiac items with a key to explain at the bottom of the page. Another idea is to serve your favorite foods in unique ways; for example, if you're a big fan of soup, serve it in hollowed-out coconuts, small pumpkins or mini loaves of bread. Giving your hors d'oeuvres a theme is another fun option. If you and your fiancé are baseball fans, for example, serve nibbles sold at ballpark concession stands, like pigs in a blanket, bite-sized burgers and soft-pretzel bites with mustard. If you're throwing a cocktail reception, tapas can be a big hit and offer a wide variety of choices. (Be sure to serve sangria!) Frites with an array of dips for dunking—or beef, chicken and shrimp satays with various sauces—can also be well received. Guests can have a great time experimenting and finding their favorites.

Q **What are some fun nonalcoholic drinks to serve at the reception?**

A Mocktails are always a great alternative to alcoholic beverages. These are variations of well-known drinks—sans the "sauce." For example, substitute grape juice (red or white) for wine to make a tasty nonalcoholic sangria. Or mix tea with any kind of juice, add some lemon or orange slices, and you've got your own version of a Long Island Iced Tea. You can also serve a Virgin Mary (add a little more pepper, Tabasco or Worcestershire sauce for extra zip). Another option is to set up a smoothie station made from a variety of seasonal fruit. Finally, don't forget sparkling cider. Come toasting time, everyone should be armed with a glass of bubbly.

Q **Do kids typically count against the per-person cost of the reception?**

A The cost of young guests varies at each reception site. Sometimes this is open for negotiation and you can strike a deal with the site manager up front, so be sure to bring it up. Other places have specific policies regarding meals. Some sites will charge you the same price for a kid's meal as they do for an adult's, regardless of the child's age. (This is something to keep in mind if you're on the fence about including children at your wedding.) Other locations might offer you a special reduced-price menu for kids 12 and under— as much as 50 percent off the regular menu price. (These places often offer kid-friendly menus with dishes that will please the younger set, like macaroni and cheese, chicken fingers or burgers and fries.) And still other venues let tykes under a certain age eat free. Once you've finalized the half-pint head count for your wedding, make sure you know what age range they fall into. (If you're not sure, shoot their parents an e-mail to confirm.) After all, it can mean the difference between a pricey dinner and a free meal.

Q **I have a significant number of vegetarians attending my wedding. We're having a sit-down dinner and can afford only two main-course selections. Does one of the meals have to be vegetarian?**

A Even if you have only one or two vegetarian friends, arrangements should be made. You wouldn't want them to try to survive on the olives from their martinis alone. At a buffet, it's easy to let guests pick and choose. For a sit-down dinner, however, you should have one vegetarian choice. Don't think of it as a meal that will appeal only to the vegetarians. A good pasta primavera, for example, should please everyone. But if you really want both your main dishes to include meat, choose a hearty pasta for the side dish. This way, it'll be available in the kitchen so the waitstaff can bring out full plates of it upon request. Give your veggie friends the heads-up

on this plan so they know to place their request rather than just stare at a plate of food they won't eat.

Q **We really want to have a cocktail reception, but we fear our guests will leave hungry, or worse, thinking we're cheap. Help!**

A These days, most cocktail receptions include several food stations with hearty fare—pasta, meat, seafood, stir-fries. If you talk to your caterer in advance about food amounts, you won't have to fret about your guests wasting away on the passed hors d'oeuvres. As for the price, most guests understand that the costs of hosting any party can add up. That said, if you're exploring a cocktail reception to keep costs under control, note the following: If your gig runs as long as a dinner party or requires extra servers, you may end up paying dinner-party prices anyway. And that would really bite!

Q **My fiancé and I don't especially like champagne. It's also very costly. Do we have to serve it at our reception?**

A You're certainly not obligated to serve champagne. However, if you're cutting out the bubbly because you and your fiancé don't care for it, no one says the two of you have to drink it. Simply have your glasses

filled with your favorite concoctions during toast time and save the champagne for your guests. If you're forgoing champagne as a means of keeping liquor costs under control, here are a few suggestions: Serve a good champagne at the beginning of the reception and switch to a less pricey label later. (Palates aren't quite as picky after the reception's been in full swing for a couple of hours!) If you decide to do without champagne completely, you can have waiters pass trays of your signature drink, a wine spritzer or a spiked fruit punch as guests arrive at the reception. Once everyone settles into their seats, they'll be armed with a champagne substitute and ready to start clinking to your future. Another option is to save the toasts until dinner is well underway. This way, you can make sure the waiters will have poured wine for all the guests. In the absence of champagne, guests will simply grab their wineglasses instead. No matter when you decide to begin the toasts at your reception, as long as your guests have a glass to raise—filled with anything—they will be happy.

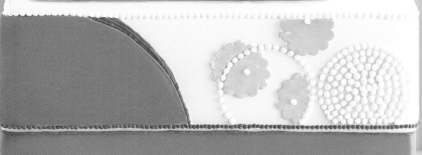

Create the *Cake*

**CRAFTING YOUR
DREAM DESSERT**

10 Ways to Get a Great Cake

KEEP IT SIMPLE. An all-white cake doesn't have to be boring—you can combine different cake shapes and unique textures to create a confection that's a standout.

THINK OUTSIDE THE CIRCLE. Cakes don't always have to be round—or perfectly stacked. In the mod confection on the previous page, a slightly skewed tower of squares and rectangles has a groovy appearance.

MAKE A STATEMENT. Don't stop at your wedding vows—meaningful words expressed on your cake are all the sweeter. Choose a smooth surface and a font that matches your invitation's.

RECREATE A GREAT DESIGN. Use your setting as inspiration, incorporating interesting architectural elements or artwork into the cake. A towering cake can have a domed top to mirror a similar ceiling in the planetarium where you hold your celebration, or the cake can feature a design copied from a stained-glass window in the church where you tie the knot.

BE INSPIRED BY THE SEASON. Let the colors and details on your cake reflect your wedding date: Try white pearlescent fondant with sparkling silver details for a winter wedding, or this sweet pastel cake—scattered with delicate sugar blooms and butterflies—for spring.

GIVE TRADITION A FRESH TWIST. Flowers are a classic cake adornment, but by using a unique color palette of brown and pale blue and funky, pop-art-style blooms, you'll give your cake a modern look.

CELEBRATE YOUR HERITAGE. For a cake with deeper signficance, borrow from your background. Research the traditional nuptial dessert from your heritage (such as a tower of cream puffs if you're French) or have your baker decorate your cake to reflect your roots. An Indian bride could have a mendhi-inspired design scrolled on her cake in chocolate; newlyweds of Irish heritage might deck their tiers in Celtic knots or Claddagh.

HAVE YOUR CAKE—AND COOKIES, TOO. The sweetest adornments for your cake may be other confections, whether you opt to create a polka-dot pattern with pastel sugar cookies or bold stripes with licorice whips.

{modern bride wisdom}

Consider the season when planning the details of your cake. An autumnal wedding may call for richer-hued adornments and dark-chocolate icing, while a summertime cake may feature strawberries.

DRAW FROM YOUR DRESS. Wedding gowns can inspire an exquisite take on the cake. This one's wrapped in gossamer-thin fondant resembling vintage lace and decorated with sugar ribbons and brooches.

CHANNEL THE KID IN YOU. Show off your whimsical side and use elements that remind you of childhood in your cake's design: An antique toy or a pretty pinwheel can serve as a charming cake topper, and striped candy sticks, lollipops and other sweet treats can adorn the rest of the confection.

{expert tip} Design the wedding cake after all of the other elements of the event have been decided so that the cake is a reflection of the overall look of the wedding.

—*Yifat Oren, event planner, Sherman Oaks, CA*

A Baker's *Dozen*

12 TIPS FOR WORKING WITH THE CREATOR OF YOUR WEDDING CAKE

Whether you're envisioning a cake that's traditional (yellow layers with vanilla buttercream) or exotic (Nutella-filled tiers or Key-lime fondant), your first move is finding a talented baker. This is how you do it, and achieve confection perfection.

Scout out your options.
Start visiting bakers about six months before the wedding and peruse their portfolios of cakes. Make sure that the photos you're seeing depict their actual work, not simply ideas culled from other sources.

Share your details.
Once you've selected a baker, tell him all about the wedding—the location, the dress, the flowers, the menu—as these details can inspire the cake's design and flavors. Bring pictures of cakes you love to show him what you have in mind. He may tweak an idea to personalize it for your wedding.

Check them out.
Don't forget to ask for the names of former clients to call, so you can make sure that other brides and grooms were happy with his work.

Start talking budget.
Most cakes are priced per serving and can run anywhere from $1.50 to $15 or more per person, depending on where you live and how elaborate and labor-intensive the sugar flowers and other decorations are.

Ask about delivery.
Many bakers include the cost of transporting and assembling your cake in their fees, but if they have to travel a great distance or if the cake design requires hours of on-site assembling, a surcharge may be added.

Discuss your storage needs.
Some frosting types—like buttercream—don't fare well in extreme heat or direct sunlight, while others need to be kept cold until just before serving. Find out from your baker approximately how long your cake can be displayed before the cutting.

Take a taste test.
The proof is in the pudding, so to speak, so try out various flavors of cake to find at least one you love. (You can choose different flavors for each of your layers to allow your guests to find their favorites.)

Consider the frosting style.
If you have your heart set on a smooth fondant finish, make sure your baker has mastered that particular style—you don't want him experimenting with your wedding cake.

Find out when your cake will be baked.
Some bakers make their cakes in advance and freeze them, then thaw them out just before the wedding to decorate. A freshly baked cake will have a lighter, airier texture.

Decide how you'll display it.
Many couples opt for more elaborate cake tables, featuring unique lighting, special linens or floral arrangements. If you want to put a focus on your cake, have your baker and floral designer or consultant talk over some options for spotlighting your confection.

Get a little reassurance.
A baker should have liability coverage to ensure that you'll be compensated if something happens to the cake, and he should be certified by the local board of health.

Get it all in writing.
Names, dates, locations, flavors, decorating style—make sure every last detail is down on paper.

MODERN BRIDE 5

Sources of Inspiration

Your flowers: For a coordinated shot of color, have each tier trimmed with the same types of flowers as those in your bouquet.

Your reception site decor: Carry over reception details—from your favors, centerpieces, the ribbons tied to the back of each chair or the setting itself—as a twist on the traditional cake topper.

Your invitations: Ask if a crest or monogram can be stamped in the icing or used as a border.

Your accessories: Is your "something borrowed" a pair of amazing chandelier earrings? Show them to your baker so he can decorate the cake with similar sparkle.

Your dress: Give your baker a swatch of lace or intricate beading from your dress, and have her replicate the pattern in icing.

To Top It All Off

While you can't go wrong with a variation on the classic bride and groom figurines, there's more than one way to complete the look of your cake. Try one of these on for size:

- vintage toppers
- wedding bells
- seashells
- family crest
- plastic palm trees
- straw dolls
- natural or silk flowers
- pinecones
- tiny lights
- picture frame with photo of bride and groom

- holiday ornaments
- toasting glasses
- figurines of pets
- mini tennis racket, skis, scuba gear, golf clubs
- replica of wedding invitation
- marzipan horseshoe with names of bride and groom on banner
- white dove figurines

BUTTERCREAM

A mix of butter, sugar and eggs that makes a delicious filling and rich icing. Watch the temperature—if buttercream isn't kept cool, it can melt.

PULLED (OR SPUN) SUGAR

Heated sugar syrup that's been twisted to make decorations. Pulled sugar makes caramelized adornments like ribbons and flowers; spun sugar creates gossamer strands, aka angel's hair. Both are impossible to transport, so they have to be created on-site.

Wedding Words

ENGAGE YOUR BAKER IN A LITTLE SWEET TALK

ROYAL ICING

A blend of egg whites and sugar that makes a thick frosting used for lace and latticework.

MARZIPAN

A rich almond paste that has a multitude of uses: It creates a smooth, fondantlike finish when wrapped around cake layers, it serves as a decadent filling and it can be used like sugarpaste to adorn the cake with fruits, flowers and other decorations.

FONDANT

A chewy, sweet sugar dough that's rolled out and wrapped around each tier, creating an ultrasmooth finish to your cake. It's ideal for receptions without a regulated temperature, as it doesn't need to be refrigerated.

SUGARPASTE (OR GUMPASTE)

A sugary dough that's used for making ribbons, flowers and other beautiful decorations for the cake. Unlike fondant, sugarpaste hardens when it dries.

WHIPPED CREAM

A light, delicious filling or frosting that is very delicate. Use it only if you can have the cake refrigerated until right before it's served.

Beyond the
Wedding Cake

A traditional tiered confection isn't the only way to top off your wedding meal. Many couples give their guests other options for dessert in addition to (or even instead of) a wedding cake. Here are a few ideas.

GROOM'S CAKE If one cake just won't be enough for you, follow an old Southern tradition and offer guests a groom's cake in addition to the traditional tiered wedding cake. As the name suggests, this cake is all about the groom—it's decorated to reflect his passions or profession, and his favorite flavors should be found inside. In most cases, the groom's cake is more offbeat and whimsical, even if the rest of the wedding is formal—we've seen cakes decked out to look like a king of hearts for a poker player or topped with sports paraphernalia for an athletic groom.

Some newlyweds serve both the groom's cake and the wedding cake as dessert, while others box up slices of the groom's cake for guests to enjoy after the party. You may want to give your single friends the scoop on a popular tradition from the past: If they slip a (wrapped!) slice of groom's cake beneath their pillow that night, they may end up dreaming of their future mate.

CAKE ALTERNATIVES If you and your fiancé are fans of a special sweet, consider serving that at your wedding—many desserts can even be stacked to approximate a tiered cake, and that impressive tower of cupcakes, tarts, cream puffs or doughnuts will definitely be a crowd pleaser. You can also offer guests fruit and a chocolate fondue fountain, or a display of pies or cheesecakes.

A SECOND SWEET Ask your catering manager to plate another dessert on the same plate as the cake slice—a mini crème brûlée, a small scoop of gelato or a trio of truffles can add an extra dimension to your wedding dessert.

{modern bride wisdom}

Give your guests a choice of treats without springing for a pastry-laden Viennese table: Have waiters place pretty trays with a selection of desserts at each table.

A little something for everyone: a cake with blood-orange, raspberry and Key-lime fillings.

Personal Flavors

Wedding cakes come in nearly any flavor imaginable, from classic white or chocolate to exotic creations like pink champagne or blood orange. So how do you pick from dozens of filling and cake options?

Consider the season. Many bakers use fresh ingredients, so certain fruit fillings or cakes may be at their best at certain times of year. A white cake with strawberry filling is best suited for spring and early summer, while a cinnamon-apple cake will give your dessert an autumnal vibe.

Keep the menu in mind. The cake flavor should work well with the items on your menu—richer flavors might work best with hearty entrées like beef, while a lobster entrée would match well with a light, buttery cake.

Offer your favorites. If you love chocolate and your fiancé's a strawberry guy, ask your baker to combine both flavors in the cake.

Preserving Your Cake

HOW TO ENSURE YOUR TOP TIER STAYS FRESH UNTIL YOUR FIRST ANNIVERSARY

1 **Arrange for someone to bring it home.** (Your mother, a bridesmaid or another trusted friend is a good choice.) If you're leaving straight for your honeymoon, let this person prep your cake for long-term storage.

2 **Stick the cake in the fridge uncovered overnight.** This will help the buttercream frosting to harden so it won't stick to the wrappings.

3 **Start wrapping.** Swath the cake in several layers of plastic wrap and a top layer of aluminum foil, making sure each layer is as close to the cake as possible. (Frigid air causes the dreaded freezer burn.)

4 **Box it up.** Most bakers provide a cake box that can transport the top tier home, then protect it from the other contents of your freezer.

5 **Be gentle when you defrost.** Don't just stick the cake on the counter—that's a recipe for drippy condensation all over the cake and frosting. Instead, reverse the entire process. Put the cake in the refrigerator overnight to thaw out before you unwrap it. Then you can put it out for a half hour or so to bring it back to room temperature before you dig in.

{expert tip} Look at the wedding cake as a "composed dessert." Each slice can have multiple layers of cakes and fillings, and a variety of colors and textures.

—*Ron Ben-Israel, baker, New York City*

Q&A

Q What are some ways to make our cake-cutting ceremony unique?

A Cutting the cake is traditionally one of the most joyful moments of the wedding for a bride and groom—not to mention a perfect photo opportunity—but it can be missed by guests who are engrossed in conversation at their tables. The best way to draw everyone in, in addition to having your bandleader or DJ announce the ceremony to gather your whole crowd, is to turn it into a unique moment that's both meaningful and memorable. Consider having a significant song played in the background; you might want to choose a tune that symbolizes an aspect of your relationship or a choice that's fun, like the '80s hit "Africa" by Toto if that's where the two of you are headed for your honeymoon. This gives the moment a more personal touch and sparks conversation among your guests, who will be interested in learning the significance from those in the know. (Everyone will quickly feel a part of your close circle.) Another idea is to use the cake-cutting ceremony as a time to honor or acknowledge a special family member or friend. To do this, have your cake displayed on a stand that belongs to this person or use a beautiful heirloom knife set to cut your cake, and mention the significance to the crowd very briefly before you start slicing.

Q How can I cut the cost of my cake without having guests notice?

A A wedding cake's price typically depends, in large part, on the amount of time and work involved for your baker. So to start, consider having yours decorated with fresh flowers rather than hand-crafted sugar flowers or other artistic ornaments, which can be very labor-intensive for your vendor to create. Scale back on intricate, over-the-top designs in favor of a simpler look; you can still have a cake with dramatic impact if you select an unconventional shape or creative colors, which shouldn't add much expense. You might also choose a rich, decadent flavor, like chocolate ganache or dulce de leche; this way, you'll satisfy your crowd with smaller slices than you would with a lighter flavor like lemon. Another subtle trick: Serve the slices on small dessert dishes with an ornate pattern or interesting shape to make them appear more substantial.

Q What's the best way to garnish slices of our wedding cake?

A A beautiful and flavorful garnish can give your wedding cake an extra fanciful touch—but you've put a lot of thought into the flavors and design of your cake, so you want to be careful not to choose anything that might detract from it in any way. And although it might be tempting to turn the cake into an over-the-top indulgent dessert—after all, this is a once-in-a-lifetime celebration—we advise that you stay away from heavy toppings like dollops of whipped cream and pools of chocolate syrup because they'll only overwhelm the slice and give it a messy appearance. Your best bets are lighter accents, like delicate swirls of fruit-based purées (strawberry sauce, raspberry coulis) or ultra-thin chocolate shavings. A dusting of cocoa powder or a sprinkling of powdered or colored sugar can also work very well. If you do want to add an extra sweet to the plate, be sure to choose something small in relation to the slice of cake, such as an assortment of fresh berries; a petite pastry, like a madeleine or ladyfinger; or a tiny scoop of colorful sorbet topped with a fresh mint leaf.

Q **How can we guarantee that everyone will love our wedding cake?**

A After careful thought and, most likely, a tasting or two, a bride and groom never want to look around the room after their cake has been served and see full slices left untouched on plates. To avoid this, many couples choose a crowd-pleasing flavor like chocolate or vanilla buttercream, perhaps with a fruit filling. But you certainly have other options if your taste runs more nontraditional. For instance, you can ask your baker to create tiers or layers in different flavors—some with the "safe" choice and others with the more exotic one (praline, raspberry-mocha or even one as daring as wasabi-infused dark chocolate; some of your guests will find it as interesting as you do!). Your servers can alternate when distributing the cake to guests, and there may be some trading among them, which is fine—this way, everyone can enjoy it. Another even more interactive option is to set up a cake bar, similar to an ice-cream-sundae bar, so that guests can customize their own slices. For this, choose a relatively neutral flavor, like chocolate or vanilla cake, and set out the slices on plates, along with an array of fun toppings: chocolate sauce, butterscotch, chocolate chips, chopped nuts, whipped cream or any others you can imagine. With free reign to "design" their own cake, your guests are guaranteed to love it.

Q **When should we serve the cake?**

A Traditionally, the cake-cutting ceremony takes place toward the end of a wedding reception, and the cake is sliced and served right after. This is perfectly acceptable, but you should understand that this timing often signals to guests that they are free to leave anytime after this point. If you'd like to put more of a spotlight on your cake, some bakers suggest that you instead serve it directly after the final course of the meal, either as the sole dessert or alongside the dessert being offered. This way, they say, the cake becomes the grand finale of the meal and is noticed and appreciated more by guests, as they're still immersed in the party at this point. Whether you choose to have your cake served earlier in the celebration or at the end, be sure you are not interrupting dancing or having plates placed on tables when a number of guests may not be in the room (if a crowd has stepped out onto a balcony or deck, for example). Your bandleader or DJ should announce the cake-cutting ceremony and afterward should invite guests to take their seats at their tables to enjoy the cake. A fun alternative is to set up an adjacent dessert lounge that guests can be ushered into after the meal. Provide more loungey seating, such as small tables with sofas and ottomans, and serve flavored coffees and teas or flutes of champagne to make the cake course even more of a festive experience.

CHAPTER 9

Pick Your *Flowers*

BOUQUETS, CENTERPIECES AND ALL THAT BLOOMS

8

Try a unique vessel for your centerpieces, like this oversized martini glass full of delicate blooms and woodsy berries: Blue Curiosa and Black Beauty roses, purple sweet pea, calla lilies and seeded eucalyptus.

Flowers can be one of the most beautiful elements of your day. Used creatively, they can add color, drama, fragrance and romance. Here's how to pull your floral look together, from finding the right florist to picking the perfect blooms.

Talent Search

HOW TO FIND THE RIGHT FLORIST FOR YOU

SCOUT AROUND. Besides checking out the center-pieces at friends' weddings, ctake note of the arrange-ments at your favorite restaurant, watch for great flowers being delivered to your coworkers and ask anyone who sends flowers as part of their job (assis-tants, event planners, etc.).

SENSE THE STYLE. Is the florist's work similar to what you're envisioning for your event? Someone who mostly does free-form centerpieces may not be the right choice to create a manicured topiary.

Florist vs. Floral Designer: What's the Difference?

Floral designer may sound like a more pretentious way of saying *florist*. But there are differences between the two designations. A florist generally operates from a storefront, where he sells everyday arrangements in addition to special-occasion blooms; a floral designer probably works out of a studio and focuses solely on events. A florist can make and deliver centerpieces and bouquets, while a floral designer may get involved with lighting and helping you choose rental linens, fur-niture and other decorative pieces to create your recep-tion's overall mood, in addition to crafting unique centerpieces and bouquets.

TALK ABOUT YOUR BUDGET. You should let your florist know up front how much you can afford. Even if you can't get the lavish orchid bouquets you wanted on your budget, your florist should have plenty of ideas for creating a similar look more affordably.

SHARE THE DETAILS. Bring swatches and photos of everything you've decided on so far—the sites, the dresses, the cake, the menu. These images will help give a picture of the wedding as a whole so bouquets and arrangements can be created to fit your wedding style.

SIGN THE CONTRACT. The contract should include your wedding date, time and location; addresses where various flowers should be delivered (you might want your bouquets ahead of time for photos at your parents' house, for example); details about the number of each type of arrangement needed; what types of flowers will be used; and the color scheme you've chosen. Try to be as specific as possible, as your florist may forget that you discussed using pale pink roses instead of hot pink.

ARRANGE TO SEE A SAMPLE. Your florist can create a prototype of the centerpiece once you've signed the contract to ensure you're both on the same page.

Your Easy-to-Use *Flower*

	THE FLOWER	PEAK SEASON(S)	AVAILABLE COLORS	ITS MEANING
	amaryllis	spring, summer	blue, pink, red, violet, white	expectation
	anemone	spring	orange, purple, red, white	splendid beauty, pride
	anthurium	spring, summer, fall	green, mauve, pink, red, white	lover
	bells of Ireland	summer, fall	green	whimsy, good luck
	calla lily	spring	many colors	magnificent beauty, elegance
	carnation	year-round	many colors	bonds of love, admiration
	coxcomb	spring, summer, fall	green, orange, pink, red, yellow	unique
	daffodil	spring	white, yellow	chivalry, regard, gracefulness
	delphinium	summer, fall	mauve, pink, purple, white	heavenly sweetness, beauty
	freesia	spring, summer	blue, orange, pink, white, yellow	innocence
	gardenia	spring, summer	pure white	joy, ecstasy

Finder A VISUAL GUIDE TO THE BEST BLOOMS FOR YOUR WEDDING

THE FLOWER	PEAK SEASON(S)	AVAILABLE COLORS	ITS MEANING
hyacinth	spring	many colors	constancy, faith
hydrangea	spring, summer	blue, lilac, pink, red, white	devotion
iris	spring, summer	blue, violet, white, yellow	promise, ardor
lily	year-round	many colors	purity, majesty, prosperity
lily of the valley	spring	white, pink, beige	happiness
orchid	spring, summer	many colors	rare beauty, ecstasy
peony	spring, summer	pink, red, white	beauty
ranunculus	spring, summer	bronze, pink, red, white, yellow	radiant with charm
rose	year-round	many colors	deep love (red), unity (white)
sweet pea	spring, summer, fall	pink, purple, red, white	blissful and lasting pleasures
tulip	spring	many colors	perfect lovers, happy years

Bouquet Basics

There are a number of different bouquet styles to choose from. Here's a description of each.

Biedermeier: Concentric rings of blooms fan out from the center of this bold, graphic bouquet, which looks a bit like a flowering bull's-eye when it's finished.

Nosegay: This classic style—a tightly packed, round bouquet of blooms—has been the most popular for years.

Pomanders and wreaths: Ball-shaped pomanders or ring-like wreaths are a fresh twist on the classic bouquet.

Arm bouquet: Think beauty-pageant winner: This grand bouquet is held flat in the crook of your arm.

Cascade: Flowers drape down from this bouquet, which came into its prime in the "bigger-is-better" '80s. Modern cascades are more compact, and don't hang to the ground.

Hand-tied: The florist simply wraps the stems with ribbon instead of inserting them in a foam-filled bouquet holder.

Biedermeier

Nosegay

Pomander

Arm bouquet

Cascade

Hand-tied

Centerpieces 101

Your centerpieces can be the most admired arrangements in your wedding celebration—guests will be staring at them for a few hours or more. But deciding what you want (Tall or short? Natural-looking or highly stylized? Flowers only or something more?) can be challenging. Here's how to pick the best arrangements for your wedding.

Consider the size of the space—and the table. A room with low ceilings calls for shorter centerpieces so the space doesn't feel cramped, while soaring spaces need tall arrangements to fill in that dead air above the table. Make sure the arrangements you choose will fit well on the tables you're using. A sprawling centerpiece may look great at the florist's, but it may make the table feel too crowded once the table settings are in place.

Choose a cool container. While simple glass bowls are nice, consider vessels with personality, like tin watering cans or antique teapots.

Include some unusual ingredients. Flowers are just one option for centerpieces. Mix it up: Use interesting fruits, greenery, and even nonfloral elements like glass "bubbles," silver beads, pretty gift boxes or faux jewels.

Go beyond the cookie-cutter arrangements. While identical arrangements throughout the room give your reception a cohesive look, they aren't always scintillating to look at. Ask your florist about varying the look from table to table, whether you opt to keep everything in the same color family but use different blooms—white roses at one table, Casablanca lilies at the next—or you decide to use variations on the color scheme, displaying pale lavender blooms at one table and bright purple at another.

Think inside the vase. Many florists are doing cool vase treatments—using citrus slices, cranberries or other interesting elements to line the inside of the vase and hide the flower stems.

Consider recycling. Breakaway centerpieces, which are groupings of several smaller containers to create a cohesive whole, can become your guests' favors at the end of the night. (Simply let them know that they can take one of the pots home.) But even if you aren't offering them as favors, look into other ways to utilize them. Call around before the big day to see if any local women's shelters, hospitals or nursing homes might appreciate the donation.

Bride to Bride

To play off of the pearls wrapped around my bouquet, our centerpiece vases will be filled to the top with faux pearls. —Catherine

Alternative Bouquets

Parasols: Colorful umbrellas can help bridesmaids beat the heat at an outdoor wedding; gorgeous handpainted silk parasols can enhance the decor of an indoor celebration.

Fans: Elegant fans work well at outdoor ceremonies, but can also be used at weddings with a retro or Asian vibe.

Candles: Glowing candles can lend a romantic touch to an evening ceremony—consider having bridesmaids carry them in glass globes to avoid any mishaps. (Sparklers are a more spectacular and summery variation on this idea.)

Muffs or purses: Give your bridesmaids a fashion accessory that's worthy of the spotlight—a plush muff for a winter wedding or a glittering handbag any time of year—and let them carry that down the aisle and beyond your wedding day.

Pinwheels or large lollipops: This is a cute idea for your junior bridesmaids or flower girl—and a fun way to show off your whimsical side.

Building the Perfect Boutonniere

Consider dressing up his lapel with something modern and masculine. Here are a few ideas for cool boutonnieres.

Think green. Interesting leaves and grasses can make a pretty bloom a little more macho—or consider using a sprig of evergreen, a braid of bear grass or a touch of dusty miller on its own.

Show off his good taste. Herbs like rosemary and mint can make fragrant additions to his lapel.

Get back to nature. Other natural objects—feathers, acorns, thistle, shells, berries—are just as lapelworthy as a rose or carnation, and may fit your wedding theme better.

Keep it basic. Skip the boutonniere altogether and simply tuck a crisp handkerchief into his breast pocket.

Focus on him. An angler groom can use an elegant lure as a unique boutonniere, while a dedicated sailor could have a bit of rope tied in an intricate knot. A touch of tartan can indicate your fiancé's Scottish heritage; a loop of Mardi Gras beads could play up his New Orleans hometown.

WHO GETS FLOWERS?

BRIDE	Bouquet
BRIDESMAIDS	Bouquet
MOTHERS/STEPMOTHERS AND GRANDMOTHERS OF BRIDE AND GROOM	Nosegay or corsage
GROOM	Boutonniere
GROOMSMEN/USHERS	Boutonniere
FATHERS/STEPFATHERS AND GRANDFATHERS OF BRIDE AND GROOM	Boutonniere
READERS	Nosegay/corsage or boutonniere
SPECIAL GUESTS/HONORARY ATTENDANTS	Nosegay/corsage or boutonniere

Sneeze-Proof Your Wedding

One in seven people suffers from hay fever—which means that a flower-filled wedding may bring them to tears (or at least itchy, watery eyes). If you have serious pollen allergies, you don't have to give up on beautiful arrangements. Here's how to work your wedding decor around your hay fever.

Look for "hypoallergenic" flowers. Some flowers release less powdery pollen, making them more bearable to hay-fever sufferers. Test them out ahead of time to make sure you can tolerate them. Options include many bouquet staples: hydrangeas, tulips, orchids, sunflowers and some roses.

Consider silks. Top-quality silks can look just as gorgeous as the real thing, and their long shelf life means you can have the arrangements made weeks ahead for a preview—and you'll be able to preserve your bouquet and centerpieces for years.

Go beyond the blooms. Today, many nonfloral elements are often used in centerpieces, including crystals, candles, feathers, brooches and even gorgeously decorated sweets. Some of these elements can work in lieu of bouquets as well.

Flower *Children*

Stylish yet sturdy accessories for your smallest attendants

Delicate nosegays and sweet wreaths won't always stand up to an eager toddler. If you've got a rowdy little one in your bridal party, consider a unique alternative to the standard floral crowns and dainty baskets.

Petal Pusher Let your little one tote her blooms in an antique carriage or wagon.

Pocket Full of Posies Fill the pockets of a pretty apron with blossoms, which your flower girl can toss in your path.

Winging It She can wear the blooms in the back, like this sweet set of rose-and-feather-adorned wings.

Floral Hair Accessories

Looking for an au naturel adornment for your big day? Blooms make a great alternative to the traditional veils and tiaras. But choosing the right flowers for the job can be tricky.

You need to choose hardy flowers that can survive without water or ones that can easily be placed into a tiny water tube (as long as your hairstyle can hide it). Orchids, roses, carnations and sunflowers are all up to the task.

If you have your heart set on a more delicate flower, consider going with silk. That'll enable you to have it made far in advance, so you and your hairstylist can practice with it before the big day. (Plus, silks will likely be lighter to wear on your head.)

Of course, deciding how to wear the blooms can be just as tricky. You can tuck a single flower behind your ear or into a chignon or other updo, or choose a wreath or headband to wear as your main adornment.

Dress Up Your Site

While many ceremony sites have beauty and elegance to spare, a few big, bold floral arrangements can make the space feel even more special.

THE ENTRANCE: A beautiful floral wreath or a lavish garland can adorn the doorway into your ceremony space, or flank the entryway with big urns bursting with blooms or a pair of stately topiaries.

THE ALTAR: These arrangements need to be on a grand scale, so your guests seated far from the action can still get a sense of the blooms. If you're marrying in a hotel ballroom or outdoors, use flowers to create a special space for your vow exchange: You can craft a canopy or a simple arch adorned with blooms. If you're marrying in a house of worship, be sure to ask where you are allowed to place floral arrangements before you and your floral designer map out your decorating plan. Some churches and synagogues have rules prohibiting flowers on the altar, for example.

THE AISLE: You can make the most momentous walk of your life even more special by embellishing the aisle. Start with something simple—pretty little cones filled with roses and tied to the ends of the rows—or go elaborate, with a lush rose-petal-covered aisle and towering floral arrangements flanking the rows. Here are a few points to keep in mind as you decide how to do it up.

● Fit your aisle accents in with the rest of the look. Sleek, modern topiaries may look out of place along an historic church's aisle.

● Measure the aisle. You'll need to leave enough room for at least two people to walk down side by side, so a narrower aisle calls for small, simple arrangements that don't take up that valuable space.

● Determine how many rows to decorate. For a smaller site, you might opt to decorate the ends of every row; in larger spaces, you can skip one or two rows between arrangements, or just adorn the aisles near the altar.

● Keep it simple. If your budget is limited, stick with simple ribbons or small arrangements and save your money for the altar and the centerpieces.

Aisle Ideas

Topiaries: These tall, sculpted plants can give your aisle a more dramatic look. To really set off the space, you can drape ribbon from one topiary to the next, or wrap each topiary in tulle to give it a softer feel.

Rose petals or leaves: Skip the aisle runner and create a more natural (and dramatic) path by having your florist create a thick blanket of rose petals, autumn leaves or other colorful foliage.

Flower-filled cones or baskets: Give this classic look a twist by encouraging your guests to toss the flowers as you walk back up the aisle.

Wreaths or garlands: Berries, foliage, flowers or decorative elements like seashells and beads can be wired into gorgeous ropes or sweet circles to adorn each row.

Candles: Give your ceremony site an ethereal glow m poles or in hurricane globes along the ground. (Just be very sure that you'll have plenty of room to walk between the candles.)

{expert tip} Choose no more than one or two types and colors of flowers to use. Too many colors and textures make everything feel restless. You should have a sense of continuity and repetition in your flowers.

—*Preston Bailey, event designer, New York City*

Make the Most of Your
Floral Budget

If you're looking to stretch your floral dollars, follow these tips:

1 **FIND OUT WHAT'S IN SEASON.** You may pay a fortune for lilacs in the fall or tulips in the summer because your florist will be paying to ship them from another hemisphere. Stick with flowers that are blooming in your locale at the time of your wedding, and you'll get more abundant and fresher arrangements.

2 **AUTHORIZE A MARKET BUY.** Consider giving your florist a little artistic (and financial) freedom: Let her pick the best flower-market bargains within your color scheme and other set parameters. That way, you'll get grander arrangements at a great price.

3 **GET BACK TO BASICS.** Exotic orchids are lovely, but simple carnations or other ordinary blooms can be made extraordinary if they're artfully arranged.

4 **BULK UP BEYOND THE BLOOMS.** Add interesting greenery and berries (bear grass, rosemary and pepperberries), small fruits (lady apples, kumquats and grapes) or even things like beads, feathers and crystal sticks to your bouquets and centerpieces. You'll get unique-looking flowers and may save money in the process.

5 **RE-USE YOUR FLOWERS.** The bridesmaids' bouquets can serve as table centerpieces, and the larger arrangements from your ceremony can flank the dance floor or adorn the buffet tables. (Just get permission first if your wedding's happening at a house of worship: They may ask you to donate your flowers to the congregation.)

6 **CHOOSE HARDIER BLOOMS, SUCH AS SUNFLOWERS AND CALLA LILIES.** Your florist won't need to order extras the way he would for delicate flowers like sweet-pea and gardenias, which can easily be damaged in transit or when being handled. Even stronger blooms like tulips and roses can show bruising if they're white, so consider using colorful flowers instead.

7 **BE BOLD.** Opt for big, dramatic flowers, such as peonies, hydrangeas and sunflowers, and your florist may need to buy only a few for each bridesmaid to carry down the aisle.

{modern bride wisdom}

When choosing the flowers for your bouquets and centerpieces, don't forget to consider what they smell like. You'll be spending a lot of time near these blooms (posing for photographs with your bouquet and sitting near a centerpiece at your table), and you should love the fragrance the flowers give off.

MODERN 5 BRIDE

Unique Ways to Use Flowers

Accessory: Yes, flowers can dress up a lapel or a chignon, but consider working with your florist to create a unique addition to your wedding ensemble—a dramatic flower boa or a beautiful lei. Use silk blooms or flowers with limited pollen to avoid damaging your dress.

Menu enhancer: Edible flowers can add a sweet touch to various dishes: Ask your caterer to dress up your salad with pansies, consider a lavender- or rose-infused sorbet for a mid-meal palate cleanser, or adorn your wedding cake with sugared violets. Just make sure that the flowers you use were organically grown to avoid pesticide residue.

Drink decoration: Flowers can be frozen into ice cubes or threaded onto straws or stirrers to add flair to your favorite cocktails. To dress up the bar, have your favorite edible blooms frozen into ice bowls or sculptures.

Favor: Have your florist set up a "flower stand" toward the end of your reception, offering several different colors and styles of stems, plus paper and twine. Guests can choose their favorites and wrap them up to go. Or send each female guest home with a tiny nosegay or a single flower as a memento of the evening.

Sendoff: Have guests toss rose petals or tiny blossoms like stephanotis to make a gorgeous (and fragrant) shower of blooms as you exit.

Q&A

Q **Do I need to have a floral arrangement on the escort table?**

A Adding flowers to the escort table can be a great way to carry your color theme through all of your reception decor, and your florist can certainly come up with some creative ideas for incorporating flowers into the display. However, flowers aren't your only option. Keep in mind that this table is often the first thing guests see when they walk into the reception so it's the ideal place to make a big impression. If your reception decor is minimal, why not display your escort cards atop a simple rock garden? Or create a sandbox for a beach-themed wedding by filling a wooden box with sand and some pretty seashells, and interspersing the cards into the display. If your wedding has an earthy or rustic feel to it or is being held outdoors, you may want to hang the escort cards from the branches of a small plant or tree. Some brides and grooms decide to turn their escort table into a tribute to family members who couldn't be with them on their wedding day. They surround the escort cards with framed photographs of loved ones—sometimes even pictures of their pets!

Q **How can I preserve my bouquet?**

A You have two options. You can have a professional freeze-dry it, which means you should drop it off with a florist as soon as possible after your wedding (the next day is ideal) or appoint a family member to do it if you're leaving for your honeymoon immediately. Or, you can dry it yourself. You've got about a 24-hour window to do this before the flowers wilt too much and won't dry properly. Start by binding your stems together with a rubber band. Even if you've got a ribbon-wrapped bouquet, you should still use the rubber band—it'll provide the grip needed to prevent stems from slipping out. Next, hang the arrangement upside down. Large Christmas-ornament hooks work well if they're sturdy enough, but you can also fashion a hook out of a wire hanger. You can affix the hook directly to the rubber band or add a small loop of string to the rubber band and attach the hook there. Hang the bouquet in a closet or dry space and make sure that nothing else is nearby that might crush the blooms. After about a month, your bouquet should be completely dried and ready for its second debut.

Q **How can I keep my groom's boutonniere fresh throughout the party?**

A Depending on the design of the boutonniere, your florist might be able to attach a small plastic water tube to the end of the bloom and conceal it with greenery. This way, the boutonniere gets the water it needs to stay fresh-looking all day and night.

If that won't work, consider choosing strong blooms known to last longer without water, such as mini sunflowers and orchids. These sturdy flowers will also fare much better should they be accidentally crushed during a well-wisher's hug or a slow dance. If you have your heart set on certain flowers that are more delicate, consider asking your florist to make two boutonnieres for your groom. Have your site manager store the spare in a refrigerator and ask him to bring it out halfway through the reception to replace the wilting one. And finally, you might want to go the silk-flower route. They can be just as beautiful as the real thing, so consider having your guy don a fake boutonniere. Trust us, no one will know the difference.

Q **Should I have my mom and sisters make our bouquets and centerpieces as a way to save money?**

A You can certainly go this route, especially if your family has a flair for floral. However, here are a few things to think about before you put your family to work: First, have they ever done flowers for a large-scale party? If not, they might find that it's more work than they bargained for. They'll need to shop for the flowers in bulk, have the space in which to store them and then be at the reception site early to set them up. Next, you should think about where you want your family to be on the day of the wedding. If they need to be standing by for photos, you might not want them busy with flower detail. And finally, since your main goal is to cut costs, be sure you have explored all of your options with your florist. A good florist should be able to work within your budget and help you find an affordable plan that doesn't involve a family DIY project.

Q **I know guests sometimes take the centerpieces home, but I was planning to use some antique jars from my own collection for the tables. How do I prevent people from running off with them?**

A Although some guests we know have been to weddings where the centerpieces were given away as added favors (either to special people or random guests at each table), it shouldn't be necessary to frisk your friends and family as they leave the building. When centerpieces are meant to be taken, often an announcement is made ahead of time—either by the bandleader or the bride and groom themselves. So chances are, no one will walk away with your jars. But let the reception staff (including the coat-check and valet attendants) and your immediate family know that all centerpieces should remain on the premises, so they can stop any overeager guests from leaving with your treasures.

Q **Is it possible to toss my bouquet at the end of the reception and still keep a few blooms for myself?**

A Absolutely. All you need to do is ask your florist to triple-tie your bouquet. Have her place two sets of ribbons around your stems. One ribbon will bind the majority of your flowers and another smaller ribbon will bind the rest. Then your florist can wrap both of those bunches together with a third ribbon. When it comes time to throw your bouquet, you just need to cut or untie the outer ribbon and you'll have instantly have two bouquets—one to throw and one to save. If you don't want to bother with separating your bouquet, then the next best thing is to simply have your florist make you a small keepsake bouquet. This way you can throw your big bouquet and take the other one home to preserve. If you're set on keeping blooms from the actual bouquet that you carried down the aisle, then just do the reverse: Toss the smaller bouquet and keep the original one for yourself. Bonus tip: Appoint a trusted friend or family member to keep track of the bouquet you want to keep. Your wedding day will be a whirlwind of activities. In all of the excitement, you don't want to risk leaving your bouquet behind.

CHAPTER 10

Select Your *Stationery*

INVITATIONS, SAVE-THE-DATES AND OTHER WEDDING PAPERIE

Bookmark
10.10.08
for
Jessica & Tom's
Wedding

Save-the-Dates

Save-the-dates ensure that guests reserve room in their schedules for the big event. So it's no wonder that they've become popular. They definitely come in handy if your wedding is on a holiday weekend, when people are more likely to make plans far in advance, or if there are out-of-towners on the guest list who need an early heads-up to book the best rates

on flights and hotels. Since these are less formal than traditional invites, you can DIY them if you don't want to hire a stationer.

Some list just the date, but if you're inviting a lot of out-of-towners, you may want to include more information: the scoop on local hotels (including the contact information for any hotels where you've set aside rooms at a group discount), a listing of cool activities that'll keep guests occupied during the downtime between celebrations, and if possible, a few details on any special events you have planned. Save-the-dates should be sent out several months before the wedding—at least six months out is best for a standard wedding, but up to a year ahead could be helpful for a destination wedding, when guests may need to save their vacation time and money for your big event and book flights and rooms well in advance.

Bride to Bride

My fiancé and I are getting married in New York City. Instead of having save-the-date cards printed, we're sending postcards with Big Apple images instead.

—Yvonne

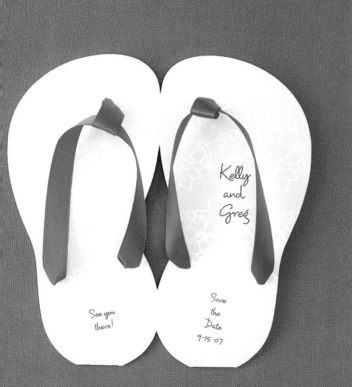

Creative Save-the-Dates

A magnet: Put your date on a magnet that guests can stick to their fridges—it'll help them remember to save your date.

A puzzle: Let guests put the pieces together to figure out your big day.

A travel brochure: If you have a lot of out-of-towners on your list, turn your save-the-date into a travel brochure, featuring local attractions and accommodation options.

A calendar: Send out calendars to your guests—with your wedding date circled in red.

A bookmark: Literary-minded couples can get their guests to "bookmark" their special date with custom-designed save-the-dates.

box style

MR. AND MRS. ROBERT FRA...
REQUEST THE HONOUR OF T...

Christine Alexandra ...
Stephen Thomas Maders...

SON OF MR. AND MRS. THOMAS REILLY ANDE...
SATURDAY, THE TWENTY-SIXTH OF JUNE, TWO
at six o'clock in the evening

BLUE HILL AT STONE BARNS
630 Bedford Road, Pocantico Hills, New York

reception to follow...

FROM POINTS EAST
Take the Cross Westches...
119 to the end. Turn rig...
1.7 miles. Make a right...
the Center and Blue Hil...

FROM POINTS WES...
Take Tappan Zee Bridge...
and turn right onto Rou...

Driving D...

630 Bedford ...

R.S.V.P.
The favour of a reply is requested
before the first of June

M _____
accept with pleasure _____   decline with regret _____

Inviting Styles

The box-style invitation: This style is all about packaging. These luxe invitations come in gift boxes and often include a present for guests—a tiny picture frame, a small bottle of champagne (with the details of the event affixed to the label) or a sweet confection—along with the invitation.

The trifold style: Single cards and simple folded invitations have given way to the trifold, which has two flaps that fold out from the center. With this style, the invitation details are usually in the center, with the response card, directions and other details tied or folded into one or both of the outer flaps. But this invitation design is also versatile enough to work for nearly any need: For multicultural weddings, couples can use the two outer flaps for the invitation, writing one in English and the other in Spanish, perhaps.

The invitation booklet: With wedding weekends becoming more popular (and extensive), many couples are replacing the traditional invitation with a full booklet, offering information on every wedding-related event, maps and directions, and perhaps even hotel info for out-of-town guests.

The three-dimensional style: It's all about texture, as couples use fabric, pop-ups and cutouts to create intricate invites.

trifold style

booklet

three-dimensional style

{expert tip} You can incorporate interesting or unexpected materials like silk, wood, ribbons or rope to give your wedding guests a preview of the reception decor.

—*Karen Bartolomei, stationer, Boston*

patterned lining

TOGETHER WITH THEIR FAMILIES

Amelia Evans Hupp

AND

Jordan Patrick Miles

REQUEST THE PLEASURE OF YOUR COMPANY
AT THEIR MARRIAGE
SATURDAY, THE TWELFTH OF JULY
TWO THOUSAND EIGHT
AT THREE O'CLOCK IN THE AFTERNOON
AUDUBON NATURE INSTITUTE TEA ROOM
NEW ORLEANS, LOUISIANA

PLEASE REPLY BY
the twelfth of June

Dinner and Dancing
AT SIX O'CLOCK IN THE EVENING
AUDUBON GOLF CLUB
NEW ORLEANS, LOUISIANA

Chic Accessories

Bellybands: These thick ribbons wrap around the middle of the invitations and are most often used with trifold invites. Look for a ribbon that matches your wedding style—such as a cheerful polka-dotted grosgrain for a casual garden celebration or rich velvet for a formal winter wedding.

Charms: Tiny metal charms—like a silver pinecone for a winter wedding—can be tied to a ribbon at the top of the invite or to a bellyband.

Patterned linings: Add interest to your envelope by lining it with paper that contains a striking design.

Wax seals: Using sealing wax with a monogram or other motif will give your invitations an antique vibe.

Embossing: Add texture and detail to your invite with a simple monogram or design that's slightly raised from the paper.

bellyband

{expert tip} The style and tone of the wedding invitation not only tell who, when and where, but also subtly convey to the recipient what sort of wedding to expect. —*Marcy Blum, wedding consultant, New York City*

{modern bride wisdom}

If you're having a formal event or hoping to create a very personalized vibe for your wedding, it's best to have the invitations hand-addressed, either by a professional calligrapher or by you and your fiancé. Many brides planning a casual wedding now use their computers to print the envelopes.

Putting It in Order

SMART ADVICE FOR CREATING A STYLISH INVITATION

1 FIGURE OUT HOW MANY YOU REALLY NEED. You may be inviting 150 people, but you'll need far fewer invitations, since you'll send a single invitation per couple or family. But pad your order with at least 15 extra invitations so you'll have some to save in a scrapbook, plus a few spares in case you add a guest to your list at the last minute. (Also, ask for more envelopes than invitations, so you can cover any mistakes you or your calligrapher make while addressing them.)

2 ORDER IN ADVANCE. Your invitations should be mailed out about eight weeks before the big event, and most stationers need plenty of time to prepare your order. Buy your invitations about four months before the wedding, and start addressing the envelopes ahead of time if you can, so you'll only have to assemble the invites and ship them out once the printed pieces are delivered.

3 DOUBLE-CHECK THE DETAILS. Most printers will send you a designed version of your invitation to proofread for errors. Have several people look over the proof to make sure the names, dates and details are correct: You'll pay a hefty reprint charge if you discover your fiancé is listed as Joan instead of John on the invitations after they've already been printed.

4 GET IT TOGETHER. Just where do all those pieces go? Any extra invitation elements go underneath a single-piece invite or inside a folded one. And when you're placing the invitation within the envelope, you want your guests to see the front of the invite as soon as they open your envelope. Voila! You're done!

5 WEIGH IN ON IT. Have a postal clerk weigh your finished invitation before you buy stamps: Many invites require extra postage because of their size.

Inside the Invitation

A PIECE-BY-PIECE GUIDE TO ESSENTIAL WEDDING STATIONERY

Directions/Map: Help your guests get to the church—and every other wedding location—on time by providing detailed instructions on how to get there. Many printers will help you draw the map, or you can crib your notes from your venue's Web site or another source; just test out the directions thoroughly before you print them to make sure they're clear.

Envelopes: The most formal invitations require three: the outer envelope, which is addressed and stamped; the inner (unsealed) envelope, which has only the guests' names written on it; and the response-card envelope, which is stamped and addressed to you, so your wedding guests can simply drop their reply in the mail.

Invitation: The main event, this can be done in a variety of creative formats, whether as a full booklet with a number of elements or as a simple card.

Pew card: Consider this a VIP pass. If you have a massive guest list and want to make sure your groomsmen give Grandma Tillie priority seating, print up enough of these for your VIPs' invitations. These important guests can simply slip their cards to the ushers, who will show them to their proper spots.

Rain card: If you're hosting an outdoor wedding, this key piece fills guests in on your backup plans, so they know where to go if Mother Nature doesn't cooperate on your big day.

Reception card: If you can't fit the reception information on the main invitation, here's where it goes.

Response card: This handy piece makes it easy for your guests to RSVP. If your caterer requires you to specify the meals your guests have chosen, you can list the menu offerings and let guests check boxes to specify their selections. Some brides have saved cash on postage and paper by forgoing the response card and envelope and creating a response postcard instead.

Extra Elements
STATIONERY BEYOND THE INVITES

Announcements: Having an ultrasmall wedding? Announcements can help you spread your good news to friends who will want to know you got married but weren't on the guest list.

Menu cards: Fill guests in on what they'll be enjoying with a gorgeously printed menu card—this makes a great memento of the occasion as well.

Place cards: If you've arranged the perfect seatmates for each guest, use these cards at each place setting to indicate who sits where.

Programs: Give guests the lowdown on the details of your vow exchange in this ceremony handout. (We've got more scoop on programs in "Get with the Program" on page 148.)

Save-the-dates: Mail these out six months or more before the big day to make sure guests mark their calendars.

Table-assignment cards/escort cards: Guests pick these up at the reception and use them to find their appointed table for the meal.

Thank-you notes: Create a uniform look for all of your stationery by ordering thank-you notes that match the rest of your pieces—or go your own way with unique stationery.

{modern bride wisdom}

We're asked all the time: Do you really need to include those little slips of tissue that many stationers provide with their invites? The answer is no. They're a throwback to years past, when a buffer layer was needed to keep the ink from smearing. If you want to use them, place them on top of the invitations—otherwise, simply toss them out.

THERMOGRAPHY

Powdered ink and heat are used to produce raised lettering like engraving without the imprint on the reverse side— or the high price tag.

OFFSET

Ink is simply put on the page in this flat printing style, like a photocopier or a computer printer. This is often used for thin, delicate material like rice paper, which won't stand up to other printing methods, or for highly detailed printing involving several ink colors or photos.

Wedding Words
YOUR GUIDE TO STATIONERY SPEAK

FOIL STAMPING

An adhesive-backed, metallic paper is applied, then stamped or embossed to create a three-dimensional design.

ENGRAVING

An etched plate presses ink onto the paper, creating raised lettering and a slight indent on the back of the card. This is the most traditional printing style for wedding invitations.

DEBOSSING

A design is pushed into the paper, creating an indent. No ink is involved, so this is usually used for something simple, like adding a special motif to the invitation.

LETTERPRESS

Just like it sounds, in this printing style, letters are imprinted into the paper. These invitations look like they're handcrafted, vintage pieces, and this style has become more popular over the past few years.

EMBOSSING

A design or monogram is pushed up from the paper, creating a textured image, but without using ink or foil to make it more prominent.

BECAUSE YOU HAVE SHARED IN THEIR LIVES BY YOUR FRIENDSHIP AND LOVE
YOU ARE INVITED TO SHARE WITH OUR DAUGHTER,

Amanda Elizabeth Lammon to *Jason Ray Morgan*

WHEN THEY EXCHANGE MARRIAGE VOWS AND BEGIN THEIR NEW LIFE TOGETHER

JUNE THE SIXTH
TWO THOUSAND AND EIGHT
SIX O'CLOCK IN THE EVENING
CATOR WOOLFORD GARDENS, ATLANTA

WAYNE & JESSICA LAMMON

RECEPTION IMMEDIATELY FOLLOWING

Directions

FROM 400/75—
TRAVEL SOUTH TO 75/85 SOUTH. EXIT AT FREEDOM PKWY.
#248C AND FOLLOW RAMP TO THE LEFT. STAY ON FREEDOM
PKWY. (STATE ROAD 10) UNTIL IT DEAD-ENDS INTO PONCE
DE LEON AVE. TURN RIGHT. FOLLOW FOR ABOUT 1.6 MILES
TURN RIGHT ONTO CLIFTON ROAD. TAKE THE FIRST
WOOLFORD GARDENS

Please reply by the seventeenth of May.

RSVP

○ WILL BE ATTENDING

○ WILL NOT BE ATTENDING

NUMBER OF PEOPLE _____

NAMES _____

_____

_____

yne and Jessica Lammon
12785 Bethany Road
Alpharetta, Georgia
3 0 0 0 4

A wedding invitation often
includes a suite of inserts, from
driving directions to an RSVP
card. Here, each item stands
out in a separate bold color.

Invitation Wording

HOW TO GET THE LANGUAGE RIGHT

THE MOST TRADITIONAL WORDING LISTS THE BRIDE'S PARENTS AS HOSTS:
Mr. and Mrs. Joseph Smith
request the honour of your
presence at the marriage of
their daughter Katharine Jane
to
John Michael Doe
Saturday, the tenth of July
Two thousand and seven
At six o'clock in the evening
St. Patrick's Cathedral
460 Madison Avenue
New York City

Reception immediately following
The Rainbow Room
Rockefeller Center
New York City

WHEN BOTH SETS OF PARENTS ARE FOOTING THE BILL (AND WANT BILLING ON THE INVITES), TRY SOMETHING LIKE THIS:
Mr. and Mrs. Joseph Smith
and
Mr. and Mrs. Thomas Doe
request the honour of your
presence at the marriage of
their children
Katharine Jane Smith
and
John Michael Doe

IF YOU AND YOUR FIANCÉ ARE THE HOSTS, THE WORDS CAN BE SIMPLE:
Katharine Jane Smith
and
John Michael Doe
invite you to celebrate
their marriage...

DEALING WITH DIVORCED PARENTS CAN BE HARD, ESPECIALLY IF BOTH PARENTS WANT TO BE LISTED. HERE'S AN OPTION:
Mr. and Mrs. William Jones
[your mother and stepfather]
and
Mr. and Mrs. Joseph Smith
[your father and stepmother]
request the honour of your presence
at the marriage of their daughter
Katharine Jane Smith...

OR TRY A LESS TRADITIONAL WORDING:
Please join
William and Mary Jones
and
Joseph and Margaret Smith
in celebrating the marriage of
Katharine Jane Smith
and
John Michael Doe

IF THE PARENTS DON'T NEED TO BE LISTED ON THE INVITATION, YOU CAN TRY ONE OF THESE:
Katharine Jane Smith
and
John Michael Doe
invite you to celebrate
their marriage...

Together with their families,
Katharine Smith and John Doe
request the pleasure of your
company at their wedding.

SOME DIFFERENT WORDINGS WE'VE SEEN:
Katharine Smith and John Doe
are getting married!
Watch them tie the knot on...

Please join us as we celebrate our
wedding day
Sunday, August 26, 2007...

Please be our guest as
Katharine Smith and John Doe
exchange wedding vows...

Generally, you request "the honour of your presence" for a wedding in a house of worship and "the pleasure of your company" for a ceremony in a secular spot, like a ballroom.

Get With the Program

A ceremony program can be anything from a simple printed sheet to an elaborate booklet that rivals the invitation for panache. However you design it, most programs offer guests this basic information.

A welcome note: Thank your guests for celebrating with you—just in case you don't get to offer more than a "hi" and a handshake on the receiving line.

Ceremony details: If there's a sweet story behind your reading selection—or if you're including a ritual that's unfamiliar to many of your guests—explain the reason you chose it. Or you can simply list the readings and songs in order, so guests can follow along.

Names of the VIPs: Your other guests may never have met your college roommate or your favorite cousin before, so list your bridal-party members, readers and other ceremony participants, and give a little background on why each person's so special to you.

Honored loved ones: The program is the perfect place to memorialize a family member or friend who has passed away with a note or even a photograph.

A sweet story or quote: Finish it off with the story of how you met or how he proposed, or a quotation or lyric that's meaningful to you. It'll help guests who know only one of you well get a better sense of you as a couple.

Bride to Bride

We had a summer wedding in a chapel that dates back to the 1850s, so there wasn't any air-conditioning. To help our guests stay a little cooler, we decided to hand out paper fans with our ceremony programs printed directly on them. —Laurie

{modern bride wisdom}

You might consider moving guests who gave cash or checks to the top of your thank-you list. They'll appreciate knowing that their gift arrived to you safely.

THANKS GIVING

While some etiquette mavens give guests a year to send you gifts (and others say only three months!), they don't allow you as much time to express your gratitude: Before the wedding, send notes no more than two weeks after the gift arrives. For gifts received at the wedding or afterward, you have more leeway—two months after your honeymoon ends.

You can send your thanks on simple note cards or ones made up to match the rest of your stationery—or have your photographer shoot a picture that can be printed on your card. (Just have it taken in advance so they can be printed before your big day.) Make your thank-yous a little more charming (and a little less taxing) with our tips.

5 FINESSE THE FINANCIAL GIFTS. "Thanks for the cash" just doesn't have a nice ring to it, so instead, thank a benefactor for his "generous gift," and give him a sense of how you plan to use it: "John and I are adding it to our savings toward a new house," or "We raised a glass in your honor at a five-star dinner during our honeymoon."

6 BE DELICATE. There are bound to be a few gifts that aren't to your taste. But even if you've already brought their gift back to the store, you need to express your appreciation of the effort and thought behind the gift. "Thank you so much for the elegant vase. We appreciate your taking the time to find us something so unique."

1 SPREAD IT OUT. Don't try to speed through 50 thank-yous in one evening. Not only will that make it seem like a never-ending chore, but your notes will suffer from the assembly-line treatment, too. Instead, aim to do 5 or 10 per day so you can take the time to write more thoughtful notes, and you won't feel like you're being punished.

2 DIVIDE THE DUTY. If your groom's sharing those plush bath towels and 1,000-thread-count sheets, he can share the responsibility of giving thanks for them. Put him in charge of sending out the notes to his friends and family members. Remember, though, that no matter who writes them, the cards should include both members of the couple in giving thanks: "Megan and I love the vase you sent us."

3 MAKE IT FUN. This isn't a college thesis—put on your favorite tunes, mix up margaritas and enjoy yourself.

4 GET SPECIFIC. Tell your guests how you're enjoying their gift—and you can even include an invitation to visit, too. As in: "Thank you so much for the wonderful waffle maker. John and I have been whipping up Belgian waffles every weekend since the wedding— we hope you'll stop by for brunch to enjoy some, too."

Q & A

Q My friend has pretty handwriting, so I asked her to address my invitations. I don't like the results. Can I ask her to redo them? Or should I have them redone by a professional?

A This is a sticky situation, but it can be solved. The key here is honesty. If you have someone else redo them without telling your friend, you will get caught (we presume she's being invited to the wedding!). So sit your friend down and tell her the invitations did not turn out the way you envisioned them. When you break it to her, emphasize that if it weren't your wedding day, you wouldn't be such a perfectionist. Then give her the option of doing them over—just be very specific about what you want this time—or of bailing out. Whatever her decision, insist that you treat her to a night on the town. If she declines a do-over, it's safe to hire someone else. If you were trying to save a little money by asking your friend in the first place, you might want to rearrange the budget to pay for a professional calligrapher.

Q Who should we plan to send wedding announcements to, and will these people be offended that they didn't get an actual invitation?

A It's impossible to predict what might offend someone—especially when it comes to planning a wedding. Someone's feelings are bound to get hurt no matter how hard you try to avoid it. Wedding announcements are sent out to people you can't invite to the wedding but who you think would still want to hear about your nuptials. Here are some possible scenarios for sending people wedding announcements in lieu of invitations: If you are having a small celebration and just can't accommodate everyone you'd like to, send wedding announcements to the folks who didn't make the guest list. Acquaintances or business associates you don't feel particularly close to but whom you still want to hear the good news can be added to the wedding announcement list, too. (Ask your parents if they have additional people who fit into this particular category.) And don't forget about long-lost friends whom you'd like to tell but who you highly doubt would be able (or want) to make the trek to your wedding. Recipients of wedding announcements should not feel obligated to buy you a wedding present.

Q My dad died several years ago, but I'd like to include him on the invitation. Is that possible?

A Yes. There's no reason you can't have his name printed along with your mom's. The best way to do this is to have the invitation come from you and your fiancé, not your parents. For example: "August Michaels, daughter of Mary Michaels and the late Charles Michaels, and Oliver Oana, son of Mr. and Mrs. Alexander Oana, request the honour of your presence..."

Q **Do we have to send out printed invitations for the rehearsal dinner and next-day brunch or can we save money and invite people via e-mail?**

A Before you decide what kind of invitation you want to send out, ask yourselves this question: What will our invitations say about our party? After all, it's the invitations that set the tone for a celebration. They should reflect the importance of your big day, and nothing says special like a formal invitation delivered by the mailman himself. If your pre- and postnuptial parties are on the informal side (such as a casual backyard barbecue or an open-house brunch), you can choose an informal design, but it's still more special to have the invitation arrive by regular mail. Here are two options that will keep your stationery costs down: Hit a local card shop or stationery store and check out the selection of prepackaged invites—you'll likely find something perfect for your casual event at a fraction of the cost of custom-printed invites. Or, consider buying festive paper and printing the invitations yourselves from your computer. We've seen computer-printed invites that are elegant

enough to have been done by a professional. Of course, if your event is super low-key and you're set on using e-mail, go ahead and create a fun Evite to send to your guests (don't just type up the information in a note). Also, be prepared to send an invitation the old-fashioned way to any guests who don't regularly check their e-mail.

Q **Should we include my fiancé's parents' names on the invitation even though my parents are paying for the whole wedding?**

A It is a nice gesture to include them, but this is entirely your call. Technically, if your parents are solely paying for the big day, then only their names need to appear on the invitation. (For example, "Terry and Carrie Farkas request the honour of your presence at the marriage of..."). If you want to include both sets of parents' names on the invite but don't want to imply that both sets are paying, simply add your fiancé's parents' names after his ("...at the marriage of Cynthia Farkas and Scott Goethals, son of Robert and Ann Goethals..."). However, if you and your fiancé feel that both sets of parents deserve top billing, by all means do it. Just make sure that both sets are okay with this before sending the wording off to the printer.

Q **I've ordered thank-you notes with my soon-to-be married name printed on them. Is it appropriate to use these to respond to early wedding gifts?**

A It's best to save those thank-you notes until after the big day. Although you're both excited about becoming Mr. and Mrs., loved ones might be a bit surprised to get a card in the mail that implies you're married before it's actually true. Also, using your future name now runs the risk of taking a little oomph from your wedding day. To thank guests for presents received before the wedding, buy some elegant note cards that are blank or feature a pretty pattern. Or, consider having some cards printed with your maiden name. After all, it's not just a handful of early wedding presents you'll need to acknowledge: There will be a slew of shower gifts—also arriving before your wedding—just waiting for a thank-you.

CHAPTER 11

Manage the *Music*

HOW TO FIND TOP-NOTCH PERFORMERS TO PLAY AT YOUR PARTY

Band or DJ?

FIND THE RIGHT ENTERTAINER FOR YOUR PARTY

YOU MAY WANT A DJ IF...

● You like to hear the original recordings. As far as you're concerned, no one can sing "The Way You Look Tonight" like Frank Sinatra.

● Your budget is limited. A top-notch DJ is generally more economical than a top-notch dance band, since you're paying for one pro, not several.

● You want to hear a wide range of music. A DJ can easily switch from hip-hop to country to jazz to suit your mood and your crowd—and if he doesn't have a particular CD you want played, you can always lend him yours.

YOU MAY WANT A BAND IF...

● You like spontaneity. If their version of "Hey Ya" has made the dance floor go wild, they can extend the tune to keep the party hot—and if a song bombs, they can quickly segue into something else.

● You want the excitement of a live performance. An amazing band will electrify your entire party—even the guests who don't like to dance will enjoy watching their performance.

● You want a more interactive, unique party experience. A live performance can put a fresh spin on the wedding standards.

MODERN BRIDE 5 Ways to Keep the Beat

Have it both ways. Kick off with a band for most of the reception, then switch to a hip DJ at midnight.

Pick your music based on your site. Choose steel drums for the beach, jazz at an old-school-style hotel and so on.

Surprise your parents. Have their wedding song played at some point during the evening.

If you can't afford a pro, make several "mood music" mix CDs. Play them during drinks, dinner, dancing, late night—and put a music-loving friend in charge of changing them. Or program your iPod accordingly and let the music play all night long.

Have a late-night sing-along. Barefoot bridesmaids singing "Lady Marmalade" can be totally hilarious.

{expert tip}

When searching for your first song, consider unfamiliar songs by familiar artists, new renditions of old favorites or tracks from movie scores.

—*Deanna Jones, orchestra leader, New York City*

QUESTIONS TO ASK

POSE THESE TO YOUR BANDLEADER OR DJ

1

What genres of music do you cover?

If you have your heart set on a lot of big-band songs or disco favorites, you'll want to be sure your band or DJ's repertoire includes your must-play tunes— or that they can learn or purchase the music before your wedding.

2

What's your performance style?

Find out how much the band's emcee or DJ talks between sets, and whether they have guest-participation events or light shows, so you can judge whether this person's style is right for your party. Also ask about their wardrobe choices—your performers should be suited up in formal-wear for a black-tie event.

3

How do you set up for the event?

If your band needs a few hours to unload equipment before the reception starts, you'll need to check with your site to make sure the space will be available to them. And if your band or DJ needs a lot of electrical power to amp up their instruments or light show, make sure that your site's system can handle their needs.

4

Have you worked at our venue before?

Every room has unique acoustics, so if your entertainer hasn't been to your site, consider arranging a time for him to check it out, so he can see where to properly place the speakers and other equipment for optimal sound.

5

Will you have backup equipment with you?

You won't want an hour of dead time in the middle of your party if an amp blows or a CD player is on the fritz.

6

Do you take breaks? If so, how do you cover it?

Most DJs play all night or have a CD of tunes they can throw on. But band members need a breather. Some bands stagger breaks, so only one or two musicians are off at a time to keep music continuous. Others take a short break every hour or two and supplement with CDs.

7

How much play time do you include?

Make sure you have the party covered, and ask about overtime fees, in case you later decide you want the band to keep playing beyond the agreed-upon time.

8

How do you get guests onto the dance floor?

Most bands have tried-and-true songs in their repertoire that pack the floor. They should explain what they'll do if they're faced with an empty dance floor during your party.

Ceremony Sounds

PICK THE PERFECT MUSICAL ACCOMPANIMENT FOR YOUR VOW EXCHANGE

Ask about restrictions. While managers at most secular ceremony sites don't care whether you walk down the aisle to Bach or The Beatles, officiants at houses of worship may limit the types of songs you can choose. Some sites may also have a list of musicians to choose from—they won't let just anyone play their instruments. Outdoor locales may have noise restrictions, so be sure to check with the site manager.

Think about the site when you're choosing music. A big cathedral needs a louder, grander sound, like an organ or trumpet, while a small chapel would be an ideal setting for a classical guitar. Outdoor weddings affect music choice as well. It wouldn't work well to have a grand piano or a harp, because their sounds travel upward. Also, if possible, keep your musicians covered, since even the slightest precipitation can alter the sound of instruments like flutes and violins.

Consider different musicians. String quartets may be the standard, but you can choose something a little unexpected—a pair of classical guitarists, an a cappella choir, or even a steel-drum band for a beachside wedding. Don't worry too much about tradition. This is your wedding. Make it as personal as you want.

Choose songs and musicians that fit with the rest of your ceremony. An offbeat rock song will seem out of place if your readings all come from Shakespeare and the Bible, and a brass band may be a bit too dramatic for a wedding held in a cozy little garden. Try to keep the ceremony as connected as possible, using the music to tell a story.

Work within your budget. If you have your heart set on a string quartet or chamber ensemble for your ceremony but it isn't proving to be an affordable option, consider hiring students from a local conservatory. They are often willing to play at much lower rates. (Be sure to watch them play before you hire them, so you know you're comfortable with their work.)

Avoid awkward silences. Start your music as soon as the doors open and have it continue as guests find their seats. Starting the ceremony late is often unavoidable so be prepared to have the music playing longer than expected.

Get the Most Out of Your Band or DJ

When you've found a pro you like, or one who's come highly recommended to you, listen to the demo tape—or, even better, go catch the band or DJ live. (Keep the size of your wedding in mind while choosing a band: Six pieces work best for 100 guests; a 10-piece band is ideal for 300 guests.) Meet with them in person to make sure you have a similar vision for your wedding. Before you pay a deposit, ask for references and check with the Better Business Bureau (bbb.org) to find out if there have been complaints filed. If there have, you may want to talk to the band or DJ to get their side of the story before making a decision.

When it's time to draw up a contract, ask whether you can explicitly state which band members will actually be playing at your wedding. While you can't be guaranteed that these people will still be available, this will at least send the signal that you're looking for a professional of a certain caliber. Be very clear about what you want your band or DJ to play and, maybe more importantly, what you don't want them to play. Let the entertainers know whether it's okay for them to take requests from guests. You'll want the band to dress uniformly, so discuss attire. Black-tie is

SONG SUGGESTIONS

CLASSICAL SELECTIONS FOR YOUR PROCESSIONAL AND RECESSIONAL

	OLD STANDBYS	FRESH TAKES
PROCESSIONAL	1. "Canon in D," Pachelbel 2. "Lohengrin: Bridal Chorus," Wagner 3. "Water Music," Handel 4. "Trumpet Voluntary," Clarke/Purcell 5. "Wedding March," *A Midsummer Night's Dream*, Mendelssohn	1. "Largo ma non tanto," Double Violin Concerto, Bach 2. "Entr'acte," *Carmen*, Bizet 3. "The Flower Song," *Lakme*, Delibes 4. "Triumphal March," *Aida*, Verdi 5. "The Arrival of the Queen of Sheba," *Solomon*, Handel
RECESSIONAL	1. "Dance of the Sugar Plum Fairy," *The Nutcracker*, Tchaikovsky 2. "Eine Kleine Nachtmusik: Allegro," Mozart 3. "Ode to Joy," Beethoven 4. "Concerto No. 1 in E (Spring): Allegro," Vivaldi 5. "Flute Sonata No. 4: Allegro," Bach	1. "Rejoicing," *Music for Royal Fireworks*, Handel 2. "Musetta's Waltz," *La Boheme*, Puccini 3. "Gavotte No. 2," Bach 4. "Brandenburg Concerto No. 3," Bach 5. "Hornpipe," Handel

always appropriate for a formal event or khaki suits for a casual wedding.

It's important to provide your band or DJ with a clear schedule of events. Set a specific time for setup—you don't want anyone interrupting cocktail hour because they're hauling in equipment. Let them know exactly when food will be served, toasts will be made, and first dances will be taken so that the night flows smoothly. Ask

them to provide music while they are on breaks so there's no downtime for you and your guests.

Don't forget to set aside (and pay for!) seats so your entertainers can eat a quick dinner. Be sure to tell your bandleader or DJ the correct pronunciation of the names of anyone being announced, including those who are giving toasts. Now rock on!

Cool Tunes for the Recessional

"The 59th Street Bridge Song (Feelin' Groovy)" by Simon & Garfunkel

"Here Comes the Sun" by The Beatles

"Happy Together" by The Turtles

"You Send Me" by Sam Cooke

"Elevation" by U2

Entertainment Alternatives

Music may be the most popular way to entertain a wedding crowd, but it's certainly not your only option. One of these may be perfect for your wedding party or rehearsal dinner.

Magician: An illusionist could go from table to table doing sleight of hand tricks with cards and small objects. Guests will still be puzzling over how he did his magic by the time your anniversary rolls around.

Dance instructors: Help your rhythmically challenged family by hiring instructors to teach guests basic ballroom, swing or line-dancing moves at the start of the reception.

Fortune teller: Ask a palm or tarot-card reader to predict your loved ones' romantic futures. (Just make sure she accentuates the positive!)

Cultural performers: Share a bit of your heritage by hiring Chinese lion dancers, an African drum troupe or a mariachi band to liven up your cocktail hour or reception meal.

Impersonator: Share your passion for the King or the Fab Four by hiring an Elvis impersonator or a Beatles tribute band to get the crowd going by doing a few numbers.

Unique First-Dance Tunes

We asked Deanna Jones, leader of the Deanna Jones Orchestra in New York City, for a list of songs your guests won't have heard a million times before.

1. "By Your Side" by Sade (A slow song with touching lyrics: "When you're cold/I'll be there to hold you tight to me.")
2. "Sway" by the Pussycat Dolls (Classic cha-cha; a great choice if you want to wow your guests with your skills)
3. "S'wonderful" by Ella Fitzgerald (Perfect for showing off your new fox-trot talent)
4. "Lovin' You" by Minnie Riperton (Simple and sexy; played live, it needs an excellent singer to pull off the high notes.)
5. "As" by Stevie Wonder (Fun tempo with beautiful lyrics)
6. "I Belong to You" by Lenny Kravitz (This song has a unique sound, plus dramatic lyrics.)
7. "All I Want Is You" by U2 (A romantic rock tune—just know that it's roughly six minutes long.)
8. "You Bring Me Joy" by Anita Baker (A contemporary song with a classic feeling)
9. "You Are So Beautiful" by Joe Cocker (For a cool twist, have it performed as a duet.)
10. "Ain't That a Kick in the Head" by Dean Martin (A fun choice)
11. "When God Made You" by Newsong with Natalie Grant (We love the lyrics, "When God made you/He must have been thinking of me.")
12. "I Will Be Here" by Steven Curtis Chapman (An alternative to "Time in a Bottle")
13. "Orange Colored Sky" by Nat King Cole (A great alternative to "The Way You Look Tonight")
14. "Love Theme (Kissing You)" by Des'ree (A slow-tempo ballad from *William Shakespeare's Romeo and Juliet*, with a mysterious sound)
15. "Love Will Keep Us Alive" by The Eagles (Perfect for classic-rock fans who like a little country)
16. "On a Slow Boat to China" by Renee Olstead (A playful classic with a sexy feel)
17. "So in Love" by Lara Fabian and Mario Frangoulis (Try this number from the film *De-Lovely* for its haunting, romantic melody.)
18. "Lovely Day" by Bill Withers (Great, uptempo song reminiscent of "How Sweet It Is")

{expert tip} Feature guests in the entertainment. Talented friends or family members can give musical performances instead of toasts.

—*Deanna Jones, orchestra leader, New York City*

$\mathcal{S}$tepping $\mathcal{O}$ut

If you and your mate haven't broken out of that old junior-high "hold and sway" method of dancing to a ballad, a few ballroom lessons may be money well spent. Here are the steps you need to take to hit the dance floor in style.

1 CHOOSE YOUR FIRST-DANCE TUNE. This will help dictate the kinds of dances you'll need to learn—a fast-paced song may call for swing, Latin or modern dance styles, while slower tunes suit ballroom classics like waltzes and fox-trots.

2 DECIDE WHETHER TO GO PUBLIC OR PRIVATE. Group classes are generally more economical, but private lessons offer you the ability to hone in on the exact dances you need to learn, and create a customized routine to your tune. (They'll also let you avoid the embarrassment of tripping in front of a room full of strangers.)

3 PRACTICE, PRACTICE, PRACTICE. All the lessons in the world won't help if you and your mate don't take a little time to try it out at home. And what's a more wonderful way to end the day than in your fiancé's arms?

The Big Songs

CONSIDER THESE TUNES FOR THOSE ULTRASPECIAL WEDDING MOMENTS

FATHER/DAUGHTER DANCE SONGS
1. "Unforgettable" by Nat King Cole
2. "Angel" by Lionel Richie
3. "A Kiss to Build a Dream on" by Louis Armstrong
4. "Isn't She Lovely" by Stevie Wonder
5. "What a Wonderful World" by Louis Armstrong
6. "Empty Nest" by Jacob's Journey
7. "I'll Be There" by The Jackson 5
8. "My Girl" by The Temptations
9. "Kind and Generous" by Natalie Merchant
10. "The Way You Look Tonight" by Frank Sinatra

MOTHER/SON DANCE SONGS
1. "Oh How the Years Go By" by Vanessa Williams
2. "Times of Your Life" by Paul Anka
3. "Your Smiling Face" by James Taylor
4. "Longer" by Dan Fogelberg
5. "In My Life" by The Beatles
6. "Forever Young" by The Pretenders
7. "Have I Told You Lately" by Van Morrison
8. "How Sweet It Is" by James Taylor
9. "Blessed" by Elton John
10. "I Hope You Dance" by Lee Ann Womack

LAST DANCE SONGS
1. "Last Dance" by Donna Summer
2. "Good Riddance (Time of Your Life)" by Green Day
3. "I Could Not Ask for More" by Edwin McCain
4. "Good Night My Love" by Harry Connick, Jr.
5. "Night and Day" by Frank Sinatra
6. "Thank You" by Dido
7. "The Best Is Yet to Come" by Tony Bennett
8. "These Are the Days" by 10,000 Maniacs
9. "Dream a Little Dream of Me" by Louis Armstrong
10. "Save the Last Dance for Me" by The Drifters

Q & A

Q How much music do I need for the ceremony?

A The length of your ceremony and the size of your wedding party will, of course, influence the amount of music you may want. In general, however, you will likely need to pick about 20 minutes' worth of introductory music to be played before you and your bridal party enter to walk down the aisle. This will give your guests plenty of time to greet one another, be seated, get comfortable and read their programs. Separate pieces should be played for each entrance: the family's, the bridal party's and then your own, as well as the recessional once the service is complete. During the ceremony itself, there will be moments for other selections to be played or sung. Work with your officiant to determine how many selections you will need, and when and how they will be incorporated into your service. Finally, before you fall in love with a particular song choice, keep in mind that some religious sites have restrictions on the types of music that can be played.

Q How can we express our cultural heritage through music at the wedding?

A Music is a wonderful way to incorporate a little bit of each family's history. Don't be afraid to add a few surprises to your day, such as a gospel choir, African drumming or specially chosen folk songs. Your guests will love sharing in this piece of your heritage. The rich tapestry of your backgrounds can be reflected not only at the ceremony but also at the reception. Why not consider incorporating a traditional dance, whether it's a tango from Argentina or an Irish jig? Consider other opportunities for introducing music as well: Scottish bagpipes could lead guests as they walk from the ceremony site to the reception site. A fife-and-drum band could welcome guests as they arrive at a Colonial-style Fourth of July festivity. Talk to your parents or grandparents to find out more about the music and dance styles of their cultures.

Q My wedding reception will be in the afternoon. From weddings I've attended, guests seem less interested in dancing in broad daylight. What can I do to motivate them to fill the dance floor?

A One surefire way to rock the house is for you and your groom to get on the dance floor first. This is your day, and guests will want to spend time with you, whether it's on the dance floor or elsewhere. If your guests are still glued to their seats, enlist the help of your DJ or bandleader. Get creative and call all couples to the floor who've been married for five years, ten years, etc. People are proud of this and will want to get up and take advantage of their bragging rights. One final note—

play a variety of music. Your aunt might still be clinging to her chair because she's waiting to hear something she actually recognizes.

Q **Our song is more of a rocker than a ballad. Should we dance our first dance to it or choose something slower?**

A If this song is the one that put stars in your eyes, then let the DJ spin it. Traditionally, first dances are slower songs, but as long as the two of you are comfortable groovin' to an audience, that's all that counts. However, if you are a little self-conscious about rocking out on center stage, then have the DJ or band leader introduce the song, briefly explain its significance to you as a couple and ask the crowd to join the two of you on the dance floor. Either way you swing it, dancing to this tune should end up ranking pretty high on your list of wedding-day highlights.

Q **I'm concerned about the noise level in the room when the band is playing. What are some ways to accommodate guests who would rather talk than dance?**

A Some couples hire two bands to allow time for quiet conversation first, followed by louder revelry. A string quartet or bass player and piano might entertain during cocktails and dinner. A band that makes you want to

jump up and dance might step in starting with dessert and continue on into the night. If you prefer to have the band there from the very beginning, just be sure to seat older guests away from the speakers, and be prepared for requests from the senior crowd to have the sound turned down a notch. You can also provide a lounge area away from the dance floor so that guests who need a little respite from the festivities can move to a comfortable sofa to chat more easily with friends and family.

Q **How can I make sure that the band or DJ doesn't play songs we don't like?**

A Many brides and grooms live in fear of hearing the "Chicken Dance" or "YMCA" played at their weddings. To make sure that bad songs don't happen to good couples, be very clear about your wishes as you talk with your band or DJ. When working on the contract with your musicians, it is just as important that you spell out what you don't like as what you do like. To be sure there are no surprises, you can create a "Do Not Play" list. In addition to citing specific songs or artists, tell your band or DJ what you think of line dances and circle dances. And it's always a good idea to give your thoughts on whether or not they should accept guests' requests. You may want to make

sure that your musical tastes aren't suddenly hijacked by your Marilyn Manson–loving cousin.

Q **We'd love to have a famous artist perform at our wedding. How hard would this be?**

A Not hard at all, if you've got a generous (some might say "unlimited") budget. Virtually any star, including biggies like Billy Joel and Elton John, can potentially be hired to perform. Prices for well-known artists begin at about $25,000 and can exceed $1 million. Aside from the hefty fee, you may also need to be flexible in terms of your wedding date— these folks are busy, after all, so if you're set on one particular star, you will most likely have to be prepared to plan around his schedule. You can start your star search by inquiring with some of the big agencies, like Creative Artists Agency, which have private-events divisions. Once you've learned your options and selected an artist to perform, be sure to have a detailed contract drawn up, specifying the exact time the performance will take place, the duration and any expectations for songs, band members and instruments. You should also be aware of all related fees you will be responsible for, such as the performer's transportation and hotel, if applicable.

CHAPTER 12

Take Your *Best Shots*

PRESERVE YOUR MEMORIES WITH GREAT PHOTOGRAPHY

How to Hire Your Photo and Video Pros

1 ASK VENDORS AND RECENTLY MARRIED FRIENDS FOR RECOMMENDATIONS. It's just as important to find photographers and videographers who are a pleasure to work with as it is to find those who produce great work.

2 DO ONLINE RESEARCH. Most photographers and videographers have Web sites loaded with samples of their work. Spend some time on the site before you set up an appointment, to make sure you like his style.

3 MEET THE PERSON WHO WILL SHOOT YOUR WEDDING. Some studios have several photographers working for them; be sure that the one who shows up at your wedding is the person whose work you saw.

4 EXPRESS YOUR STYLE. Give an idea of your preferred ratio of photojournalistic, candid shots to posed pictures, and how much of the wedding should be shot in black and white vs. color.

5 ASK ABOUT EXPERTISE. Some photo and video pros have specialties, such as hand-coloring or black-and-white photography or documentary-style videos. Find out what he's mastered—and whether you want him to do that for you.

6 GET PROOF. Don't look solely at a best-of collection of photos or videos—ask your photographer to show you the entire proof book from a recent wedding, and your videographer to show you one of his recent videos. That way, you can get a more complete sense of how your wedding will be covered.

7 FIND OUT HOW HE WORKS. Thanks to technological advances, photographers and videographers have a wider range of tools available than ever before. They can shoot your wedding digitally or on film, and can often pick up sound and visuals without resorting to using huge microphones, strobes or lights. Ask your pros how they handle recording in low light or at a distance so you can decide whether their methods may be too intrusive for your taste.

8 ASK FOR BACKUP. Find out about your pro's contingency plans. Does he have an assistant who will come to help out on the wedding day? Does he have another photographer or videographer who can fill in if he has an emergency and can't make it? Does he have an extra set of cameras in case of any malfunctions?

9 DISCUSS THE PRICING. Most photographers and videographers offer packages, which include a certain amount of coverage on the wedding day, and some prints and/or an album after the event. If a package isn't quite perfect for you, see if you can make changes to it—perhaps you'll want two 5 x 7 shots in lieu of the big 10 x 13 mantel picture, or you'll decide to skip the extra copies of the video so you can have a longer, edited version instead.

10 GET EVERYTHING IN WRITING. You'll want to make sure every detail, from the approximate number of shots being taken to the wedding date and locations, is clearly stated in your contract.

{modern bride wisdom}

Ask your photographer to recommend a great videographer. He'll help you choose an expert who produces quality work— and who works well with him, so neither pro misses a shot.

Should You Go Digital?

Many photographers and videographers now offer the option of shooting on film or digitally—and plenty shoot digital exclusively. Here's the lowdown on both formats to help you decide which one's right for you.

DIGITAL

Want to see the photos of the ceremony before the cocktail hour begins? That's one of the biggest benefits of digital photography, which will allow your photographer to do things like create a slideshow of your ceremony photos to show during your reception, or give you access to the proofs almost right away. Digital images are very easily manipulated, as well, so your photographer can transform a color photo to black and white. Years ago, digital cameras didn't offer the same image quality as film (prints were prone to fading sooner than regular film, and there was that dreaded delay before the camera actually took the shot), but the technology has rapidly caught up, and today's high-end professional cameras offer quality that's nearly on par with traditional film cameras.

FILM

This "old-school" way of creating images is still with us, in large part because film captures truer colors than digital can. Shooting on film may mean you have to wait a little longer to see your proofs, but if you're all about the color, it may be worth it.

What to Include in Your Contract

☐ **Wedding date, time and locations:** Make sure your contract lists the address for every destination and approximate times your photographer or videographer will need to be there. He may not realize that you want to take some shots at your parents' house before the wedding, for example.

☐ **Agreed-upon coverage:** Some photographers shoot a certain number of rolls, others for a certain amount of time. Either way, get this in the contract so you know you're both on the same page.

☐ **Final product:** Find out exactly what the fee will cover. Will you get just the proofs and have to order images and the album à la carte, or will the package include an album and several prints for framing and sharing? Even if your photographer offers a set package, you may be able to negotiate the components of that package.

☐ **Due dates:** You'll want to document when payments are expected and when you can expect to see proofs and final prints. With digital photography, some photographers can let you see images instantaneously; with traditional film, many will have a proof book ready for you once you've returned from your honeymoon.

Wedding Words

LEARN THE LINGO BEHIND THE IMAGES

BACK-LIGHTING
The method of lighting the photographer's subjects from behind, creating a soft glow around them.

CONTACT SHEET
A sheet containing tiny versions of the images from a roll of film.

MATTE
The satiny, shine-free finish to a print.

RETOUCHING
The process of removing red-eye, blemishes and other problems with the images through editing software.

CROP
The process of trimming an image to focus on a particular subject, remove a bad background or otherwise improve it.

PROOFS
These are all the shots your photographer took, with little or no editing done. You'll need to go through these to select your favorite shots.

MONTAGE
A compilation of several photos or short bits of film that create a "best-of" highlight video of your wedding day.

DOCUMENTARY
An increasingly popular form of wedding video, which includes interviews with the couple and other key people, along with highlights of the wedding day.

NATURAL LIGHTING
The lighting that's available, without any artificial light, candlelight, etc.

STRAIGHT SHOT
A video that includes just the basic coverage of the wedding day, with no interviews or additional elements.

Formals Done Fast

DON'T WASTE YOUR WHOLE DAY STRIKING A POSE. HERE'S HOW TO GET YOUR GROUP SHOTS DONE IN RECORD TIME.

DO CONSIDER TAKING THEM BEFORE THE CEREMONY. You won't have other people (or the allure of cocktails and hors d'oeuvres) distracting your bridal party—so you'll have a little more time to get them done.

DON'T WING IT. Write up a list of the must-get shots, and go over it with the photographer ahead of time to figure out if it's doable in the amount of time you have allotted. If not, consider scaling back to the bare essentials and asking your photographer to increase his candid coverage instead.

DO START BIG. Get the biggest groups done first—your entire clan, his college pals—so you can send those people back to the party fast. That way, you don't have the added confusion and distraction of a crowd of people milling around.

DON'T TRAVEL. Unless it's really important to you, skip the trek out to that perfect stretch of beach or a tour around town shooting at a dozen different locations. Just find one pretty space near either the ceremony or reception site.

DO ENLIST HELP. Ask an efficient friend or family member who knows most of the key people to gather the groups and seek out anyone who's missing—that way, you won't end up sending out five separate search parties for the groomsman who got away.

DON'T LET YOUR PHOTOGRAPHER GO IT ALONE. A photographer's assistant can serve as a second snapper or help load film and wrangle overexcited flower girls into place, making the photo session go more smoothly.

MODERN BRIDE 5

Top Photo Ops

The anticipation shots: This includes images such as your wedding dress (before you put it on), the reception tent enveloped by the morning fog or the empty ballroom.

Recessional: An action shot at the ceremony of you and your new hubby walking back up the aisle as the crowd beams.

Your first dance: Ideally, this image should be taken from an elevated position: the stage where the band performs, a balcony or even from the top of a ladder.

The memorable moments: Your dad making his toast, the groom looking on lovingly, the best man dancing with the flower girl and so on.

A perfect ending: A shot of the two of you as you're leaving the wedding—looking out of a car window, perhaps, or walking down the hotel's steps.

{modern bride wisdom}

Wedding videos today don't always have fade-ins, photo montages and other expected elements. Some videographers now use a mix of media (Super 8 and 16mm film with video, for instance) and employ a swift, MTV-like editing style.

Bride to Bride

We set up a display table that contained not only the usual photos of our parents', grandparents' and great-grandparents', weddings but also mementos: my grandmother's veil, Todd's grandparents' cake topper and his parents' cake knife. —Laura

{modern bride wisdom}

Make your wedding-day weather a part of your photos. Your bridal party can pose beneath colorful parasols on a sunny day, or you can have your photographer capture your groomsmen having a snowball fight at your winter wedding.

{expert tip}

A pre-ceremony photo session is the best way to have a fun, stress-free day. You can go straight from the ceremony to the cocktail hour without the break for all the posed photos.

—*Lisa Lefkowitz, photographer, San Francisco*

MODERN 5 BRIDE

Creative Ways to Use Photos

Pew decorations: Hang framed photos of you and your fiancé along the aisle for an ultrapersonal decor element.

Guest book: Ask a friend to snap Polaroids of your guests as they enter the reception, then have guests sign the edge of their prints. You can later paste the photos into your guest book for a perfect memento of the day.

Favor: Search through your collections of old photos for shots of you and/or your fiancé with each guest. Frame these, and give them out to guests as a special reminder of their relationship with you.

Cake topper: A framed photo of you and your mate can be the perfect finish to your wedding cake.

Thank-you note: Choose a favorite shot from your wedding day to insert in the envelope along with your thank-you note.

Get Great Photos

BE SURE YOU CLICK WITH YOUR PHOTOGRAPHER. Skill and talent are important, but so is chemistry, since you'll be spending the entire day with this person. You are more likely to let your true smile come out if you feel comfortable and relaxed around the photographer. If you find the photographer even slightly annoying during a short meeting, imagine how you'll feel after five hours with him.

KEEP IT CAREFREE. The formal photo session doesn't have to be torture. Opt for nontraditional shots that allow personalities to shine through—the groomsmen hoisting the groom on their shoulders, for instance, or something as simple as the bridal party trotting toward the camera will ensure that no one can keep a straight face. Crack jokes and laugh with your party members, and that natural, joyful glow will show up in your wedding photos.

VARY YOUR POSE. Standing still will only make you look stiff, so make sure you move your head and body between shots. Your photographer might even suggest doing something active, like dancing, during the formal photo session. Go with it—these shots will make your wedding album far more interesting.

BE NATURAL. During your reception you might be tempted to strike a pose every time you feel a camera on you. Don't. Candid shots are a great way to capture your genuine emotions. Whether you are laughing with friends, embarrassed by the best man's speech or caught kissing your groom, you'll cherish the pictures of you being you.

DON'T LET THE WEATHER GET YOU DOWN. Rain on your big day is supposed to be good luck. (Yes, you've heard it a million times.) You might not have heard that it also makes for gorgeous photo-ops. Grab a couple of big umbrellas and head outside to shoot some pictures in the rain. A romantic black-and-white photo of you and your groom kissing under one umbrella with raindrops pooling at your feet could end up being one of your favorite shots.

PLAN OUT THE DAY. A little organization goes a long way to ensure you get the photos you want. Your photographer should know how to keep the picture-taking on track, but to make sure you get all the important photos, give him a list of your "must-have shots" beforehand. (Use our Photo Checklist on the next page.)

INCORPORATE YOUR LOCATION. You picked where you are going to wed for a reason. Whether you are getting married in a bustling city, a serene countryside or a calming beach, incorporating the natural environment around you (people, buildings, trees, etc.) will make your photos more colorful and playful.

STEP INTO SOME GOOD LIGHT. Light is a photographer's most valuable tool. Late-afternoon sunshine is the best for photos—it'll make you and your party positively glow. If you can't wait until then, opt for a spot in the shade, which will help you avoid excessive squinting.

STAND UP STRAIGHT. Keeping your shoulders back, arms loosely bent and neck elongated will ensure you never get caught from a bad angle. Practice this runway-model stance that makes everyone look thinner: Stand with one foot in front of the other and slightly bend your front knee. Then lean your upper body back just a little.

GLAM IT UP. Nothing conveys elegance like black-and-white photos. It's a great medium for documenting emotional moments and bringing the mood into focus. Bonus: Black and-white film also masks skin imperfections.

{expert tip} If you are going to take family portraits before your ceremony, start dressing two-and-a-half hours before, and be ready to take these shots an hour before the ceremony. —*Marcy Blum, wedding consultant, New York City*

Photo Checklist

GETTING READY

- ☐ The dress, the shoes
- ☐ Bride's bouquet
- ☐ Bride getting ready
- ☐ Bride and mother
- ☐ Bride with bridesmaids
- ☐ Groom
- ☐ Groom with father
- ☐ Groom with groomsmen
- ☐ Extra shots:

_____

_____

_____

FORMAL PORTRAITS

- ☐ Bride alone, groom alone
- ☐ Bride and groom
- ☐ Bride/groom with attendants
- ☐ Flower girl and ring bearer
- ☐ Wedding party
- ☐ Bride/groom with parents
- ☐ Bride/groom with siblings
- ☐ Bride with mother and grandmother
- ☐ Groom with father and grandfather
- ☐ Bride and groom with bride's family
- ☐ Bride and groom with groom's family
- ☐ Bride and groom with both families
- ☐ Extra shots:

_____

_____

_____

CEREMONY

- ☐ Exterior and interior of the site before guests arrive
- ☐ Wedding programs
- ☐ Guests arriving at the site
- ☐ Bride arriving at the site
- ☐ Parents and grandparents being seated
- ☐ Wedding party walking down the aisle
- ☐ Groom waiting, before processional
- ☐ Ceremony musicians
- ☐ Bride and escort(s) walking down the aisle
- ☐ Groom watching bride walk down the aisle
- ☐ Bride and escort(s) parting at the end of the aisle
- ☐ Wide shot of altar during ceremony
- ☐ Bride and groom saying vows
- ☐ Bride and groom exchanging rings
- ☐ The first kiss
- ☐ Bride and groom's recessional
- ☐ Bride and groom outside, with guests
- ☐ Bride and groom getting into car
- ☐ Bride and groom in back seat
- ☐ Extra shots:

_____

_____

_____

RECEPTION

- ☐ Exterior and interior of the site before guests arrive
- ☐ Table setting
- ☐ Menu card
- ☐ Centerpiece
- ☐ Guest book
- ☐ Escort-card table
- ☐ Bride and groom's table
- ☐ Wedding cake
- ☐ Favors
- ☐ Bride and groom arriving
- ☐ Bride and groom with guests
- ☐ Food stations, bar at cocktail hour
- ☐ Guests at tables
- ☐ Bride and groom's first dance
- ☐ Toasts
- ☐ Bride and groom during toasts
- ☐ Father-daughter dance
- ☐ Mother-son dance
- ☐ Musicians
- ☐ Guests dancing
- ☐ Cutting the cake
- ☐ Extra shots:

_____

_____

_____

_____

_____

_____

_____

_____

Picture-Perfect Extras

We've seen so many fun ideas for keeping and sharing the memories from weddings. Here are some creative ways to capture the moment.

Photo Booth: Rent one through a local company or have your photographer set up a backdrop in a spot where guests can strike a pose. Make sure you get doubles of the pictures: You can send one home with the guest, and keep the other one as a memento of your wedding.

Table Cameras: Let your guests catch moments you might miss. Disposable cameras can be found in cool color schemes to match your wedding decor.

Surprise Slideshow: Give guests an instant replay: If your photographer shoots digitally, ask him to upload photos into a slideshow program and set it up on a screen near the bar or dance floor during your reception.

Love Story Video: Have your videographer interview you and your fiancé on camera—and perhaps even some of your friends and family members—before the big day to share the details of your courtship and proposal. He can use the interviews and photos you provide to create a short video of your love story, which you can show at the rehearsal dinner or during the reception.

Sketch Artist: Some couples hire artists or illustrators to create renderings of key moments of their wedding—a unique, artistic way to remember their big day.

Build a Better Album

After the wedding comes the tough part—editing down a mountain of great proofs into the key images that encapsulate the feeling of your wedding day, and figuring out exactly how to display them. Here's how to gear up for the challenge.

Decide how you want to tell your story. Some couples like to showcase only 25 or 30 images that capture the most telling details of their special day, while others opt to use more images to tell their wedding story in a more complete way.

Choose your album style. Albums come in all shapes and sizes, and some couples even opt for an alternative, such as a set of matte prints stacked in a beautiful box. You can get the traditional leather-bound book, or select an accordion-style album with photos printed on both sides. Your album style will impact how many and what types of proofs you choose—for instance, you'll likely choose only 20 to 25 photos for a photo box, while a big, traditional album could fit as many as 75 to 100 smaller images.

Determine your level of involvement. You can control the entire album, choosing which photos will appear on each page and what size to make them, or you can simply choose the photos to be used and let your photographer select the photo sizes and layout.

{expert tip} To help prints last, keep them in an archival-quality photo album and don't expose the prints to sunlight or moisture.

—*Faith West, photographer, Philadelphia*

Q&A

Q My fiancé wears glasses. I am worried that the flash photography will reflect off them and ruin our pictures. How can I ensure beautiful photos?

A Wedding photography has advanced by leaps and bounds, so the reflection should not be a problem. However, it doesn't hurt to stack the deck in your favor. Have your fiancé invest in glasses with anti-reflective coating, and encourage your photographer to use natural light whenever possible. To be safe, you may want to have a clause added to your contract stating that reflection from the flash will be retouched free of charge. You can also simply ask your fiancé to remove his glasses for some of the pictures. (He won't know what he's smiling at, but hopefully the pictures will capture only his good looks and not his confusion.) If you opt for this, though, keep in mind that your fiancé will look different without his glasses. You fell in love with some-one who wears glasses, and it's impor-tant that your wedding pictures reflect that. (No pun intended!)

Q We want to have photos of both the rehearsal dinner and the after-party. Is it okay to rely on friends and family, or should we hire a professional?

A You could go either way on this one. If your budget can accom-modate a photographer for these extra events, you'll have peace of mind knowing that a pro is on board to roam around and capture everything on film. (He might even be able to customize a cool album for you and your groom of photos from all the other celebra-tions.) With a photographer on hand, there also won't be any question as to whether the photos will come out or if everyone important to you—grandpar-ents and college pals alike—will be represented. However, there's some-thing to be said for the supercandid, amateur photos most of your friends and family would likely snap. If your rehearsal dinner and after-party are going to be laid-back and informal, pictures that aren't so perfect will reflect the fun time guests had. Beforehand, spread the word that you're going to be relying on everyone to take pictures. You can either invite friends and family to use their own cameras or buy disposables in bulk, so you're ready to capture every moment. It's also smart to enlist the help of a trusted friend to collect the disposables at the end of the night.

Q How can I speed up the photogra-pher so I can eat, drink and be merry?

A Be prepared to cast superstition aside and take the bulk of your pictures with your groom, his family, your family and your attendants before the ceremony. Although it makes for an even longer day, snapping photos of your wedding party a couple of hours before the ceremony will guarantee you more fun time later. If you and your fiancé don't want to sneak a peek at each other prior to the "I Dos," prepare a list of each formal photo you want taken after the ceremony. Designate one list keeper and have her organize groups of people so they're photo-ready as soon as the previous group is finished. You can also build in some extra time—no more than two hours—before the reception starts.

Q **My parents divorced years ago, but they still don't get along. What do I do when it's time to take the family picture?**

A To keep the awkwardness on your big day to a minimum, discuss your anxiety about picture time with both parents beforehand. Also, plan out exactly which groups of people will be shot and in what order, and share these groupings with your parents ahead of time to make sure there are no surprises. To avoid the added tension of having your guests watching the session, take your formal photos during the cocktail hour when everyone else will be busy mingling and enjoying the food and drink. If your parents are willing to pose in a photo together with you, take this picture first—to get it out of the way—then follow it with a photo of you with your new husband and both parents. Your siblings (and

their spouses and children, if they have them) can also jump in for a family picture. After these three shots are done, send Dad away to join cocktail hour while your shoot resumes with Mom's family, then start again with Dad's clan. If a photo with both parents isn't possible (or even desired), make a plan so that neither parent needs to stand around and watch the picture-taking; ask a close relative to make sure your mom or dad is comfortably in another part of the room. By the way, try using your photographer to ease this process as well. He's probably used to this sort of scenario, so share your concerns with him ahead of time and ask for ideas on how he might approach the various groupings. If nothing else, he can keep the shots moving quickly, which will help keep the mood light. Remember, no matter who's in the picture, the focus will always be on you and your groom.

Q **How do we rent a photo booth for the reception? Is it expensive?**

A Finding a reputable photo-booth-rental company is much like hiring your other wedding vendors. The best way to start your search is to ask family and friends for their recommendations. They'll be able to tell you about their experiences at events they've attended. Make sure you get the answers to these questions: Was

the booth in good working order? How did their photos come out? Was the operator professional? Of course, if you're working with a planner, she probably knows of some good companies from parties she's organized in the past. Your next best bet is to do a search online. Most vendors service specific geographic locations (the size of the machines makes them difficult to transport great distances). Some, however, are nationwide or have sister companies that work together as a national network. Unless you're marrying in a very remote location, it shouldn't be difficult to find a company to work with. When shopping around, be sure to ask about what kind of booth you can get. Classic or vintage booths produce strips of four or five small images, while more modern digital booths create larger 4" x 6" pictures. Rates vary anywhere from $1,000 to $1,800 and up, depending on the type of booth you request, the distance it will have to travel and the length of time you are planning to be using it. In most cases, your fee will include unlimited pictures and an operator to set up, take away and supervise the use of the machine.

CHAPTER 13

Be Good to Your *Bridesmaids*

ALL ABOUT YOUR GIRLS—AND HOW TO KEEP THEM HAPPY AND HELPFUL

Party Politics

DECIDING WHO GETS THE BRIDESMAID NOD

If you don't want to end up with a gaggle of girls at the altar, you'll need to cut your potential list down to the essential people. But how do you make the cuts? Here are some things to think about.

Do discuss plans with your fiancé before you ask anyone to be an attendant. You don't want to decide to keep the party small after you ask your 10 best friends to be bridesmaids.

Don't feel you must return the favor. You aren't obliged to include every gal who's asked you to be her bridesmaid.

Do take difficult personalities into consideration. Your pal who always sees the glass as half empty may end up being a real downer to you and the rest of the party.

Don't worry about evening out the party. You don't have to have perfect pairings gliding down the aisle. Some 'maids can have a guy on each arm, or some of the guys can walk down the aisle on their own.

Do try to be sensitive to any tension between your friends. If two of your pals aren't on speaking terms, don't have them both in the party. Give one or both of them another role, like performing a reading or overseeing the guest book instead.

Don't feel like you have to include everyone you know. You may have pinky-sworn that you'd be in each other's wedding parties when you were 11, but if you haven't spoken to your grade-school pal since grunge went out of style, she'll understand if you don't fulfill that promise.

Do choose your 'maids based on inner beauty. The aisle isn't a fashion runway, so pick your bridesmaids based on their relationship to you, not on aesthetics.

{modern bride wisdom}

Don't limit yourself when you choose your wedding party. If you're especially close to your brother or have a male best friend, have him stand on your side of the aisle. And there's no rule that says Mom can't be a matron of honor, too!

Bridal-Party Duties

If you're not sure what your bridesmaid or maid of honor can do for you, check out these tasks normally assigned to party members.

BRIDESMAIDS

● **Lend a hand with the planning.** If you need a second opinion on the table linens or a few friends to help you tie ribbons to favors, your bridesmaids can handle it. Just don't take advantage of your pals—asking your attendants to help you assemble invitations is okay; having an attendant address 200 invitations isn't.

● **Plan and host a shower and bachelorette party.** Your attendants will be the masterminds behind these key prenuptial parties.

● **Serve as a sounding board.** When your fiancé forgets to get you his friends' addresses (again) and you're feeling frazzled after a full day of tackling your to-do list, your bridesmaids can be the ones you vent to.

● **Greet guests at the wedding and mix and mingle.** Your party girls can be, well, party girls, chatting up the other invitees and helping ensure the dance floor's always hopping.

MAID OR MATRON OF HONOR

● **Lead the bridesmaids.** As the head attendant, she'll oversee the shower plans and make sure you stay sane through the planning.

● **Give a toast.** Your maid of honor can raise a glass to you and your groom at the rehearsal dinner or the wedding.

● **Be your right-hand woman on the big day.** She'll hold your bouquet during the ring exchange, make sure your train doesn't twist and grab you a drink from the bar when you're too busy greeting guests to head there.

'MAID MONEY

Your bridesmaids will be footing most of the bill for being part of the party. The bride typically pays for the bridesmaids' bouquets and thank-you gifts, and will often host a special bridesmaids' luncheon right before the wedding. The rest of their expenses—dresses and accessories, hair and makeup for the big day, shower and bachelorette party, travel and accommodations, and, of course, shower and wedding gifts for you and your mate—usually come out of their pockets.

But that doesn't mean you can't help your attendants out if you have the resources. Some brides decide to splurge on manicures for everyone the day before the wedding or hair and makeup sessions on the wedding day. Some cover the costs of their attendants' attire, from dresses to shoes.

If, like most brides, you can't quite afford to help in that way, at least be mindful of their budgets. Choose a bridesmaids' dress that is affordable, or let them pick their own, so they can buy one at a price point that feels comfortable to them. Help them find reasonably priced accommodations (or a pullout sofa at your sister's place!) and don't suggest a pricey shower at the chicest eatery in town.

MODERN BRIDE 5

Grand Gestures

Showing appreciation for your 'maids goes a long way toward keeping them happy for the big day.

Treat your 'maids to a pre-wedding massage. Make the spa experience more festive by serving a little champagne.

Spend some quality time together. Catch up with each girl separately or in a group over coffee or lunch in the weeks before the wedding.

Take special pictures. Before the ceremony, ask the photographer to get shots of you with each 'maid. Later, mail the girls the photos with their thank-you notes.

Buy their accessories. Giving the girls shawls, shoes or even jewelry to wear at the wedding is a thoughtful gesture.

Hire a hairstylist or makeup artist. She can tend to your 'maids, so they feel as beautiful as you do.

{modern bride wisdom}

Make sure that none of your requests are extreme. It's one thing to ask your bridesmaids to get their hair and makeup done—it's quite another to force a short-haired pal to get extensions so she matches her long-tressed fellow party members.

{expert tip} Give your bridesmaids wonderful gift certificates for dinner for two— either at a restaurant or for a personal chef to cook a meal for them.

—*JoAnn Gregoli, event planner, New York City*

Perfect *Presents*

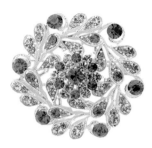

GREAT GIFTS FOR THE GALS

1. Monogrammed cosmetics bags filled with lots of beauty goodies, like luxury skincare products, makeup brushes and travel-sized toiletries

2. Necklaces, bracelets or earrings in their favorite colors

3. Monogrammed keepsakes, such as picture frames, photo albums, jewelry boxes, silver key chains or jewelry

4. Spa treats for pampering: plush bathrobes, comfy slippers, eye masks

5. Monogrammed tote bags teeming with beach accessories: sunscreen, books or magazines, water bottle, sarong, sunglasses, hat and flip-flops

6. Clutch purses or preppy Bermuda bags, depending on their style

7. Mani-pedi gift certificates to be redeemed at their leisure

8. Elegant wraps or shawls to wear during the wedding

9. Classic movies on DVD, boxes of microwave popcorn and bags of candy sold at theaters (Milk Duds, Dots, etc.)

10. Antique-looking silver-plated vanity sets (brush, comb and mirror)

{modern bride wisdom}

You don't have to give all of your bridesmaids the same thing. Play to their individual tastes: a stack of good books and a bookmark for your literary pal, margarita ingredients and a set of glasses for your friend who loves to entertain, and scrapbooking supplies for your crafty sister.

For the Flower Girl

Fun gifts for young attendants

- tickets for, or an IOU promising, an event she'll love: a trip to the ballet or a musical, or a zoo-and-ice-cream-parlor date
- a pretty, kid-appropriate necklace with her birthstone
- a "bride" doll
- art supplies—crayons, washable markers, etc., and a little carry case, so she can bring it to the reception to entertain herself.
- her own "big girl" purse, with a monetary gift toward some new toys or her college savings
- her flower-girl dress and accessories
- Candy Land game and a pail full of candy

MODERN BRIDE 5

Sweet Showers

Share these fun ideas with your 'maids.

Garden Party: Celebrate nature by holding the shower in a friend's backyard. Tuck blossoms and sprigs of lavender into the napkin folds. Serve fresh-from-the-garden foods such as seasonal vegetables, herbed grilled chicken and sun-kissed iced tea.

Afternoon Tea: It's girly and grown-up all at the same time. Lace linens with floral accents are perfect for the tables. Borrow china from friends to create an eclectic mix of cups and saucers. Serve finger sandwiches, scones with jam and clotted cream, petits fours and, of course, tea.

Sweet Shoppe: Top your tables with bouquets of oversized lollipops and bowls of bright-colored candy. Place a gourmet candy bar at each guest's place setting. Offset the sweets with some savory treats like ice-cream-cone- and lollipop-shaped hors d'oeuvres and trays of light sandwiches, mixed fruit, and garden and pasta salads.

Film Festival: Choose classic movies as inspiration for your table decor (*Pretty in Pink*, *Casino*, etc.) and see if guests can guess the flick. Hot dogs, chicken fingers and french fries give a nod to the concession stand, along with mini boxes of Junior Mints and Raisinets, and bags of popcorn.

Wine and Cheese Tasting: Hold your shower at a local winery or turn a home into a tasting room. Set up wine-and-cheese stations throughout your space, and include some brief description cards next to the selections. Lunch can include salads topped with grilled chicken or steak and roasted vegetables. Consider ice-cream parfaits served in wineglasses for a sweet ending.

Bride to Bride

I bought my bridesmaids necklaces to wear on the wedding day, but I also bought plain black tank tops and "monogrammed" them using silver iron-on sequin letters, and then sewed silver beads around the necklines. It was a chance for me to express my love for my amazing friends. —Jeannie

The Bachelorette Party

Help your bridesmaids plan a last hurrah that's built for you.

- **Tell them what you want.** You don't have to plan the whole thing (you do have another party on your agenda, don't you?), but it's helpful to give them some general suggestions: whether you want the party to be wild or mild, if you want to hit the spa or a favorite hotspot. This is key if you're hoping for a party that's a little out of character for you: a demure bride who wants a stripper-filled send-off should definitely let her friends know.

- **Help your bridesmaids bond.** If your attendants don't know one another well, they may have a hard time teaming up to plan your party. Arrange for get-togethers early on, just after you've gotten engaged, so your college roommate and your work buddy can forge a friendship before they have to arrange the bachelorette bash.

- **Keep it affordable.** Don't insist on the most expensive spa in town or a lavish Vegas weekend if all your pals are fresh out of college and struggling to get started.

Guest Who?

Your bridesmaids will likely turn to you for help with the shower guest list. Make sure all of your attendants, and your and your fiancé's family members—moms, sisters, aunts and grandmothers—make the list, then give them the names and addresses of any other friends you would like included. Just remember that those who are invited to a personal shower must also make the wedding guest list. (You don't have to worry about inviting your entire office if they throw you a shower at work.)

{modern bride wisdom}

When it's time to open presents, create an assembly line to keep things moving. One bridesmaid can hand presents to the bride to open while another can record the name of the gift giver and what she gave. A third can create the traditional "bow bouquet" for the rehearsal.

COOL SHOWER ACTIVITIES

Here are more ideas to mention to your girls.

Photo Fun: Ask guests to bring pictures of themselves with the bride or groom. As they arrive, insert their photos into a pretty album. Then add the album to the gift table.

Recipe Book: Buy some recipe cards from a stationery store and slip one in with each shower invitation. Ask guests to share their favorite recipe, then create a cookbook to present to the bride at the shower.

Pop Quiz: Gather information about the bride from her family and friends, and create a quiz to be taken during the shower. The guest with the most correct answers wins.

Bridal Bingo: Pick up M&M's or Hershey's Kisses to use as playing pieces and order bridal bingo cards from bride bingo.com or blissweddingsmarket.com. Appoint a bridesmaid to run the game and call out the numbers. Play a few rounds to give more than one guest the chance to win.

Mad Love: Inspired by Mad Libs, write out the bride and groom's courtship story. Then take out a handful of nouns, verbs and adjectives from the story and replace them with blank lines. Pass out copies and ask guests to fill in the blanks with whatever wild words come to mind. Award prizes for the most creative and funniest versions.

What to Do on Your Big Night Out

- Belt out your favorite ballads karaoke style at a local bar—or DIY it at a pal's home with a rented machine.
- Show your team spirit: Have a tailgate bash in the stadium parking lot, then head inside to watch the action at your favorite team's game.
- Go upscale with a swanky wine-tasting party—serve up gourmet cheeses on the side, and hire a sommelier to explain the varietals you'll sip.
- Have an old-fashioned slumber party. Serve spiked smoothies and shakes with a few Twinkies and Ring-Dings on the side, throw *The Princess Bride* in the DVD player and giggle about guys as you give each other manis and pedis.
- Go the bawdy route, and hit the local strip club or have your gal pals hire a male stripper to perform at your party.
- Relax and say *spaaah*. Spend a day at the spa with your gals, indulging in relaxing and re-energizing treatments.
- Live like a high roller in a larger-than-life hot spot like Las Vegas, Miami or Atlantic City. Jet off for a nonstop party weekend featuring hot cocktails, cool clubs—and maybe a chance to test your lady luck.
- Get campy—rent a cabin (maybe not one that's too rustic!) or even pitch a few tents and savor some s'mores around the campfire with your favorite friends.
- Eat, drink and be married—gather the girls for a gourmet tasting menu at a fabulous five-star restaurant.
- Learn when to hold 'em or fold 'em at a poker party with your friends. Hey, you might even score a little extra spending money for your honeymoon.
- Head out on a quest—let your friends set up a scavenger hunt for the evening, with silly tasks to complete and items to find, whether you need to dance on top of the bar or get a single guy to give you his phone number.
- Learn something new together. Sign your friends up for a striptease or belly-dancing class, or take a jewelry-making or cooking lesson. Reward yourselves afterward with a fabulous meal and a champagne toast.
- Be entertained: Score tickets to a concert, comedy show or musical, then go somewhere cool to recap the evening over drinks and dessert.
- Take a walk down memory lane. Hit your hometown or your college campus and visit all of your old haunts. Burn a CD of your favorite tunes from the era to provide a soundtrack for the evening. Whether you decide to recreate your high-school hairdo is up to you.
- Cue up—hit the local pool hall to see if you can beat your bridesmaids at billiards.
- Satiate your sweet tooth at a dessert party. Serve spiked coffee drinks and savor every rich mouthful of your favorite treats. (Note: Plan this party a few weeks before the wedding so you can all indulge without wondering if your dress will still fit come wedding day.)
- Shop until you drop. Visit your favorite boutiques to stock up on lingerie and other goodies for the honeymoon. Some stores will even close down for a private party for you and your gals, where you can sip champagne and search out the perfect bikini for the beach.

Bride to Bride

My bridesmaids wanted to rent a lake house and a pontoon boat for a weekend, which would have been fun, but would have left out some girls who didn't have a few hundred bucks to drop on a weekend. I nixed that so I could spend time with all of my friends together. That's what bachelorette parties should be about. —Nicole

Q & A

Q **My bridesmaids are scattered across the country. How should we shop for their dresses?**

A Your safest bet is to shop at stores that have locations nationwide. This way, if you find something you like, you can send your 'maids out to try it on. After all, most dress anxieties occur if a bridesmaid doesn't get to try the dress on before it lands on her doorstep. The next best thing is to search for your styles via the Web; log on to a dress designer's site and choose your favorite styles, then direct your gals to the site to check them out. Once you find a winner, all you need are dress measurements from everyone and you're all set. Even better, most Web sites refer you to stores in the region that carry the dress. Another option: Drop color swatches in the mail and have your bridesmaids shop on their own. As long as you give them some parameters for styles and lengths, they should be good to go.

Also, don't worry if they can't find a dress to match the swatch exactly. Varying shades of the same color palette can look very pretty standing in a row. The most important thing is for everyone to be comfortable with what they're wearing and feel content. And if you keep your 'maids involved in the choices, happiness is pretty much a sure thing.

Q **When I told one of my bridesmaids the cost of her dress, she freaked and said she didn't know if she could afford it. I wasn't planning on paying for my bridesmaids' dresses. What should I do?**

A If the wedding is months away, sit her down for a financial heart-to-heart. Be up front with her about all of the upcoming costs: As a bridesmaid, she might be expected to chip in for the bridal shower and bachelorette party, and there are possible travel expenses. Then give her the option to back out of the bridesmaid business, making sure she knows that you won't take it personally. Tell her you understand that the responsibility comes with a pretty big price tag, but that it means a lot to you to have her in your bridal party and you want to work it out if possible. If the wedding is just weeks away and she is reacting to the cost as you are placing the dress in her hands, consider springing for this bridesmaid's dress.

Q **Would it be alright if I have two maids of honor?**

A Of course! It's your party, and you can have as many maids of honor as you want. But you'll want to set your dynamic duo off in a special way so guests understand the distinction. You might have them wear slightly different dresses from the rest of your bevy of bridesmaids. This could mean a different color, different style or the same color and style with a shorter or longer hemline. Or simply have the two of them march down the aisle together—this way there's no mistaking that they both hold the top spot in the wedding party. If you're having a bridal-party dance at the reception, instruct the best man to take a turn around the dance floor with both girls (separately of course—no football huddles necessary!). Finally, ask your two main 'maids to each say a few words or even give a joint speech at the reception. And don't forget to give your photographer the heads-up on this great photo op.

Q One of my bridesmaids is pregnant and wants to bow out. What should I do?

A First you need to find out why your friend wants to bail. If she feels bad because she won't be able to dress the part, you've got options: If she'll be only a few months' pregnant by your wedding date, a seamstress might be able to let out a bridesmaid's dress enough to fit her; if your maid will be very pregnant on your wedding day, give her a swatch of the other 'maids' dresses and ask her to look for a maternity dress (or have one made) in the same color; or have all of your maids wear the same color, but in different patterns. If your

friend's afraid she'll stand out too much in your wedding pictures, fear not. Your photographer can arrange people around her so her belly's not front and center.

If your friend still feels she just isn't up to the task, reassure her it's okay to back out and that you appreciate her initial interest in acting as a 'maid. Dub her "Honorary Bridesmaid" and get a corsage to seal the deal.

Q Do I need to ask my fiancé's sisters to be bridesmaids? Should my fiancé invite my brothers to be groomsmen?

A Including future in-laws in the wedding party is always a good idea. After all, you want your soon-to-be family members to feel special and snubbing them could start you off on the wrong foot. However, depending on the wedding-party size you were envisioning, you might need to rethink asking other family members or friends to be your best guys and gals. If you're set on keeping your wedding party on the small side, don't worry. There are several other important ways you can include loved ones in your big day. You might want to ask them to pass out the wedding programs, do a reading during the ceremony or make sure that the guest book gets signed (a good task for a gregarious soul). Also, regardless of the roles these special folks end up playing, make sure you've

given them corsages and boutonnieres to wear on the big day to denote their VIP status.

Q How can I tell a good friend that she won't be one of my bridesmaids?

A In awkward situations like this, make sure your friend hears the news early and directly from you, not through the grapevine. Ideally you'll have an obvious explanation that will make her feel a little better: You're having family members only or just your oldest friends. You can also offer her another role in the day's festivities. Regardless, make sure you reaffirm your friendship by saying something like, "I care about you and hope this won't come between us. It's important to me to have you at my wedding." Then just give her time to deal with any disappointment and move forward, shifting the conversation to what's happening in her life.

CHAPTER 14

Guide Your *Groomsmen*

HOW TO ORGANIZE AND OUTFIT THE MEN IN THE BRIDAL PARTY

BEST MAN

Lead the groomsmen. The best man acts as the head of the rest of the group—and as the mastermind of the bachelor party.

Serve your groom. Consider this guy your groom's wingman, helping out in whatever way he can before and during the wedding day: holding on to your marriage license for you, transporting your suitcases to your wedding-night suite or even giving your guy a ride to the ceremony site.

Keep track of the wedding bands. Put your best man in charge of safekeeping the rings until the exchange. (Don't even think about tying your actual rings to that ring-bearer pillow!)

Deliver a toast. The best man traditionally leads off the toasting at the wedding reception. For the keys to a fabulous, well-received speech, see "The Best Man's Toast" on page 195.

Hand out the tips. Many couples put the best man in charge of the wedding-day dough. Give your best man the tips in marked envelopes.

Tasks for the Groomsmen

The guys in the wedding party have a few responsibilities to complete to fulfill their mission. Here's what your groomsmen and best man can do.

GROOMSMEN

Help plan and attend the bachelor party. As your fiancé's closest pals, these guys will be the main members of your groom's bachelor-party posse.

Escort the guests to their seats. If you have any special requests—like seating the grandmothers in the first row with your parents—be sure to brief them before the big day.

Serve as arm candy for the bridesmaids. Many couples have their bridesmaids and groomsmen walk arm in arm both up and down the aisle.

Great Gifts

Show your gratitude to the guys in the party with these perfect presents

1. Monogrammed billfolds, money clips, cufflinks or flasks
2. Pairs of tickets to an upcoming sporting event or concert in their city
3. Subscriptions to a wine/dining magazine and bottles of wine
4. Series of personal-training sessions at a local health club
5. Ties with motifs that are appropriate to them
6. Greens fees for a local golf course, golf lessons with a pro or a box of monogrammed golf balls
7. Monogrammed dopp kits filled with luxury skincare, shaving and haircare products, as well as grooming tools
8. Books of coupons for free car washes or a gift certificate to have the car detailed
9. Personalized humidors with a selection of hand-rolled cigars or bottles of premium single-malt scotch
10. Deluxe army knives, so they're prepared for any emergency
11. Sleek sunglasses (perfect for an outdoor wedding)
12. Gift certificates for massages at a local spa
13. Boxes filled with their favorite movies and snacks (think James Bond flicks and Junior Mints)
14. Gift subscriptions to an online movie service like Netflix
15. Their drinks of choice, whether microbrews or vodka for martinis, plus fancy glasses to enjoy them in

Well Suited

CHOOSE THE TUX STYLE THAT'S BEST FOR YOUR GUY

IF HE'S...

Tall and slim

He has plenty of options. He can go modern, as with a single-breasted four-button jacket, or stick to a traditional double-breasted tux with broad shoulders and a narrower waist. For the most flattering silhouette, your groom should opt for a wider shoulder with peaked lapels; double-breasted styles are the best for adding a little bulk. With tall guys, it's especially important to make sure their jackets and pants are the perfect length.

Tall and husky, or muscular

It's best to go for a clean, minimalist look. A shawl lapel (a smooth collar with no notches) helps create a sleek line that minimizes a bigger build. He should avoid double-breasted styles and pleated shirts, as they tend to add unwanted volume to the midsection. Instead, opt for a single-breasted, one- or two-button jacket. A vest is a great alternative to a cummerbund because it draws attention away from the waist. As for color, black is ideal for its slimming qualities. Lighter colored suits, especially white and tan, aren't necessarily his best options. He can keep his look proportional with a fuller bow tie or a wider tie.

Short and slender

He can create an elongated look with a single-breasted jacket with buttons that hit around the natural waist. The more white space you can see from the necktie to the first button, the taller he will appear. If he wants to look a little broader, he can also opt for peaked lapels or a double-breasted jacket. He might even ask the tailor for a little extra shoulder padding. Smaller bow ties are the best accessory for him.

Short and stocky

The trick to creating an elongated silhouette is a single-breasted jacket with a shawl lapel, a smooth collar with no notches. He should choose a jacket with one or two buttons that fall around the belt line to make his torso appear longer and leaner. A jacket with a natural shoulder line will also help him look slimmer. He should choose a vest over a cummerbund to draw attention away from his waistline. If his neck is wide, his shirt and tie or bow tie should not appear too constricting.

Fit to Be Tied

Figuring out if the formalwear fits right can be a challenge: Is the jacket too tight, or would a bigger size make your groom look like a member of the Talking Heads? Are those pants looking a little high around his waist? And should the edges of his shirtsleeves be sticking out like that? Here's how you'll know your groom has a perfect fit.

THE JACKET Your guy should be able to move his arms comfortably, and the jacket's shoulders should line up with his shoulders. The sleeves of his jacket should cover the wrists when he has his hands at his sides.

THE SHIRT You should see a hint of the shirtsleeve along his wrists—about a half inch of it when his arms are at his sides. The collar fits if you can slip two fingers into it.

THE PANTS Formalwear pants are designed to sit a bit higher than suit or casual pants, so they should be further up on his waist than normal. At the hem, there should be a small "break" over the shoe: The pants should pool slightly on the top of the shoe in the front and hit the top of the heel in the back.

Your groom's personality can show in his tux choices—whether he's in basic black or all in white.

{modern bride wisdom}

Make sure the guys all try on their rental tuxes before they leave the shop. You don't want to find out an hour before the ceremony that the best man's jacket is way too small.

Buy or Borrow?

Should your groom splurge and keep his wedding ensemble, or follow the lead of the majority of guys, who rent their formalwear?

This is a common question. Here's how to decide: If you or your fiancé get invited to a fair number of formal events, it may be worth the investment for him to purchase his own tuxedo. But if your social calendar requires more T-shirts than tuxes, then renting is your best bet.

Tux Alternatives

Planning a not-so-formal event? Here are a few options for dressing the guys.

White dinner jackets with black trousers

Black, gray or blue suits

Striped seersucker suits

Khakis with navy blazers

Linen pants and shirts

Linen suits

Bermuda shorts with jackets

BOW TIE

This is the traditional tux tie, which looks like a bow at the neck.

CUMMERBUND

A wide, beltlike sash worn at the edge of the pants. Make sure the pleats are worn facing up.

PEAK LAPEL

The top of the lapel points up and out.

Wedding Words

LEARN THE FORMALWEAR LINGO

DOUBLE-BREASTED

The coat overlaps in the front, and two sets of buttons hold it in place.

MORNING COAT

A black or gray jacket originally worn for morning horse-riding. Also known as a cutaway, the front cuts away to a curved pair of tails.

FOUR-IN-HAND TIE

Also known as a "long tie," this is similar to a traditional suit tie and has become a hot choice in formalwear.

NOTCHED LAPEL

You can see a notch cut out of the lapel close to the collarbone.

SHAWL LAPEL

The entire collar is rounded, right to the lapel.

SINGLE-BREASTED

Just one set of buttons holds this jacket closed.

VEST

Vests have become the most popular accessory—opt for a full vest instead of the backless rental vests if your guy will likely take off his jacket before the party's over.

TAILS

In the back, the coat trails down into two long tails. This is the most formal type of coat.

THE BACHELOR PARTY

The strip-club bachelor party is becoming more of a stereo-type and less of a reality. Truth is, many guys aren't really thrilled about the idea of hanging out with "dancers" all night. So if your groom would rather have a less, um, intimate party, here are some cool ways he can celebrate the final days of his bachelorhood.

He may want to tailgate before heading to an event of his choice—a football game, NASCAR race, concert or comedy festival. The guys can pack classic munchies like buffalo wings, nachos and hot dogs or elevate the party with some gourmet goods like beef filets, grilled shrimp and seared tuna.

If they like to get in on the action rather than watch from the sidelines, a full-on tourney of the groom's favorite game is a guaranteed bonding activity. Whether it's paintball or pinball, volleyball or video games, they can put together a bracket and then battle it out.

If golf is his game, they can take the clubs and head to a familiar course for a few rounds. Or they can go for a guys' grand tour and transport the whole group to a golf-friendly destination like Arizona, California or Hawaii.

Trying out a much-talked-about restaurant can be a relaxing way to spend time with the guys. One possible itinerary: Make reservations for a night full of prime cuts at a swanky steakhouse, then move the party to the cigar lounge for stogies and scotch.

Then again, a Vegas getaway might be right up their alley. The boys can try to bust the bank at the casino, hit up trendy restaurants or take the party out on the town with nights of craps, clubs and cocktails.

If they're not the gambling kind but still want an action-packed getaway, they can go for a ski weekend. The guys can spend the days skiing or snowboarding and the nights chilling in the lodge, playing cards, smoking cigars and throwing back a few drinks.

Or, for something a bit more one-with-nature, they might want to pack up the tackle and poles, bring a cooler full of their favorite brews and head out on a fishing expe-dition. Or maybe they'll nix the fish and commune with nature over a relaxing weekend of camping. It's up to them how authentic they want their experience to be: They can rough it in tents and sleeping bags or go the luxury route in a fully stocked cabin.

Then there's the option that's almost the anti–bachelor party: keeping it low-key with a funny movie marathon. It can be a trip down memory lane with old-school classics like *Caddyshack*, *The Jerk* and, of course, *Bachelor Party*, accompanied by pizza and beer.

Groom to Groom

Help your best man come up with something you'd like to do—after I talked to mine, he planned a perfect bachelor party: a weekend of swimming and hanging out in Vermont. —Mike

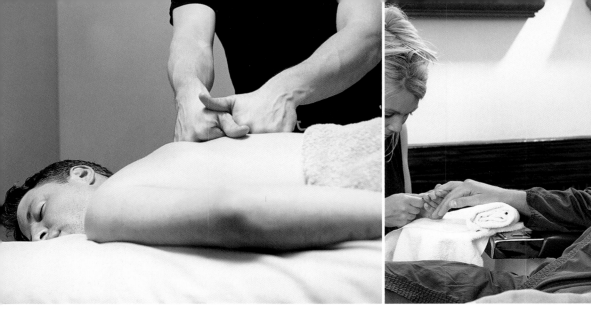

Good Grooming

HOW TO GET YOUR GUY LOOKING GORGEOUS FOR THE BIG DAY

Book a spa appointment for him. Most spas offer more manly versions of the treatments you'll be getting, so arrange for both of you to get a facial, manicure and pedicure—and follow it up with a relaxing massage.

Give him the right tools. Most men will tolerate a few new additions to their grooming arsenals: a top-notch shaver with attachments to help him trim hair on the back of his neck, a good cleanser and moisturizer, a strong sunscreen and a set of tweezers to eliminate any signs of a unibrow.

Offer incentives. If your groom's a little less than willing to be pampered, reward his efforts with a massage—or anything else he likes.

Guy Gear

Create a tote with some of these essentials and hand it over to the groomsman least likely to forget it at the hotel.

- your wedding-day schedule
- cash for tipping/ emergencies
- contact list of vendors and wedding VIPs
- his cell phone
- paper and pen
- handkerchief or tissues
- pain reliever
- antacid
- nail clippers
- eye drops
- contact-lens case and solution
- extra undershirt
- shoe-polish kit
- sandpaper (to scuff up slippery soles)
- stain-remover wipes
- comb
- lint roller
- spare cufflinks
- buttons
- sewing kit
- travel shaving kit
- styptic pencil (for treating shaving nicks)
- breath mints or mouthwash
- dental floss
- light snacks
- bottled water

The Best Man's Toast

WOW THE CROWD WITH A FIRST-CLASS WEDDING SPEECH

Brides-to-be are often worried about their best man's toast. To ensure that his words are thoughtful and appropriate (and don't call to mind the toast scene from *Old School*), check out our list of toasting Dos and Don'ts. Then pass it on to the best man. He may be grateful for the guidance, and you just may sleep better at night.

DO start off by introducing yourself and thanking everyone for attending. (You may also want to thank the couple's parents if they're hosting the event.) Explain your connection to the groom and tell a funny (but tasteful) story or two about your friendship. Skip the inside jokes. You may find them utterly hilarious, but the rest of the audience will be utterly bored.

DON'T forget to talk about the bride and why she's the perfect match for your buddy. Tell a quick story about the first time you were introduced to the bride, or how you knew the groom was falling for her. Make your words personal, as if they couldn't possibly be used to describe any other couple.

DO feel free to riff on the groom's table manners, fashion sense, culinary skills, physical fitness and singing and dancing prowess (or lack thereof).

DON'T mention any of the following: ex-girlfriends, former "player" status, alcohol or drug use, violence, anything sexist or anything negative about the wedding or family members.

DO talk about what a bright future they'll have and wish them lots of luck in their life together. You may want to throw in a little relationship advice from personal experience or other sources of wisdom such as quotations, song lyrics, poems or passages from secular or spiritual literature.

DON'T forget a conclusion. Raise your glass and ask the audience to do the same. (All but the bride and groom will raise their glasses with you.) Look directly at the happy couple, say "Here's to Amy and Brian," and take a sip from your glass.

DO practice. You'll feel much calmer when delivering the toast if you know it well. Make sure it's no longer than three to five minutes. Go for quality over quantity—even a one-minute speech can be a home run if it's heartfelt, so make your words count.

DON'T have more than one drink before toast time. You can start the party after you've given your speech.

DO use notecards to remember your main talking points. Stiff cards are better in shaky hands than flimsy sheets of paper. Try not to read your entire toast from the cards.

DON'T rush. Take a deep breath and look around the room before starting your speech. This will keep you from racing through your first words.

DO pause if you get a laugh. Wait until it dies down before moving on to your next unbelievably witty line.

DON'T lose confidence if one of your funny bits misses its mark. You may be the only one who noticed, so just keep going and don't give it a second thought.

{modern bride wisdom}

Worried the best man will forget the rings? Consider entrusting them to your parents' care, then having them slip the bands to him before the ceremony begins.

Q & A

Q **My fiancé really wants his sister to serve as his "Best Woman." Is this sweet…or weird?**

A It's sweet! We see all kinds of unique takes on the best-man and maid-of-honor roles these days. We've heard of grooms asking a woman they're close with (such as a sister) to be their best woman, best maid or even groomswoman. And by the same token, a bride may choose to ask her brother or best guy friend to stand up for her as her man of honor or bridesman. The only potential complication that may arise with your future sister-in-law is when it comes time to plan the bachelor party, which is generally the best man's responsibility. Depending on what your fiancé would like the itinerary to be, his sister may not want to attend, much less plan it, so they'll have to work that out. If you're a little uneasy with the fact that a best woman isn't the norm, try to look at it this way: Isn't it nice that you're marrying someone so thoughtful that he'd happily break tradition to convey how much his sister means to him?

Q **When it comes to the bachelor party, who pays for what? How are the costs divided among the groomsmen?**

A Generally speaking, everyone who attends the bachelor party is responsible for equally dividing the costs and also covering the groom's expenses. This holds true whether it's a small event involving just the wedding party or a huge blowout including lots of guys. (We've seen plenty of bachelor-party guest lists that even included friends and work colleagues who weren't invited to the wedding.) To make sure everyone is on the same page and there are no misunderstandings later, the best man or other bachelor-party organizer should give all guests a cost estimate along with the party details, either by phone or e-mail. There is one exception to the "everyone pays for the groom" tradition, though: When the bachelor party turns into a guys' getaway—to Vegas, to an out-of-town ballpark, etc., and especially if this trip was the groom's idea—he may want to offer to pay his own way, thereby reducing the amount his friends and family will have to come up with.

Q **Is there a difference between a groomsman and an usher? And if there is, how do we decide who should have which role?**

A Many people think the terms *groomsman* and *usher* are interchangeable, but they're actually not. A groomsman is an active participant in the wedding ceremony. He stands up for the groom at the altar; he'll walk up the aisle during the recessional with one of your bridesmaids. He may escort guests down the aisle—particularly VIPs such as the grandparents of the groom—but he may also proceed straight to the front of the altar and join the groom. An usher's responsibilities occur before the ceremony: He may greet guests, hand out programs, alert guests to reserved seating and, yes, usher people to their seats. During the ceremony, he sits with the rest of your guests (albeit toward the front, close to family). It's certainly not necessary to have both groomsmen and ushers; the groomsmen ought to be able to help seat your guests, then head to the altar just before the ceremony begins. However, if you and your fiancé have many men you'd like to include in the wedding but are trying to limit the size of your wedding party, then consider having the two groups. As for who has which role, you'll want close family members and friends as your groomsmen, while the others (those just outside the inner circle, such as your fiancé's brother-in-law) can serve as your ushers.

Q **Should the best man wear anything different to distinguish himself from the rest of the groomsmen?**

A It's a nice thought, but probably not necessary. In fact, it might even cause confusion among those guests who don't know your wedding party well. If they see one man in a different-colored tie than everyone else, for example, they might assume he's the groom. If you'd really like to differentiate your best man, though, consider getting him a boutonniere that's not like the ones the rest of the guys will be sporting: Maybe the groomsmen have red roses on their lapels, and the best man has a white one. (In that case, it's a good idea to make sure your groom wears a boutonniere that's different from both of those.) Or, for a completely different way to give this special guy his moment in the sun, turn to your wedding program. When you list his name, you can add a line about his connection to you and why he means so much to you (and then do the same for the maid of honor, of course).

Q **One of our groomsmen, a friend of my fiancé's, has a lot of unruly facial hair. Can I ask him to clean up before our wedding?**

A You can, but the better question is, would you really want to? First of all, he may be planning to do this on his own. You don't want to insult him by assuming he wouldn't try to look his best as a member of your wedding party. So your first step should be to enlist a fellow groomsman you're friendly with—or the groom himself—to casually find out if he plans to shave for the wedding. If you learn that he thinks he looks just fine the way he is, then you have a choice to make. You can speak up or encourage your groom to do the deed. (If you do, the key is to make your request short. Try something like, "Would you do me a huge favor and trim back the [mutton chops/Fu Manchu/handlebar 'stache] for all the photos that will be taken over our wedding weekend? It would mean so much to me.") Or you may decide to let this one go. After all, you and your groom asked this friend to be in your wedding party for his inner qualities, not how he looks in pictures. You can also consider treating all of the guys to a haircut and shave on the day before the wedding.

Q **Should my fiancé buy his best man a different gift than what the rest of the groomsmen are getting?**

A This is optional, but it can be a thoughtful gesture. Just be careful not to make the gift conspicuously more lavish than the ones you're giving the rest of the guys, particularly if you plan to distribute them all at one time (which is usually how it's done, specifically at the rehearsal dinner). And resist the idea of giving the best man a gift that's simply an upgrade of the one you're giving everyone else, since that's an obvious sign that his present cost more.

CHAPTER 15

Gift Your *Guests*

A GUIDE TO WELCOME BASKETS, FAVORS AND MORE

Ernie & Barbara
August 10, 2007

Favors can themselves become part of your reception decor. Prettily wrapped boxes can be stacked to create a centerpiece of gifts.

Before You Give

FAVORS AND WELCOME BASKETS ARE NICE TO HAVE, BUT NOT ESSENTIAL. HERE'S HOW TO DECIDE IF YOU WANT TO OFFER THEM TO YOUR GUESTS.

As with any decision, it's helpful to weigh the pros and cons when considering whether to incorporate gifts for guests into your festivities. There are a number of reasons why you may want to provide them; for one thing, it's a nice way to thank your friends and family. Many will have traveled hundreds or thousands of miles to be with you as you take this big step—and most came bearing fabulous gifts to honor you on your big day. You may want to offer a token of appreciation—a small but sweet way to acknowledge the thoughtful things your loved ones have done for you.

FAVOR FACTORS

Preparing gifts also presents another opportunity to express your personal style on your big day. Through favors, you can share one of your favorite things with loved ones—whether it's your grandmother's famous chocolate chip cookies or fancy soaps from a beloved bath shop. And they can be a great reminder of your celebration: When your guests put that special ornament up on the tree or enjoy the bath salts you gave out, they'll think about the great time they had at your event.

On the flip side, there are some disadvantages to gifting your guests—the biggest one being that it can add unnecessary expense. We've all been to weddings where most of the favors were left behind at the end of the evening. In those cases, that portion of the budget could have been better spent elsewhere. But the more thought and personality you put into your gift, the more likely it is to be cherished. With that in mind, you should also consider your workload before beginning to plan the perfect gift; it may be more than you can handle at the moment. If you can barely manage to squeeze in time with your fiancé between your long work hours and your never-ending to-do list, you may not have the time to brainstorm and execute a clever favor. And when you're already overwhelmed, taking one thing off your to-do list can be a real lifesaver.

A WARM WELCOME

Welcome baskets are a gracious way to greet your wedding's out-of-towners. Unlike favors, which are typically handed out at the reception, these gifts tend to be given to guests when they arrive at the hotel. But figuring out what to give—and how to present it—can be a challenge. When coming up with ideas for the contents, consider what makes your city or town unique and incorporate elements of those things. Also, especially for a destination wedding, think about what makes you feel comfortable when you travel (slippers? sweets?) and include those items to pamper your guests. And remember, welcome gifts don't have to rival awards-show gift baskets—a small container of homemade cookies can be just as nice.

Once you've decided on the contents, start gathering the individual items early on and then order the containers you'll put them in (to ensure you get the right size). When you have everything, create a sample to make sure it all fits. Leave yourself enough time to personalize each welcome basket with the recipient's name—not just "Guest of the Smith-Jones wedding"—as it'll make them feel much more special. Finally, think about how and when your guests will receive the gift. If requested, most hotels will distribute baskets upon check-in, which is fine—but if your hotel or B&B will leave them in the room, this is an even nicer touch. (Ask if there is a charge for this service.)

Guest *Gift Guide*

START EARLY. No one wants to be assembling welcome baskets or favors the night before a wedding. Choose your gifts at least a month or two before the big day, and make sure they're packaged and ready to distribute as soon as possible, unless you're giving out fresh-baked goods.
INCORPORATE YOUR THEME. If you've developed a wedding motif, continue it through your welcome baskets or favors—offer your guests a decorative corkscrew at a vineyard wedding, for example, or Key-lime cookies at a tropical-themed affair.
CONSIDER THE OTHER DETAILS. Everything from your reception site to your wedding flowers can inspire a great gift—consider giving gilded votive holders at a wedding in a grand ballroom or tulip bulbs in planters if tulips are the predominant flower in your centerpieces.
GIVE WHAT YOU LOVE. Your guests will probably adore your favorite chocolates just as much as you do.
FIND YOUR LIMITS. Budget can be a big factor in your favor and welcome-basket decisions—if yours is tight, consider giving one gift per couple instead of per guest (display it with the escort cards) or find something you can easily (and inexpensively) make yourself, such as offering guests small pear-shaped candles adorned with tags bearing the phrase "A perfect pair."

Welcome-basket Checklist

Make sure your basket includes:

☐ a brief welcome note
☐ a copy of the wedding-weekend itinerary, listing locations and times for all events
☐ contact information for a local friend or family member who's serving as the out-of-town coordinator
☐ a detailed map or directions to each event
☐ a small snack or treat

MODERN BRIDE 5

Welcome-Basket Themes

Color Coded: Match your wedding decor. For red, pack a scarlet bucket with cherry soda, red licorice and a crimson candle.
Season's Greetings: Take cues from the calendar: In winter, fill a mini sleigh with hot-cocoa packets; in summer, stuff a kids' sand pail with a floppy hat and a pair of sunglasses.
Local Flavor: Stock a cool tote with a hometown snack, a map marked with great insider spots to check out, a subway or bus pass, and a list of fun facts about the area—for instance, let 'em know that Chicagoans don't use the term "Windy City."
Opposites Attract: You're a vanilla girl, he loves chocolate? Fill two-compartment baskets with your faves on one side, his on the other.
Perfectly Pampered: Give guests the royal treatment by tucking body lotion, a facial mask, tea and slippers in with a pretty towel.

Fun Foodie Favors

Snacks and treats are always a hit. Our faves:

- candied apples
- teas
- fruit jams
- cookies
- jars of honey
- hot chocolate and marshmallows
- peanut brittle
- truffles
- gingerbread cookies
- mini cupcakes
- bottles of flavor-infused oil
- Jordan almonds
- chocolates—shaped like hearts or your monogram
- bottles of sparkling cider
- jelly beans in your wedding colors
- muffin mix

- Red Hots candy
- gumballs
- M&M's
- petits fours
- flavored popcorn
- sugar cookies
- yogurt-covered pretzels
- striped candy sticks
- miniature bottles of your favorite liqueurs
- macaroons
- bottles of hot sauce
- maple candy
- donuts
- bottles of wine
- striped lollipops
- meringue kisses
- bottles of maple syrup

Perfect Presents

These favors are unique or useful, or both:

- paper parasols
- fragrant soaps
- miniature wooden sailboats
- copper-dipped leaf or shell ornaments
- decorated masks
- scented candles
- mini snowglobes
- potted flower bulbs or packets of seeds
- potted plants or herbs
- vases in your wedding colors
- decorative picture frames

- scratch-off lottery tickets (with a lucky penny for scratching)
- customized CDs
- silver-plated ice-cream scoops
- paperweights
- flip-flops
- sandalwood fans
- painted chopsticks
- miniature books of poetry
- beaded bookmarks
- personalized golf balls
- sets of postcards
- trinket boxes

Favor Bars

The best favors don't always come prepackaged: Many couples are setting up specialty bars, where guests can pick their favorites from a selection of goodies to take home with them as a customized treat. The bonus? No late-night bag assembly for you. Plus, guests get to pick and choose what they like. These are some of our favorite options.

Breakfast Bar: Send everyone home with a little treat for them to enjoy the next morning. Let your guests pick from an array of delicious pastries and bagels, which can be packed into small bags or boxes for safe transporting home.

Candy Bar: Have your favorite treats displayed in pretty glass jars; guests can scoop their favorites into cellophane bags. Consider candies that complement your color theme such as Red Hots, strawberry Starbursts, pink lollipops and red licorice.

Dessert Bar: Stock a table with a selection of treats: cream puffs, mini pies, petits fours, chocolate-dipped fruits and slices of wedding cake, which guests can pack into pretty bakery boxes.

Flower Bar: Your florist can put out a variety of fresh blooms. Place each variety in its own tub of water. Provide guests with brown paper and string for wrapping, and they can create their own fresh arrangements to bring home.

Beauty Bar: Display a variety of pampering bath and body items guests can collect in mini crates or canvas bags. Just be sure you include a few guy-friendly options, like lip balm, sunscreen and a nonfloral-scented soap, so your male guests can indulge, too.

Double-Duty Favors

With a little creativity, favors can often serve more than one purpose at your party. Here's how to get the maximum impact.

Use them as escort cards. You can tie a tag with a guest's name and table assignment onto nearly any gift. Rows of snowflake ornaments, for example, can look beautiful on the escort table. Or use favors as place cards at the table.

Turn them into centerpieces. Dress up your tables with prettily packaged favors stacked on tiered trays, or a grouping of potted plants or flowers that guests can take home. Just put a little card on each table explaining that guests are welcome to a gift from the centerpiece when they're ready to leave.

Give out favors guests can use at the wedding itself. Consider providing guests with something that'll help them stay comfortable at your event: pairs of flip-flops at a beach wedding, wraps at an outdoor evening event, or parasols to protect against the sun at an afternoon wedding. If you make the favors part of the table setting—nestled into your guests' napkins or placed on their chairs or their plates—they'll have them as soon as they sit down.

Create a personalized parting moment. Use favors to stylishly bid your guests farewell: Have waiters hand one to each person, or have a separate table set up near the exit where favors can be displayed with a sign that says "Please Take One" while you and your husband stand at the door thanking everyone for coming.

Favors can be used as placecards at each seat

Cool Containers

Sometimes, the packaging can be part of the gift itself. We've got five great ways to present your guests with their gifts.

Tote bags: Use colorful canvas totes to help guests carry larger gifts, like beach towels, flip-flops and sunscreen.

Food containers: Try Chinese takeout containers, pink cardboard bakery boxes or vintage popcorn boxes to hold your favorite treats.

Paint cans: Fill clean, unused pint-sized paint cans—available at your local Home Depot or paint store—with M&Ms, jelly beans or flavored popcorn in your wedding colors. Add a decorative label or monogrammed sticker.

Flower pots: Go beyond the expected seeds, bulbs or plants—fill a decorated flower pot with floral-scented soaps, flower-shaped cookies or another themed gift.

Plexiglas boxes: Simple, clear boxes can be bought in shapes and sizes to fit any gift—and dressed up with colored tags and ribbon to fit any decor.

Your presence was a sweet gift. June 6, 2008

Send-off Snacks

In lieu of guest gifts, many couples are opting for "send-off snacks," to be served as everyone leaves the party. The best options are foods that are portable and easily served from a cart. A few to try:

- ice cream or gelato
- donuts
- warm chocolate-chip cookies and a "shot" of milk
- hot pretzels
- hot dogs
- Italian ice
- popcorn
- flavored coffees or hot chocolate
- ballpark foods like cheesesteaks or knishes
- cones of french fries
- cotton candy

{modern bride wisdom}

If your site offers valet parking, consider asking the valets to place favors on guests' dashboards when they retrieve their cars. Make sure the favors are resistant to heat or cold.

Bride to Bride

My fiancé and I are huge baseball fans, so we're giving bags containing Cracker Jack, baseballs with our favorite team's logo, and our own custom-made baseball cards that will include our pictures and our "stats" (names, when we became engaged, wedding date and location, etc.). —Jennifer

Q&A

Q **Do hotels usually deliver welcome baskets to the guest rooms for free?**

A Some hotels may offer this service without charging you, but most venues will issue a fee (usually starting at around $3 per room). You might negotiate this rate depending on the number of welcome baskets to be delivered, or you could try working out a deal based on all of the business you are providing the hotel for your wedding weekend. (You can also ask whether you, a friend or relative, or your wedding planner can deliver the baskets instead—but very often the hotel won't allow this due to security concerns.) Another option that's fairly common for weddings is to leave all of the welcome baskets at the front desk and ask that they are handed over to guests as each checks in. This is often done for free, but there are some downsides. For one, a guest feels more pampered to find the welcome basket displayed nicely in the room or hanging decoratively on the doorknob than he would having it handed to him as he's already weighed down with all of his luggage. Also, there is a chance that the front-desk staffer won't remember to give the welcome basket in some instances, especially during busy moments. However, if you are looking to have your welcome baskets distributed for free, this may be your best, or only, option.

Q **Does every guest really need a favor, or can we give out one per couple?**

A It's certainly a nice touch to give a favor to every guest, whether by leaving one at each place setting or displaying them on a table, inviting everyone to take the favor as they depart—but by no means is it a necessity. Favor costs can add up, so if you're working with a tight budget, this is an area where you can easily cut back. Your first step is to rule out favors meant for individual use, such as lollipops. Better choices are items that are easily shared, such as a pie-baking kit in a small sack (which can be a group activity), a decorative box of popcorn (enough for two people) or a picture frame, which can hold a photo of the couple. To make it clear to guests that there is only one per couple, you can attach the favor to seating cards, which usually contain both guests' names if they are to be seated together. Placing the favors on a table can be trickier, as guests may assume there is one for everyone, and it's not easy to tactfully tell your crowd otherwise in a sign. It's also not advisable to leave a favor on every other plate at the table as this will give the impression that something is missing. So if you cannot attach your favors to seating cards, consider arranging them on a table and asking your bridal party or family members to gracefully distribute them to couples on their way out.

Q We're donating to charity in lieu of giving out favors. What's the best way to let guests know?

A Charitable donations have become increasingly popular at weddings today. Whether you and your groom are giving back at your wedding to memorialize a family member or friend, or to support a charity that has meaning to you both, there are many ways you can share this information with all of your guests. First, you could mention this in your welcome toast or speech; for instance, if you are donating in memory of a relative, it'd be nice to share a brief anecdote or description of this person so that guests can get a sense of what this act means to you. Another idea is to place a note at each guest's place setting, where a favor might typically have been, or even to include a brief statement in fortune cookies, which are fairly inexpensive. If you do distribute a note, describe the charity you are supporting and include some information about its significance to the two of you. Some organizations, such as the American Diabetes Association, offer couples preprinted table cards explaining the decision to donate and how this contribution will help the charity. Other organizations provide visuals that are an immediately recognizable symbol of the charity and therefore do not require much explanation, such as yellow wristbands from the Lance Armstrong Foundation and pink wristbands in support of breast-cancer research.

Q I'm having an eco-friendly wedding. Can you suggest cool favor ideas?

A "Green" weddings are an increasingly popular way to tie the knot, and as a result, there are a number of fun, eco-friendly favor ideas on the market, from recyclable flower vases to patterned bookmarks made of plantable paper. Seed kits are a huge hit at weddings—you can customize them by wrapping them in pretty paper to match your wedding colors and attaching a tag that reads "Love Is Blooming." You could also give plants themselves: Pick up seedlings from a nursery, wrap the pots with printed ribbon, handwrite a note inviting guests to plant them, and display the small trees on a wooden table or in a wheelbarrow or other rustic vessel. Organic treats also fit the green theme. Check out wine companies like Bonterra (bonterra.com) and Appellation Wine and Spirits (appellationnyc.com), which offer many organic varieties that can be dressed up with a pretty sheer wrapping and a customized label to serve as your favors. Food is always a well-received gift, too, so you might consider organic snacks or sweets, like gourmet chips or brownies. Present them in boxes made of recyclable paper and filled with colorful biodegradable "ecofetti" confetti (ecoparti.com).

Q We'd like to give away the centerpieces as extra favors to guests. How do we do this?

A At the end of your wedding, many guests may be wistfully eyeing your centerpieces but not feeling comfortable enough to ask if they can take one home, so actively giving them away is a thoughtful idea. Before the wedding, you and your groom can create a list of the guests you'd like to gift and then personally let them know. (Appoint a relative or friend to remind them of this on the wedding day.) If you don't have specific guests in mind, you could hold a sort of contest to give away the centerpieces as "prizes." Under each guest's plate, slip a tag with a number printed on it. One of the numbers should be the same as the table number. At some point during the party, have your bandleader or DJ instruct guests to look under their plates to find their numbers and determine who the winners are. If you are simply looking for a way to ensure your centerpieces don't go to waste and you aren't set on giving them to guests, consider having them collected at the end of the party and reused (the way they are, or refashioned) to decorate tables at your next-day brunch.

Plan the *Other Parties*

EXTEND YOUR CELEBRATION WITH THESE WEEKEND EVENTS

Inviting the Guests

HOW TO SPREAD THE NEWS ABOUT YOUR PRE- AND POSTNUPTIAL PARTIES

While there's a certain protocol associated with wedding invitations, it can be harder to figure out how to tell your guests about the other parties you're hosting. Depending on your situation, one of the following options may be right for you:

Include it in the wedding invitation. Some brides turn their wedding invitations into elaborate booklets, with information and response cards for each part of the celebration, from the rehearsal dinner to the brunch. This is a great way to ensure that you'll get good responses to your invites.

Send out a separate mailing. If you're planning a rehearsal dinner with a really fun theme—a backyard luau, a football tailgate—consider sending out a separate paper invitation with the scoop, so guests can also get a sense of what that party will be like.

Post your notice. If you've created a wedding Web site, include information about these pre- and postnuptial events: Your guests can simply e-mail you a quick yes or no through your site.

Keep it casual. For these more laid-back events, giving guests a heads-up via e-mail or phone can also do the trick.

The Bridesmaids' Luncheon

Your bridesmaids will be supporting you through your entire engagement, from that gigantic guest-list crisis to the quest for the perfect favors. So what better way to thank them for their help than an intimate little get-together right before the big day?

The bridesmaids' luncheon is usually held in the days leading up to the wedding, either the week before the wedding or on the afternoon of the rehearsal or wedding itself. And it doesn't necessarily have to be a luncheon—it can be a casual pizza-and-pasta dinner, a formal tea with sandwiches and dessert, or a champagne brunch at your favorite restaurant.

Obviously, your bridal party is on the must-invite list, but you may also want to invite your mother and your groom's mother, and any sisters or sisters-in-law who aren't already in the wedding party. Consider this party a perfect opportunity to celebrate many of the special women in your life.

The Rehearsal Dinner

This can be thought of as the opening act for your main event—a less formal, slightly smaller get-together that allows your family and friends to meet and greet one another before the big day. It's also a great opportunity to do something completely different from your wedding reception. If you'd wanted a steel-drum band, Mexican food or make-your-own sundaes at your reception but it just wasn't going to work, try it at this event. The rehearsal dinner is your chance to let your creativity flow.

The details can be as laid-back or as luxe as you wish, though you'll want to mix it up a little—in other words, don't have a steakhouse rehearsal dinner if filet mignon is going to be the main course at your reception. And while the parents and siblings of the bride and groom, the members of the bridal party and their dates are all must-invites, you can make the guest list as large as you want; many couples opt to include out-of-towners and other VIPs for a grand rehearsal dinner that rivals the reception in size.

This party is traditionally hosted by the groom's parents the night before the wedding, but some couples throw it themselves (especially if the parents are footing the bill for the wedding), and some opt to have it two days before the wedding, so they don't have two big events in a row.

{modern bride wisdom}

Want to break the ice at your rehearsal dinner and ensure that guests will have an even better time at your wedding? Seat guests family style, alternating folks who know each other with folks who don't. Giving them a chance to mingle outside of their social circles means your aunt could be close buddies with your groom's best pal by the end of the night.

MODERN BRIDE 5

Rehearsal-Dinner Ideas

Outdoor Barbecue: A grilled feast possibly followed by a game of softball is an inexpensive, relaxed and easy-to-prepare party for groups both large and small.

Seaside Clambake: Lobster and clams on the sand at sunset is a deliciously low-key and informal treat. Add a bonfire and s'mores for a sweet ending to the evening.

Sports Night: Baseball-stadium boxes are a fun party spot for all ages. Have ballpark faves like hot dogs and beer served.

First-Date Celebration: Chances are, the place was romantic enough to inspire the two of you. Let that same spirit infuse your dinner. Hold the party at the site of your first date and name tables after other spots that are meaningful to you.

Hoedown: A country-themed bash, complete with a square-dance caller, will keep guests entertained. Serve Southern favorites like fried chicken and cornbread so guests can do-si-do the night away.

THE AFTER-PARTY

The celebrating doesn't have to end when your reception comes to a close. If you and your fiancé are night owls, plan a postnuptial gathering for your friends and family members.

If you plan an official after-party, you'll want to pick up the tab for your guests, though for more casual, impromptu events—like a last-minute decision to head to the hotel bar or the best man's hotel room for a nightcap—your guests can spring for their own drinks.

If you'll be hosting something official, look for a great venue. Some couples have their post-reception celebration in a more intimate space within their reception site; others look for a VIP room in a nearby pub or bar, or a late-night "specialty" space, like a karaoke bar or pool hall. You can make it really elaborate, with a special late-night menu of tapas, desserts or a favorite midnight snack, or simply offer whatever's on tap at the bar of choice.

After-Party Ideas

Good Sports: Play up your competitive side by enjoying a few games with your guests: pub favorites like darts or billiards, board games from Trivial Pursuit to Cranium or a few frames of midnight bowling at your local alley.

Just Desserts: Set up a sweet buffet with all of your favorite treats, and let guests sip port and dessert wines as they gather around a pianist playing loungey tunes.

Late-Night Nosh: Get a jump start on your post-wedding brunch and serve mini versions of brunch favorites: petite quiches, Danishes and bagels with mimosas and Bloody Marys.

Tapas and Tunes: Set up a karaoke machine so guests can serenade one another as they snack on a tapas spread featuring olives, cheese, bread and other savories.

Cozy Campfire: After an outdoor or beach reception, gather around a campfire for s'mores and conversation.

{modern bride wisdom}

If you want to have an after-party, it's safe to assume that it will appeal most to the younger crowd. Use your bridal party to spread the word and give the time and place.

The Day-After Brunch

To get a little more quality time with your friends and family members before everyone hits the road, consider hosting a brunch the following morning.

Usually, the bride and groom throw this party in conjunction with their parents—it can be anything from a breakfast of bagels and donuts in your parents' backyard to a lavish omelette-and-Belgian-waffle spread in a swanky restaurant. Either way, you can't go wrong; your guests are sure to appreciate the gesture—and the meal. If you're inviting a lot of out-of-towners, consider a venue in or near the hotel where they're staying to minimize their transportation needs.

If you're leaving for your honeymoon that day, just remember to book your flight for late in the afternoon or evening, so you'll have plenty of time to mingle and sip mimosas before you have to head to the airport. Most brunches are planned to accommodate as many guests as possible—starting early for those who need a quick bite before they head home, and going into the early afternoon so your late-rising buddies have a chance to attend as well.

{modern bride wisdom}

Have some fun with the seating at your pre- and postnuptial wedding parties—offer open seating, where guests find a spot wherever they like, or try a "blind" seating arrangement, where guests pick a number out of a hat and sit at the corresponding table.

Keeping Active

You've gathered all of your favorite people together for the weekend, so make the most of it. Between the rehearsal dinner and the post-wedding brunch, plan a few other fun activities for you and your guests. Here are some of our favorites.

- golf outing
- spa day
- softball or volleyball tournament
- karaoke party
- bowling bash
- billiards party
- picnic or barbecue
- clambake
- cocktail reception
- tour
- cruise
- game night

Bride to Bride

For our wedding, we chose a hotel that offers a complimentary brunch for guests (so we're discreetly saving money on our send-off brunch). The restaurant will reserve a section for us, and they'll keep a count of our brunch guests, deducting from the bill the number of hotel guests from our party. —Alyson

Q & A

Q **My fiancé and I are having a formal engagement party. Should we open our presents at the party or wait until we get home?**

A Unwrap the presents when you get home. It prevents hurt feelings (someone who gave you a modest gift may feel outdone by the more extravagant presents you receive). And besides, for most of your guests, especially the men, watching you open presents is as much fun as watching you get your nails done. Instead, use this party as an opportunity to celebrate with your friends and relatives (and possibly introduce each other's family to one another for the first time). It's best to save the oohs and aahs of public present opening for the gals at your bridal shower.

Q **If I invite someone to my shower or bachelorette party, do I have to invite her to my wedding?**

A Unless you are having a small "family only" wedding, you'd better believe it. Would you invite friends for cocktails and then tell some they can't stay for dinner? This is the same deal. Consider your shower or bachelorette party as an extension of your wedding weekend. If your friend makes the A list for one of the parties, she needs to be invited to all of them. Showers and bachelorette parties are not opportunities to "pack 'em in" so that you can keep the guest count down on the expensive wedding day. Your friend will definitely be offended if she's made to feel like a part-time celebrator in your wedding festivities.

Q **My fiancé and I aren't having a rehearsal. Do we still need to have a rehearsal dinner?**

A Despite its name, a rehearsal dinner is more than just grabbing a bite to eat after the rehearsal. Hosting a pre-wedding event gives you the perfect chance to spend a little more quality time with family and friends before the real frenzy of your celebration begins. Also, rehearsal dinners are a great way to greet out-of-town guests when they arrive. It makes them feel welcome and shows them that their efforts to travel to your wedding are genuinely appreciated. So go ahead and skip the rehearsal if it's not necessary, but don't skip an opportunity to get together with family and friends. Call it a "welcome dinner" instead. If budget is an issue, consider this: The groom's parents often offer to host this event in the couple's honor. If you're paying for the shindig yourselves, just be sure to set a reasonable budget and stick to it. Scout out some inexpensive but fun local restaurants, or consider a backyard barbecue (and we offer more ideas on the next page). Neither option should put a big dent in your overall wedding budget.

Q My fiancé and I were hoping that his parents would pay for the rehearsal dinner, but they haven't offered yet. How do we bring it up?

A Asking for money is never easy. However, there are ways to finesse it without sounding like you're just trying to hit up your future in-laws for cash. One approach is to ask them if they are planning on hosting the rehearsal dinner. "Hosting" implies "paying for" without having to actually come out and say it. If they say yes, turn over the guest list to them and let the party rest safely in their hands. If your future in-laws aren't big party-throwers, they may still offer to foot the bill but leave the party planning up to you. Another way to approach the money issue is to ask your in-laws if they want to make a contribution to your wedding. If they throw a check your way, then you can decide whether or not you want to apply their cash gift to your rehearsal dinner.

Q We'd like to invite our out-of-town guests to the rehearsal dinner, but have to keep the costs down. What are some affordable ideas for a larger party?

A One of the most inexpensive ways to play host to a large party is to hold it at the home of a close friend or relative. Fire up the grill, set out some tables and folding chairs, add some lawn games (croquet, badminton, etc.) and you're all set. Or better yet, talk a relative with a pool into hosting the gig and invite guests to bring their suits. Another option is to hold your affair at a public park. The park fee will be nominal, and you can either grill up burgers and hot dogs or enlist family and friends to participate in a potluck-style dinner. If you'd rather have your party at a restaurant, consider renting out the back room of your local pizzeria. It's an affordable (and tasty) way to feed a lot of people.

Q We want our out-of-town guests to have enough to do during our wedding weekend, so we've come up with all kinds of activities. But we don't want anyone to feel pressured to participate. How do we make this clear?

A By saying exactly that. Provide the weekend's itinerary in the form of a schedule that you leave in each guest's hotel room, as a wedding newsletter or as an update to your wedding Web site. And at the very top of the itinerary, begin with a quick note from you and your fiancé explaining that all of the activities are optional and that everyone is welcome to participate in as many or as few as they'd like. When you're coming up with the schedule, try not to organize anything that requires or depends on a definite head count, such as a reservation at a restaurant. This way you won't have to worry, either. The best approach is to name a time and place and let the guest list unfold from there—for example, "10 a.m.: Kayaking at the lake" or "4 p.m.: Museum tour." That said, certain activities are likely to require a minimum number of participants—such as a hula lesson—so when that's the case, try to enlist a group of siblings, cousins or friends to make an appearance.

Q We can't afford a next-day brunch. Can we skip it?

A Most guests are happy enough to be invited to the main shindig. They certainly won't pass judgment if you decide not to throw a party after the party, and you're under no obligation to do so. So if a brunch would push you over budget, simply forgo it. That being said, a simple bagel and cream-cheese spread at your parents' house may be within reach and can give you and your new hubby a second chance to visit loved ones. As an alternative, tuck a list of great local breakfast spots into your guests' informational packets. They'll appreciate the tips and will get the message that they're on their own for brunch the day after your wedding.

CHAPTER 17

Make Everyone *Happy*

TIPS TO HELP YOU BE A TOP-NOTCH HOSTESS

Please kick off your shoes and get comfortable!

Ways to Be Gracious

Your wedding may be your day, but it's a good idea to keep all of your guests in mind as you plan your festivities. Follow these tips as you're planning your big days and you'll have people raving about your wedding for years to come.

1 **GIVE "AND GUEST" A NAME.** Don't know the name of your cousin's steady beau? Make a quick call to your aunt or your cousin to get the spelling so you can put it on the invitation—that'll make him feel even more welcome.

2 **MAKE SURE THEY'RE IN THE KNOW.** Guests want to be made aware of key details about the wedding so they have an idea of what to expect and what to wear. While the style and formality of the invitation will give them a clue (engraving and formal wording equals a fancy event; an invite with a whimsical butterfly emblem promises a more offbeat celebration), spell out anything unusual about the wedding: Guests will appreciate knowing to wear flats and less-dressy attire to an outdoor wedding, or to eat a light dinner before a dessert reception.

3 **TELL THEM HOW TO GET THERE.** At most weddings, there's a sizeable set of guests who may not know their way around town—and nothing spoils that celebratory mood like wandering for an hour looking for the right street sign. So include good directions with your invitation, and stash a few extra sets at the ceremony site, so guests who forgot to pack the originals can find their way to the reception.

4 **DON'T LEAVE GUESTS TO FEND FOR THEMSELVES.** If there are a few hours to kill between the ceremony and reception, make sure they'll be occupied. Some couples set up a hospitality suite at the hotel or arrange for a friend or family member to host some out-of-towners for soft drinks and light snacks before the party starts.

5 **HELP THEM MIX AND MINGLE.** Odds are, this is the first time your favorite college professor, your officemate and your great-grandmother are in the same room together—encourage these special people in your lives to get to know one another. There are plenty of ways to encourage interaction: Host pre- and postnuptial events that help people break the ice, like a Brides vs. Grooms softball tourney; use a "blind" seating method for your rehearsal dinner, where guests draw table numbers from a hat, to mix everyone together; and plant conversation starters at the reception, such as having your emcee ask trivia questions about you and your mate, or having your dinner served from stations to encourage guests to mingle to the max.

6 **DON'T MAKE THEM PAY AT THE PARTY.** You wouldn't ask your friends to pay per beer at your Super Bowl bash, so don't ask them to do it at this celebration. If you can't afford a full bar, see page 103 for some cheaper options that don't fall into the cash-bar category. And unless your family has included the "money dance" for generations, don't make guests pay for the pleasure of dancing with you— it'll make your celebration seem like a ploy for cash.

7 **KEEP YOUR GUESTS' DIETS IN MIND.** Alert your caterer to any special dietary needs that your guests may have, from nut allergies to being a vegetarian. He can help you figure out how to accommodate them, whether you add a third entrée option to your sit-down dinner or have special meals prepared for these guests.

8 **DON'T CATER ONLY TO YOUR CROWD.** You'll definitely want your dance floor to be hopping—but be considerate of guests who would rather sit and chat. Ask your bandleader or DJ to set up his equipment to minimize the volume off the dance floor, or set up a separate lounge where guests can relax and catch up. Ask your entertainers to play music that spans the generations because you'll have guests of all ages at your event.

9 **SPEND TIME WITH EVERYONE.** Your guests may have traveled hundreds or thousands of miles to be with you on your wedding day—make time to say a quick "Thanks for coming" to each of your guests who made the effort. And minimize the amount of time you spend getting pictures done: A formal photo session is a poor substitute for having fun with your guests.

Bride to Bride

I wrote a personal note to each of our guests explaining why they were important to my fiancé and me. They found their notes with their place cards as they entered the reception. —Diane

Child's Play

Here are some foolproof ways to keep the little ones happy at your reception.

Plan a kid-friendly menu. Ask your caterer to modify your entrée or create a new dish that'll appeal to pint-sized appetites: Your 5-year-old nephew may turn his nose up at filet mignon, but a burger and fries will be a hit.

Hire some help. Give the parents on your guest list the night off, and hire sitters to entertain your youngest guests with games, toys and art projects. If you want to really go the extra mile, hire an entertainer—a magician, a balloon artist or a storyteller—to make the night special for the children.

Set aside a space. If there's room in your budget, ask if your site has a separate place where the kids can play. That way, the children can run wild without disturbing the grown-up fun you have planned.

Keep them entertained. Create a kit for each child to help keep him occupied—and away from that enticing tower of cake. Offer up crayons, paper and stickers and suggest that he create a special piece of art inspired by your wedding—you can even arrange to have the results displayed at the end of the reception. Board games or a deck of cards with instructions for a simple card game (like Hearts) can keep older kids from getting bored.

Play favorites. Tell your bandleader or DJ that there will be little ones in attendance, and have them throw a few songs from the Disney collection onto the playlist.

{expert tip} Keep guests comfortable: For hot-weather weddings, pass out fans. If it's cool, offer pashminas. And if it's sunny, give them parasols.

—JoAnn Gregoli, event planner, New York City

Help Out-of-Towners Have Fun

Make their stay more affordable. Hopefully, you'll be able to get your guests a discounted rate by blocking off rooms at a local hotel, but even that "bargain price" could be a budget breaker for some of your guests. One solution: E-mail some of your single guests to offer to help them find a roomie to split the cost of the hotel room with them, or ask some of your local friends and family members if they'd be willing to open their homes and their sofa beds to a few of your pals.

Keep them occupied. Plan a few special events for guests who've traveled so far for your big day. Consider inviting them to the rehearsal dinner, or throw a post-wedding brunch the following day. (Check out chapter 16 for more on these bonus bashes.)

Give them a lift. If your wedding events are scattered around the area, out-of-towners may have a hard time getting their bearings—or even using a rental car to take them from here to there. Consider hiring a shuttle service or bus to transport your out-of-towners from your chosen hotel to the wedding events. (Score extra points by having the bus service offer a brief tour of local sights during any lag time between your ceremony and reception.)

Bride to Bride

I mailed a set of travel instructions to out-of-town guests well in advance to make their plans easy to coordinate. To help keep their expenses down, I arranged discounts for them with an airline, rental-car company and hotel. —Lisa

Seating *Made Easy*

1   **Map it out.** Many sites will provide you with a diagram of the setup so you can plot out the best spots for certain guests. Your younger guests may merit spots by the dance floor, for instance, as they're more likely to be dancing and less likely to be bothered by a loud sound system. Elderly guests may appreciate a spot close to the restrooms or the buffet tables or stations so they don't have to walk too far for the essentials.

2   **Avoid extra drama.** Don't seat Aunt Bertha near Uncle Bert if they haven't spoken for the past decade. You can work on reuniting them at a less important occasion.

Make sure everyone knows at least one person at the table. Putting all of your single friends together may make them feel uncomfortable if they don't know each other. They don't need their singleness being broadcast to the rest of the guests. —Sarah

3 **Create lively conversations**. Avoid the impulse to seat all those hard-to-place people at one big table—your groom's Star Trek–loving college roommate probably doesn't have a whole lot in common with your hippie-chick pal from yoga class. Instead, try to find people they'll enjoy talking to: Your yoga pal may be intrigued by your Uncle Pete's tales from his days following the Grateful Dead. You might even want to fill your friend in on her seatmates ahead of time, since you may not have a moment to explain the connection that day.

4 **Be considerate of your bridal party.** You can avoid longing glances across the room by letting your bridesmaids and groomsmen sit with their dates. You and your groom can sit at an intimate table for two or join your party people (and their dates) at a big table.

5 **Get some help.** Ask your parents and his to help you arrange their friends—you won't necessarily know who should sit together.

6 **Vary the table size.** Standard tables generally seat eight to 10 guests, but many sites now offer tables in larger and smaller sizes—perfect for creating a big, boisterous gathering of your college buddies, or letting your childhood friends catch up at a cozy table of six.

The Receiving Line

Worried about spending the entire party meeting and greeting your guests? Follow these practical suggestions to have an efficient receiving line.

Keep it small. Don't have the entire wedding party greet guests—your bridesmaids and groomsmen can mingle with the crowd while you and your parents serve line duty.

Keep it moving. Don't take 10 minutes to catch up with your out-of-town pal while the rest of your guests wait for their turn to congratulate you—give your friends a quick hello and let them know you'll meet up with them later on.

Do it early. If you don't want your guests standing in a line, head right back in to your ceremony site after your exit to release them row by row from the ceremony. That way, guests can stay seated until it's their turn to say a brief hello, and then head to the reception.

Try a more casual approach. Consider going from table to table during the dinner to meet and greet your guests instead of holding a traditional receiving line. You may miss out on most of the meal, but you'll be able to work your way through your invitees at your own pace (and perhaps a little faster than you would by greeting each person individually).

Want your guests to write more than the standard "Congratulations" or "Best wishes" in your guest book? Ask them to instead share their definition of love or predictions for you as a couple.

The Guest Book

A DESIGNATED PLACE WHERE ALL OF YOUR GUESTS CAN SHARE A SENTIMENT CREATES AN INDELIBLE MEMORY OF YOUR BIG DAY

Bound book: The most common option is an elegant, traditional-style notebook, which is placed on a separate table for guests to inscribe throughout the evening.

Note cards: Individual cards can be placed at each table or stacks can be piled on one table, and several guests can sign at once.

Postcards: Have your guests write their best wishes for you on pretty picture postcards, then put your maid of honor in charge of mailing you a few each week. You'll be receiving sweet reminders of your wedding day for months to come.

Polaroid pictures: Ask a few friends to man the guest book, snap Polaroid shots of your guests, then paste them into the book. Your guests can add sweet notes near their photos.

Large, matted photo: Let guests sign the matting around a photo, then frame and hang the finished product in your home as a lasting reminder of your wedding day.

A coffee-table book: Choose a gorgeous book with images related to your wedding theme or location—such as great wineries for a vineyard wedding—and let your guests sign the pages. You can leave this book out on the table and flip through everyone's well wishes often.

Video: Skip the book altogether and go with a digital-age version. Set up a video camera and you'll capture not only your guests' favorite stories of you and their best wishes, but also the personalities of each of your guests.

A special object: Consider choosing a more three-dimensional take on the guest book—for example, a tablecloth or platter that guests can sign with markers, which you can use for special occasions, or a set of ornaments for your Christmas tree. If you're a sports-loving couple, have baseballs signed, then display them in your house.

How to Handle
Sticky Situations

A SINGLE FRIEND ASKS WHETHER SHE CAN BRING A DATE.
Solution: If your guest list is too tight to allow single guests to bring escorts, simply say so. "I wish we could, but we just can't fit another person into the party" is a gracious way to turn down her request. But you'll need to acquiesce if the date is her longtime beau—he should have been invited in the first place.

A GUEST INSISTS ON BRINGING THE KIDS TO YOUR ADULTS-ONLY RECEPTION.
Solution: Start by reminding her that it's an adults-only affair, so there will be no other children and no child-friendly activities to keep her little ones occupied. If a sitter shortage is to blame, try to help her find child care—recommend a trustworthy teen to take charge of her kiddies. And if she still insists she can't attend without her children? Say something like, "Well, we're really sorry that we'll miss you on our big day—I hope we can get together soon."

THE RSVP DATE HAS COME AND GONE, AND A HANDFUL OF GUESTS HAVEN'T RESPONDED.
Solution: Start calling or e-mailing to follow up on any missing responses as soon as the date has passed—and assume that their response simply got lost in the mail.

A COLLEGE FRIEND HAS BEEN KNOWN TO DRINK A FEW TOO MANY—AND BECOME BELLIGERENT.
Solution: Ask a trustworthy mutual friend to keep the potential heavy drinker in check by encouraging him to mingle far from the bar. It may not be a bad idea to have someone point the guy out to the bartenders at the start of the evening, so they can subtly try to limit the liquor served to him.

YOU'RE SURE YOUR COUSIN IS THE TYPE WHO WOULDN'T FORGET A GIFT, BUT IT'S BEEN A FEW MONTHS SINCE THE WEDDING, AND YOU HAVEN'T RECEIVED A THING.
Solution: Send the guest a nice note thanking him for coming to your wedding. If he has sent a gift that got lost in transit, your thank-you note will clue him in that something's awry, and he can remedy the situation.

MODERN BRIDE 5

Thoughtful Gestures

Have your waiters pass trays of wine and sparkling water as the reception begins to avoid crowding at the bar.

Stock restrooms with beauty products your guests might need over the course of the evening.

Create a cozy lounge space away from the dance floor where guests can linger and chat over coffee on comfy couches.

If your wedding is outdoors, provide small flashlights for guests to get to their cars—and umbrellas in case of rain.

Provide shuttle buses to take guests back to their hotels so there's no chance of anyone drinking and driving.

Q&A

Q **I really want my wedding to be a dressy affair. But I'm afraid that if I insist on black-tie attire, some people won't want to come. Should I?**

A If you've got your heart set on a celebration that resembles Oscar night, go for it. Most guests will be happy to dress the part. Just keep in mind that for the men who will need to rent tuxes, this can mean an additional cost. For the women, a formal wedding may mean that they have to pony up for an appropriate dress. If you add these expenses to the cost of a present and travel arrangements, it could get pricey for them to see you tie the knot. However, no one on your guest list is being forced to wear a tux or ball gown—men can wear dark suits instead when black-tie is called for, and women can dress up in a semi-formal ensemble with glamorous jewelry and accessories. If you're afraid your guests won't understand this option, you can always indicate "black-tie optional" on the invitation. Although some guests will bow out of the tux option, plenty of people will still participate in your Academy Award–style fantasy.

Q **We expect our guests to enjoy themselves… and probably drink a lot. What can we do to make sure they get home safely?**

A Weddings are a great excuse to eat, drink and be merry, and let's face it: Every bride wants her reception to be the best party ever. But as the host and hostess, you and your new husband are responsible for seeing to it that guests consuming alcohol are taken care of after the revelry ends. If you have guests staying at a hotel, find out if the hotel offers a shuttle service that will transport your guests from the property to the reception site and back. It's not uncommon for this to be offered, and sometimes even at no cost. You can also rent a bus or van to drive guests to the hotel after the event. Have the phone numbers of local cab companies available and easily accessible throughout the evening for anyone who lives locally. Tell your DJ or bandleader to make an announcement that transportation will be available to guests. You can also ask your bartender to keep an eye out for the warning signs that a guest may have overly imbibed—and give the barman a point person (maybe a parent or close family friend) to report any such cases to. Talk to your friends before the event and encourage them to assign designated drivers and carpool to the event if possible. Of course, you'll want to provide a wide range of nonalcoholic beverages, as well as coffee all night. Also consider closing the bar a little before the reception ends and putting out a send-off snack—whether it's an old-fashioned hot-dog or pretzel stand or a spread of finger foods. Some couples host after-parties with a smaller buffet of munchies, as guests will have probably danced off their dinner by that point.

Q **We're having a flower girl and a ring bearer in the wedding party. Who should pay for the outfits?**

A The children's parents traditionally foot the bill for the ensembles, unless you're feeling extra generous and want to offer to do the buying. (So don't pick a little Vera Wang unless you know the parents can afford it.) At the very least, offer dresses in two or three price ranges. And remember, you're responsible for providing the flower-girl basket and ring-bearer pillow—and if you're having the flower girl wear fresh flowers in her hair or scatter rose petals as she walks down the aisle, they're on your tab, too.

Q **I don't want to put my single gals on display for the bouquet toss. What are my options?**

A Go a different route altogether. Have your DJ or bandleader ask your guests who believes they've traveled the greatest distance to attend your wedding. Then narrow this group down to the person who actually did cover the most miles, and present that jet-setter with your bouquet. Another idea is to invite all married couples within the crowd to the dance floor.

Then have the DJ ask everyone who's been married for more than five years to keep dancing and for everyone else to stop. Then have him ask for people who've been married for 10 years to keep dancing, and dismiss everyone else. Continue until you eventually identify the longest-lasting duo in the room (something to aspire to!), and then flower them with love.

Q **My parents are inviting a lot of people I have never met before to my wedding. Are there any good tricks to remembering people's names?**

A Absolutely. One of the most effective methods of remembering a name is to simply repeat it aloud right after you are introduced. For example, upon meeting Elaine, you should say, "It's nice to meet you, Elaine." Also, try to slow down your introductions, because taking a few extra moments to look into someone's eyes and shake her hand will up your chances of creating an impression in your own mind. Another tip: Make a connection between this person and another who has the same name. For instance, think to yourself, "Elaine has really curly hair, just like Elaine on *Seinfeld*," or "Elaine has skinny legs just like Elaine in my yoga class." It's the number of connections and the time spent making them that will help keep your new acquaintance's name fresh and dis-

tinctive in your mind. And finally, don't forget that when it comes time for you to make your rounds to the tables at the reception, you already have a cheat sheet—the seating chart. Before the big day, spend a little time studying who's sitting where so you'll have a head start. Plus, you've probably already seated your parents' friends based on their association with your parents (Dad's golf buds at table four, Mom's book club at five, etc.). So when you approach the table, some names (those your parents have mentioned) should already be familiar to you and thus, easier to remember. If you do end up forgetting a name or two, don't sweat it. Guests understand that you're a busy bride in the midst of a fast-moving day and will certainly cut you some slack.

CHAPTER 18

Get Married Away

**PLANNING A WEDDING
IN A DISTANT LOCATION**

Why wait until after the wedding to get away from it all? For a destination wedding, you'll invite your favorite people to join you at your dream locale for a mini vacation—and to watch you wed in style. While these used to be popular for second weddings or no-frills nuptials, many couples now throw these parties in their favorite getaway spots.

A getaway wedding is often the perfect option for couples who don't have a clear-cut place to get married because their families are scattered around the world, or who want to keep their guest list small—when you're asking people to travel thousands of miles, you're likely to have only your very nearest and dearest by your side. Here's how to get it off the ground.

Pick Your Place

HOW TO FIND THE RIGHT LOCALE FOR YOU

There's a whole world of possible wedding destinations out there: beaches and mountains, cities and countrysides. Consider these points to come up with the location that suits you best.

Think about your favorite places. Create a list of destinations you've visited together, or your most beloved vacations from your childhood. And if your fiancé proposed on a gorgeous Hawaiian beach, why not make it official on that same strip of sand?

Incorporate your passions. Whether you and your fiancé are ski buffs or enjoy exploring exotic cultures, you can find a perfect spot to reflect your interests.

Consider your guests. A Tahitian wedding will be gorgeous—but if the trip's too pricey for most of your friends and family members, you may end up marrying alone. And think about the difficulty of reaching your destination: Your grandmother may not be comfortable taking a six-hour flight to your ceremony.

Factor in your budget. In addition to the usual flowers, dress, catering and cake for your wedding, you'll be paying for your own travel and, often, other wedding-weekend events for your guests.

Research the marriage laws. Some countries have residency requirements and other restrictions that could make it impossible to tie the knot legally, so you may have to limit your options. Keep in mind, though, that if this is the case at your dream destination, you could always have a brief legal ceremony at home, then hold a vow affirmation and reception at your destination.

Check the weather forecast. Be wary of planning your wedding during your locale's hurricane or rainy seasons—see our chart on page 240 to determine when you'll have the best chance for good weather for your celebration.

Cool Spots to Tie the Knot

Hawaii: This tropical paradise and top honeymoon destination gives you plenty of resorts to choose from (and you don't have to worry about exchange rates and passports).

Las Vegas: While you can still be wed by Elvis at a drive-through wedding chapel, many Vegas resorts are creating wedding packages that appeal to people looking for a more traditional ceremony and reception.

Caribbean: Planning a wedding on most of these islands is a cinch, thanks to all-inclusive packages, tourist-friendly marriage laws and truly gorgeous settings.

Europe: Ancient castles and cathedrals, charming villages and sophisticated cities serve as a rich backdrop for a getaway wedding here. (Be sure to check on the legality of the ceremony, however.)

Mexico: Balmy weather, easy travel and a vibrant culture make Mexico an attractive wedding destination.

{expert tip} Allow plenty of time: When working with vendors on island resorts, "island time" may prevail and things may move more slowly than you would imagine. —*JoAnn Gregoli, event planner, New York City*

Planning Across the Miles

If you're a continent away from your wedding locale, coordinating all those details can be a bit of a challenge. This is how to make the planning as easy as possible.

Determine your wedding size. You and your groom can go it alone, invite along a few friends and family members, or ask 200 of your nearest and dearest to join you at your getaway wedding. The number of guests you want may affect the locale you pick for your wedding as well as the amount of time you'll need to plan.

Get a coordinator. It'll be tough to track down the best wedding pros—and stay on top of all those details—from hundreds or thousands of miles away, so finding someone who knows your destination inside and out will be a huge

help. Many resorts have a coordinator on staff whose services are included in their wedding fee. You could also work with an independent consultant or even a travel agent who specializes in weddings.

Consider keeping it simple. You've already chosen a top-notch wedding location, so if handling all of the logistics from afar seems overwhelming, know that you don't have to worry about crafting an elaborate party plan. You can make it easy on yourself by choosing a caterer who can also make your cake and a band who can take you from the ceremony to the last dance, for example, and by using simple white linens from your caterer instead of fussing over rentals.

Ask your pros for help. Your caterer will likely be able to recommend a great baker if he doesn't make cakes himself.

Use the Internet. E-mail makes it easy for pros to send out photos, contracts, playlists and other essentials as attachments. You can submit questions anytime, day or night—especially helpful when you're planning a wedding in a vastly different time zone.

Make a visit. If you can, travel to your destination at least once so you can get the lay of the land, meet face to face with key vendors, and feel more comfortable that plans are progressing as you wish.

Get it in writing. This is even more important for a long-distance affair, when you may not be able to see sample centerpieces or taste the menu in advance. Make sure the contracts are as specific as possible about what you want (plumeria for the leis instead of orchids, for example), so you can be sure you're both on the same page.

QUESTIONS TO ASK

FIND OUT WHETHER YOUR RESORT CAN CREATE YOUR DREAM WEDDING

1. Where can we wed?
Many resorts can offer you several different locations on their property, and may even be able to set up your wedding elsewhere for you, whether you want to get married on a boat or in a nearby park.

2. What happens if it rains?
Since most destination brides want their weddings outdoors, find out how the resort handles bad weather. Some have indoor spaces where you can tie the knot, and others keep you under cover in a tent.

3. What's included?
Some wedding packages cover just the officiant and the setting, while others include everything from a champagne toast to dinner for 50. Make sure you find out what you'll get for a basic rate, and what add-ons you want will cost.

4. Are there day fees?
If your guests opt to stay at another resort nearby, you might be charged extra for the use of amenities while they're at the resort for your events.

5. What about refunds or insurance?
Find out what happens if you need to cancel. Will you get the deposit back if the resort can rebook or if the reason is something beyond your control, such as a hurricane? Some resorts have policies that cover you financially if a big storm cancels your wedding plans, or you can purchase wedding insurance independently.

6. Is there an on-site coordinator?
Not only can this person give you a short list of great vendors to use for your wedding day, but she'll be able to key you in to cool tours or outings for your guests, little-known amenities the resort can provide—and can even help coordinate your travel plans.

7. Will you provide a discount for a block of rooms?
Many resorts offer group discounts for large parties—so if you're inviting more than a dozen guests, odds are they'll get a reduced room rate, and you might even get a free room for bringing in so much business.

8. How many other weddings will be going on that weekend?
A sizeable destination wedding may book up a small resort for an entire weekend, but a small party at a large resort may end up being one of several going on there. Find out how they handle multiple brides, and make sure you're comfortable with their method.

Guest Travel Tips

MAKE SURE YOUR LOVED ONES HAVE AS WONDERFUL A TIME AS YOU DO

Notify them well in advance. Save-the-dates should be sent out as soon as the destination and date are booked—you'll want to give guests at least three months to reserve their vacation time, set a travel budget and make their plans, though six months or more is ideal.

Use one travel agent. Find an agent who specializes in destination weddings or group travel to help you get great packages from airlines and hotels for your guests. Send out the travel agent's phone number with your save-the-date and put it on your wedding Web site to simplify planning for your guests.

Set aside a few suites. When you're blocking off rooms, stick with mostly doubles, but reserve a suite or two. Some families on your list may appreciate the extra space.

Sell them on it. Want to guarantee a great turnout? Make sure your communications about your wedding showcase why you love your chosen destination. Tell them about the amenities at the resort, your favorite restaurants and activities and nearby attractions they can check out. They can turn your wedding into the perfect excuse for a mini vacation.

Give them a packing list. If your resort has a dress code at dinner or if you're planning some activities, you may want to send an e-mail or note with suggestions on what to bring— some resorts require men to wear jackets at dinner, for example, or you might want guests to bring hiking boots if you're planning a mountain walk as one of your wedding events.

Give them a warm welcome. Consider planning a little cocktail party or get-together when most of your guests are scheduled to arrive so everyone can catch up with one another. And consider having a welcome basket waiting in your guests' rooms, with a few goodies to help them enjoy their stay, a directory of where each guest is staying and a full itinerary.

{modern bride wisdom}

Consider buying your favors and welcome-basket goodies at your destination to avoid having to worry about shipping and customs headaches.

Who Covers the Costs?

As the hosts of this grand event, you'll need to spring for the actual wedding events—the rehearsal dinner, ceremony and reception—plus your own airfare and accommodations. Many couples also spring for a few other get-togethers, like a welcome party or a sunset cruise.

Your guests—including members of the bridal party—should expect to pay for their own travel expenses and meals and entertainment outside of the wedding-related activities.

A wedding away makes for some great photo ops. Make sure your photographer captures a sense of the place.

Destination-Wedding Style

CHOOSING THE RIGHT ATTIRE FOR YOUR CEREMONY

Keep it simple. Consider the ceremony setting when you choose your dress—a long train will be a real drag over sand, and delicate lace might catch and tear on a rocky landscape. For the guys, linen suits or a linen shirt with khakis may be more appropriate for a beach wedding than a formal tux.

Look for packable styles. Fabrics like chiffon and taffeta are light enough for a beach wedding and can fit into a small bag—and they'll be much easier to steam on-site than a thick satin gown.

Think about your accessories. Will your shoes sink into the grass or fill with sand? Barefoot can be beautiful under the right circumstances. Consider the wind factor when choosing accessories as well. Veils can really fly in a high wind. Shoulders may need a protective wrap at night.

{modern bride wisdom}

Incorporate elements of the local culture into your celebration—exchange leis during your ceremony if you're marrying in Hawaii, use tropical flowers for a wedding in the Caribbean or give out maple candy as favors in New England. Using indigenous elements for your wedding will give it local flavor.

Post-Wedding Celebrations

PLAN AN AT-HOME PARTY AFTER YOUR NUPTIALS AWAY

If many of your friends and family members can't make it to your wedding destination—or if you've chosen to make the ceremony an ultra-exclusive affair—you can still have the big celebration after you get home from the honeymoon. This party can be a casual backyard barbecue or a full-on, lavish reception, and can be held right after you get back or a few months into your newlywed life (you could even use cool postcards from your getaway as the invites). Here are a few ideas to make this post-wedding bash wonderful.

Give them a recap. Show the video or a photo slideshow of your ceremony—it'll make a great conversation piece during your cocktail hour or dinner.

Dress to impress. Consider wearing your wedding dress again for this celebration: Since you'll get to wear your gown twice, you'll have even more reason to splurge!

Add a little flavor from your destination. Bring home great souvenirs to give your guests as favors—wooden maracas from Mexico, bottles of jerk sauce from Jamaica—and find a caterer who can recreate some of your favorite dishes from your wedding locale.

Q & A

Q **We're concerned that attending our destination wedding will be very costly for friends traveling solo. Is there anything we can do?**

A Sure. Start by sending out an e-mail to all of your friends who are making the trek themselves to see if anyone's interested in pairing up with other singles to share costs. If they are, give them each other's contact information (names, phone numbers and e-mail addresses). For friends coming from the same region, you can suggest they share rides, gas charges and rental-car expense if necessary. If the bulk of your single friends are coming from different places and a travel buddy won't work, ask them if they're interested in bunking together in the same hotel room to save a little dough. For an even cheaper room (and possibly board), see if any friends and family who live near your wedding locale and have a spare bedroom are willing to play B&B hosts for these friends. If so,

include their contact info as well in your e-mail. Basically, all you need to do is put these cost-saving options out there. After that, it's up to your pals to take the ball and run with it.

Q **How far in advance of our wedding should we arrive?**

A You should make sure that you arrive at least a day or two before your guests descend on the location. This will offer you not only a few quiet moments, but also time to get acclimated to your surroundings. If there is a time difference, you want to be over any jet lag so you can truly enjoy your day. Arriving in advance also gives you the ability to check on how your plans are going and tend to any last-minute details or decisions. Depending on the laws in your location, you might need to be in the country a certain number of hours or days before you can be officially married there. (Be clear on

those rules well in advance.) If you do have a few days to yourselves, however, just make sure that you don't log too many hours in the sun prior to your wedding. You don't want to risk having a sunburn on the big day.

Q **How do we explain to our parents that we prefer a destination wedding to a traditional at-home affair?**

A For parents who had always imagined their little girl marrying in the backyard, the idea of a destination wedding can at first be off-putting. Your parents may worry about the expense and time involved, as well as the guests who might not be able to join you. They may also predict that long-distance planning will be difficult and frustrating. In reality, destination weddings have become more and more popular with couples every year, in large part due to the ease of planning. Many resorts even offer their own wedding planners. Come prepared for these reactions when you meet with your parents to discuss a destination wedding. First let them know about all the positives: a beautiful location, great weather, the ability to spend more time with guests and the convenience of hosting all your events in the same place. If you have already researched some locations, your information can help dispel your parents' fears. Maybe you've discovered a package deal, for example, that includes free nights at the hotel because you're having your wedding there. Remind them that guests pay their own way, so a destination wedding does not necessarily drive up costs. If they still feel they need a way to celebrate at home with a bigger crowd, you might consider a compromise: a small destination wedding for close family and friends followed by a larger cocktail or dessert reception back home later.

Q How can we cater to guests with disabilities at a destination wedding?

A Before you choose your location, keep those guests in mind. Will transferring to a tiny plane prove difficult? Is the resort you are considering set up to handle guests with disabilities? Are you exchanging vows in a remote location or on uneven ground? A good travel agent or wedding planner can help you to identify the sites that are accessible to all. Once a location is chosen, a wedding planner in your own area or on-site can continue to help you to make everyone comfortable. Make sure that the hotel is aware of any guests with disabilities so that an appropriate room can be reserved. Look at a map of the resort so you can determine how far away they will be from all the activities and try to get them as close as possible to the central hub. As you make each plan, keep these guests' comfort in mind and it should all work out fine.

Q How can I determine the best way to transport my gown?

A Begin by discussing your plans with the bridal salon where you purchased your gown. They may be able to pack the dress so that it arrives with minimal wrinkles. Many brides prefer to carry the dress on the flight with them. If this is your preference, be sure to call your airline in advance to find out if this is possible and to ask their advice. Depending on how voluminous your dress is—and how full the flight is—you may be able to have an attendant hang it for you in a closet. However, there is also the chance that it will have to be stowed in an overhead compartment. No matter how your gown is transported and how nicely it has been packed, it will still need to be steamed to rid it of the wrinkles that invariably occur in transit. Most hotels have steamers you can borrow (definitely check in advance) that are far better for freshening your dress than an iron is.

Q How can we carve out time for ourselves when there are so many guests around?

A Just because you're all together doesn't mean that you have to be all together all the time. Consider booking yourselves into a nearby hotel for part of the time if you really want to separate yourselves. Otherwise, be sure to arrange some off-site activities for your guests that will leave the two of you blissfully alone back at the hotel. Or, you two can travel off-site for an intimate lunch or dinner à deux. Most guests will stay only a few days, so you typically do find yourselves on your own private honeymoon by the end of the week. Consider hopping to another part of the island or to a nearby island to guarantee that at least some of your honeymoon will be just the two of you.

CHAPTER 19

Plan Your *Honeymoon*

FIND YOUR IDEAL GETAWAY WITH OUR GUIDANCE

This is the trip you've dreamed about forever, and these are your first days spent together as husband and wife. The wedding is behind you, and you get to simply bask in the glow of being married. So you want your honeymoon to be a true escape—whether that means touring a city, going on a cruise, taking a safari or hanging out on the beach. But there's a lot that goes into making your ultimate fantasy a reality. Read on to pick your ideal locale, book the most romantic retreat and have an unforgettable honeymoon.

Get Started

Not sure how to begin making the plans for your ultimate romantic getaway? Here's how to create your itinerary.

First of all, plan ahead. You'll probably want to start booking your trip about six months out—that will give you plenty of time to research and find the perfect getaway. To begin, figure out how much time you have to honeymoon. Count up your vacation days—and don't forget to subtract any time you'll take off to prep before your nuptials. This can actually factor heavily in your honeymoon plans: If you have only a week off, you may opt to stay closer to home to avoid losing most of your time in transit.

Next, determine your honeymoon personality. Think about what you really love to do on vacation: For many newlyweds, postnuptial bliss is just a perfect stretch of sand where they can laze the day away, while others need a bustling nightlife or a long list of adrenaline-packed activities to keep them entertained. If you and your husband-to-be aren't quite on the same honeymoon wavelength, try to find a happy medium: A beach resort with a world-class golf course—and a world-class spa—may bring both of you bliss.

Now, factor in your budget. No one wants to start her married life deeply in debt, so determine how much you can comfortably spend and find a suitable destination within those limitations. (Don't rely on cash gifts from your wedding to bankroll your getaway, as you may receive less money than you'd expect.) You may be heading to Tampa instead of Tahiti, but you'll look back on your honeymoon just as fondly.

Then it's time to start researching. Check out travel guides, magazines and Web sites to determine which destinations appeal most to you. For more individualized advice, call or visit a local travel agent to help you narrow down your options.

PRACTICAL CONSIDERATIONS

Get your papers in order. Traveling to most of the U.S.'s North American neighbors used to involve bringing your driver's license. But stricter regulations mean you'll now need passports—and some destinations, such as Antigua and the Galapagos Islands, require that your passport be valid for several months beyond your travels. To visit some countries—including Australia, India, the Maldives and Indonesia—you need to get tourist visas either from their embassies before you leave or pay for one when you arrive at your destination. Check out travel.state.gov a few months before your honeymoon so you have plenty of time to handle paperwork long before the big day.

Research the health recommendations. Nobody wants to get sick on a honeymoon—that's why it pays to check out your destination on the Centers for Disease Control's Web site, cdc.gov, to research any health issues you may face. In some tropical or developing countries, you may need immunizations or medications to protect against diseases like typhoid fever and malaria; for other locales, it's a matter of decreasing your risk of contracting common parasites—and traveler's diarrhea—by drinking only bottled water and avoiding raw produce.

Do as the Romans do. It's wise to do a little research into the customs of your destination to avoid offending anyone. For instance, some countries frown on public displays of affection, so you'll want to keep your newlywed nuzzling in check; in others, something as simple as pointing or giving the OK symbol with your thumb and forefinger can be considered rude.

Book Smart

1 DON'T TAKE THE FIRST PRICE YOU FIND. A little legwork before you book your flights or hotel rooms could save you a lot of dough. Check out Web sites like Kayak, Sidestep, Expedia or Travelocity to quickly compare prices from several companies. For your accommodations, skip the toll-free reservation line: After you have a price quote, call the hotel to see if they can beat the rate—sometimes the hotel's managers have the ability to reduce rates or upgrade rooms if their hotel has a lot of vacancies for your date.

2 GO OFF THE BEATEN PATH. Top honeymoon destinations often cost top dollar, thanks to their popularity. Start searching for less obvious (but just as charming) alternatives—Moorea instead of Bora Bora in the South Pacific; Prague instead of Paris. You'll not only save money, but you'll also enjoy a destination that not everyone's been to (yet).

3 REWARD YOURSELF. Sign up for a credit card that offers hotel points or frequent flier miles for every purchase you make, and use it to put down all of those wedding deposits. You can cash in those points later for a first-class upgrade—or a free night's stay. (Just be sure you can pay off the credit card in full each month, or you may end up paying more in interest than the points are worth.)

4 AVOID PEAK TRAVEL TIMES. Head to your chosen destination outside of its peak season (summer in the tropics, winter in Europe) and save a bundle on your trip. Even simply changing your flights—from ultrapopular weekends to less coveted Wednesdays—could net you significant savings on airfare.

5 FLAUNT YOUR NEWLYWED STATUS. Tactfully let everyone from the front-desk clerk to the maitre d' know you're honeymooners—you never know when you might score a free upgrade, a gratis bottle of champagne or another special treat as a result.

6 WORK YOUR CONNECTIONS. You may be able to get better rates on everything from car rentals to accommodations through alumni associations, credit-card networks or auto insurance—or even your company's corporate travel office.

{modern bride wisdom}

Make sure you book your flight in your maiden name. You may be a newlywed, but your license or passport will still show your old name—and your ticket and photo ID need to match.

When-to-Go Guide

YOU'VE SET THE DATE, NOW SEE IF THE WEATHER IN YOUR DREAM HONEYMOON

	JANUARY	FEBRUARY	MARCH	APRIL	MAY	JUNE
BERMUDA	69°/61°	68°/60°	69°/60°	71°/63°	75°/68°	81°/73°
	Cooler temperatures, fewer crowds, lower rates at the majority of hotels and resorts			Temperatures start to rise	Comfortable, clear weather and abundant but be aware that they are possible from	
CARIBBEAN/ CENTRAL AMERICA	83°/73°	84°/73°	84°/74°	86°/77°	87°/78°	88°/78°
	Great weather, larger crowds and highest rates, so book hotels and resorts well in advance			Good weather, lower rates at many hotels and resorts		Expect a mix of lower rates at resorts
WESTERN EUROPE (Italy, France, Greece)	46°/37°	46°/37°	55°/40°	64°/45°	71°/52°	75°/57°
	Cool temperatures, lower rates; some coastal and island resorts may be closed			Nice weather, but European students tend to crowd top sights		Summer season: highest hotel rates
FLORIDA	72°/59°	73°/60°	78°/64°	81°/66°	86°/69°	88°/75°
	Best time to visit: dry and clear in both Miami and Orlando, but hotel and resort rates are high				Comfortable temperatures, but good chance of rain in Orlando	
HAWAII	80°/65°	80°/65°	81°/67°	82°/68°	84°/70°	86°/72°
	Rates are high and hotels book up early, but it's also the rainiest time, so expect afternoon showers			Dry season: the best time of the year to visit; lots of sunshine with fewer crowds at hotels and resorts		
LAS VEGAS	57°/37°	63°/41°	69°/47°	78°/54°	88°/63°	99°/72°
	Winter season: cool daytime temperatures with occasional showers; evenings can be brisk			Best time to visit: comfortable daytime temperatures and cool nights		Very, very hot: 100°, limiting
MEXICO (Caribbean & Pacific coasts)	86°/70°	86°/70°	88°/71°	90°/72°	90°/73°	90°/76°
	Great weather, large crowds and high rates at most resorts; book well in advance			Fewer crowds, great weather and good rates		Hot, rainy season: lower at coastal resorts
SOUTH PACIFIC (Fiji, Tahiti, Cook Islands)	86°/74°	86°/74°	87°/74°	87°/73°	85°/72°	84°/70°
	Wet season: warm and humid with chance of rain; cyclones possible				Dry season: clear skies, low humidity book hotels and resorts well in advance;	
AUSTRALIA/ NEW ZEALAND	93°/65°	93°/65°	90°/63°	72°/58°	67°/52°	61°/49°
	Summer in the Southern Hemisphere: temperate to the south, steamy up north			Fall brings milder temperatures, fewer crowds; good time to visit the reef and rain forest		
AFRICA (Kenya/Tanzania & South Africa)	77°/60°	78°/60°	79°/60°	75°/58°	70°/57°	68°/54°
	Hot and dry in Kenya/Tanzania; warm in Cape Town, South Africa		Rainy season in Kenya/Tanzania; hot and wet in the game-viewing areas of South Africa until April			Best time to visit: and less foliage)

☐ SUNNY SKIES AHEAD   ▨ FAIR AND FAVORABLE   ☐ BRING AN UMBRELLA

DESTINATION FITS THE BILL

JULY	AUGUST	SEPTEMBER	OCTOBER	NOVEMBER	DECEMBER
85°/77°	86°/78°	84°/76°	80°/72°	75°/67°	70°/63°
crowds, so book hotels well ahead; hurricanes rarely hit the island, June through November				Temperatures start to cool down	
88°/78°	88°/78°	88°/79°	87°/76°	86°/74°	84°/73°
sun and rain;	Traditional rainy season: some resorts close for renovation; hurricanes possible on some islands			Good weather and good rates	Great weather; book ahead
80°/68°	85°/68°	76°/60°	65°/52°	55°/45°	50°/40°
lots of crowds; locals vacation here too;		Fair weather, less crowded and slightly lower hotel rates		Cooler weather; some coastal and island resorts may be closed	
89°/77°	89°/77°	87°/76°	84°/73°	79°/69°	74°/62°
Hot, humid weather with chance of tropical storms in Miami and frequent showers in Orlando; expect lower rates at hotels and resorts				Some showers are still possible	Peak season starts: hotel rates high
87°/73°	88°/74°	88°/73°	86°/72°	84°/70°	81°/66°
lower rates and	Hot weather: daytime temperatures have been known to soar above 95°		Dry season: lower rates	Rates are high even though it's the rainiest time of the year	
104°/78°	102°/77°	94°/69°	81°/57°	66°/44°	57°/37°
afternoon temperatures routinely top outdoor activity		Best time to visit: comfortable daytime temperatures and cool nights		Winter season: cool daytime temperatures; evenings can be brisk	
91°/76°	91°/76°	90°/75°		88°/73°	86°/71°
rates usually	Hot, humid, rainy season: hurricanes are possible on both the Caribbean and Pacific coasts			Good weather and rates	High season: book ahead
82°/69°	82°/68°	83°/69°	84°/71°	85°/72°	85°/73°
and abundant sunshine with noticeably bigger crowds; expect to pay the highest rates of the year				Wet season: warmer, more humid with probable showers	
63°/49°	67°/52°	72°/56°	72°/56°	74°/61°	85°/63°
Winter brings cooler temperatures; still a good time to visit the reef and rain forest			Spring temperatures are mild; there's lots of sunshine in Sydney, Melbourne and Auckland		
67°/50°	67°/50°	69°/53°	74°/54°	74°/59°	75°/60°
cool, dry season in Kenya/Tanzania and winter (drier weather means good game-viewing in the wildlife areas of South Africa			Rainy season in Kenya/Tanzania and the game-viewing areas of South Africa; warm and sunny in Cape Town		

Popular Honeymoon *Hot Spots*

A BALMY BEACH, A COBBLESTONE CITY STREET, A RAIN FOREST ADVENTURE—FIND YOUR IDEAL HIDEAWAY AMONG THESE FAVORITE DESTINATIONS

HAWAII Any honeymooner can find something to love on Hawaii's string of practically perfect islands: There's the year-round balmy weather, the stunning black-sand beaches, the snorkel-perfect coral reefs and lava tubes, and rugged volcanos and rain forests just waiting to be hiked, biked and explored. Glamorous types can savor the posh shopping in Wailea or the glitzy scene on Waikiki Beach, while surfer dudes can catch a wave on Maui's famous North Shore.

TAHITI This South Pacific paradise blends natural splendor—rugged green peaks, crystalline lagoons—with a touch of French flavor. Overwater bungalows are the accommodations of choice, and aquatic adventures like feeding sharks and snorkeling help you get up close and personal with life below the lagoon's surface.

ITALY The Italians seemingly invented romance, and you'll still find plenty of it here: in the echoing songs of the Venetian gondoliers, the charming cliffside towns along the Amalfi Coast and the millennia-old ruins of Rome.

MEXICO Our southern neighbor offers something for everyone, from the wild nightlife in places like Cancun and Los Cabos to the world-class snorkeling and ruins that run along the Riviera Maya.

FIJI Thousands of tiny islands make up this friendly South Pacific nation, where intimate resorts dot the pristine white sands and emerald-hued peaks. It's a snorkeler's dream destination, with shallow, coral-filled lagoons to explore.

ANGUILLA There are very few chain hotels on this secluded, one-stoplight desert isle—instead, intimate resorts line miles of tranquil, talcum-powder shores that are perfect for strolling or just relaxing.

ST. LUCIA The grand Pitons are the crowning glory on this tropical paradise, but lush rain forests and world-class snorkeling also help St. Lucia claim its place as a top honeymoon destination.

BERMUDA Mix a bit of British charm with a string of blush-pink beaches, and you'll get this unique tropical isle—just a short hop away from the East Coast. Golfers can take on one of its eight top-notch courses, while scuba divers can check out the spectacular wrecks just off shore.

FRANCE The French culture is simply built for romance—cozy conversations over café au lait or champagne in quaint bistros, countryside picnics of baguettes and brie, a grand view of Paris sparkling beneath you from atop the Eiffel Tower or a stroll along the legendary sands of the French Riviera.

COSTA RICA Ecotourism was born in this lush wilderness, and nature-loving newlyweds flock here to meet spider monkeys, leatherback turtles and scarlet macaws in their natural habitat. (Adrenaline junkies can get their kicks here as well, whether they prefer rafting, hiking or biking.)

Pick your paradise:
Where will you be
for the first few
weeks of the rest
of your life?

Island Hideaways

Not really ready to limbo with hundreds of other honeymooners? These are a few romantic retreats where you can get away from it all—including other tourists.

Exumas: This sleepy strand of Bahamian isles offers top-notch snorkeling and fishing on its turquoise seas—and plenty of deserted beaches perfect for soaking up some sun.

Nevis: Engage in this serene island's national pastime—limin'—by chilling out on its sparsely developed beaches or soaking in the geothermal mineral springs that made Nevis a top spa destination as far back as the 18th century.

Santorini: In this Greek paradise, you can take a break from resting on serene black- and red-sand beaches to explore whitewashed cliffside towns and ancient Minoan ruins.

Virgin Gorda: Tucked away in the British Virgin Islands is this treasure, where many beaches and resorts are reachable only by boat. Here, the beaches each have a unique personality, from the boulder-strewn majesty of The Baths to the grand coral gardens of Mountain Point.

Lanai: Escape the crush of Hawaiian honeymooners on this serene 16-mile-wide strip, the smallest of the five islands, known as "The Pineapple Isle."

SHIP SHAPE
WHY A CRUISE MAY BE YOUR IDEAL HONEYMOON

It's an ultraconvenient way to hit the hot spots. On these floating resorts, you get to hop around from one great destination to another without having to drag your luggage from hotel to hotel.

A cruise ship can be a destination in itself. On many of the massive ocean liners, you can have a fabulous vacation without ever setting foot on shore—testing out luxe spas, upscale eateries and activity options like surf pools and skating rinks can keep you busy for an entire trip.

There's a ship out there for everyone. You'll find everything from behemoth boats offering rock-climbing walls and other activities for adventurous types, to luxe liners stocked with martini bars and gourmet cuisine for epicureans. Even privacy-minded newlyweds can find intimate ships where they'll set sail with only a handful of other guests and hit out-of-the-way spots that huge cruise ships can't touch.

You can visit any destination you desire. As long as it's not landlocked, odds are you can find a ship traveling to your favorite port of call, whether you're dying to set sail on the South Pacific, the Mediterranean or Alaska.

Packing Tips

Airlines and cruise ships often limit the amount of luggage you can bring—and you'll want to leave a little room for those great souvenirs you'll pick up. Here's how to travel light.

Know the dress code. Some destinations and resorts are more formal than others: You may need to dress up for dinner, or put on a cover-up as soon as you step off the beach. Cruise lines may have formal dinners or theme parties that could influence what you pack.

Research the regulations. The rules about what's allowed in carry-on luggage are always changing, so get the latest scoop on the Transportation Security Administration's Web site (www.tsa.gov) before you end up losing your favorite fragrance at a security checkpoint.

Make a list and check it twice. Create a thorough packing list a few weeks before the wedding, then keep adding to it as you remember other essential items.

Leave yourself some wiggle room. Fold an extra tote bag into your suitcase that you can fill with souvenirs for your return trip.

Limit your palette. Stick with a single color scheme, so you don't have to bring extra shoes and accessories for several different outfits.

AMERICAN PLAN

(aka Full Plan or Full Board): The hotel is including breakfast, lunch and dinner each day in its quoted price.

ALL-INCLUSIVE

Generally, this indicates that everything you'll use at the resort—your room, meals and activities—is included in one flat price. It can be a great option for couples who want to know up front what they're spending. But make sure you check the fine print, as some all-inclusives charge additional fees for premium activities like spa treatments or golfing, or ring up your bar tab separately.

Wedding Words

TRAVEL TERMS YOU NEED TO KNOW

MODIFIED AMERICAN PLAN

Two meals per day are included in the room price—usually breakfast and dinner.

SHOULDER SEASON

The few weeks right before or after a travel destination's peak season, when rates are lower and the crowds are sparser, but you'll still be likely to have good weather.

GRATUITY

(aka tips or service fees): Many all-inclusives wrap this into the flat fee you pay, and restaurants and resorts in many parts of the world already include this in the charge. (You can still tip an additional amount if the service is truly exceptional.)

EUROPEAN PLAN

The hotel's rate includes only the room—no food.

RACK RATES

The published, "official" price of a hotel room— though you can often get a price that's discounted below that.

VIEW

A room that has an "ocean view" looks out on the water, but the view may be partially obstructed—or only visible if you peek around the corner of your balcony.

FRONT

A room that's "oceanfront" or "gardenfront" faces right out onto the water or the landscaping, so you get a great view.

Q & A

Q **Who is typically responsible for paying for the honeymoon?**

A These days, who pays for which wedding expenses varies substantially on a couple-by-couple basis, but tradition would tell you that the groom or groom's family covers the cost of the honeymoon. The reasoning is that it helps balance out the budget if the bride's family is paying for the bulk of the wedding itself. But if both families and even the bride and groom are contributing to the reception costs, as is increasingly common, it's not unusual for the honeymoon to be another shared expense. Sometimes grandparents or other extended family members—maybe a great-uncle or godmother—offer to pitch in. And of course, some couples take on the entire burden themselves, especially if they are older and more financially established. A trend that's gaining popularity is the concept of a honeymoon registry (see the next question), which allows your

wedding guests to contribute toward the cost of the trip as gifts.

Q **We're considering registering for our honeymoon. How does this work?**

A Honeymoon registries enable guests to buy you a piece of your dream vacation—such as a couples spa treatment or romantic dinner at your resort, or even a portion of your plane tickets. The concept is similar to a traditional wedding registry: You select experiences or a cash contribution via a company's Web site (some recommended sites include distinctive honeymoons.com and thebigday.com) or a resort chain (Starwood, Marriott, Sandals and Disney offer registries). Most honeymoon registries make it easy for guests to shop (online or via phone or fax), and many offer cool extras—like posting an itinerary with descriptions and photos you choose, or sending announcements and personal-

ized gift cards after an order is placed. But know that some services charge a setup and handling fee of up to 15 percent, though often you can choose whether to have individual givers foot the bill or have it deducted from your total gift amount. Even with the charge, this can be a smart way to save money if you're paying for your honeymoon. Plus, family and friends may be willing to spoil you with something super-lavish—like an upgrade to your hotel's presidential suite—that you would never justify splurging on yourselves.

Q **Should we use a travel agent?**

A There are definite advantages to booking your honeymoon with a travel professional. First of all, this is probably the most expensive and meaningful trip you'll be taking so far, so you don't want there to be any loose ends or glitches. Working with an agent dramatically decreases the chances of things going wrong, since it's her job to ensure everything's taken care of. And if something does go awry, her first priority is fixing it—so that yours doesn't have to be. But of course, this kind of personal attention comes at a price. Some agents now charge a consultation fee based on where you're going and how much time and effort making the arrangements will entail. Keep in mind that the relationships many agencies have with travel partners—from cruise lines to hotel chains to airlines—may get you better rates than booking on your own, so you just may break even.

Q When should we leave for the trip?

A Many couples underestimate how exhausted—both physically and emotionally—they may be when their wedding festivities finally end. For that reason, it could be worth waiting a day after your wedding night to fly out (i.e., Monday, if your wedding is on a Saturday). This way, you'll have 24 hours to relax, recover and rehash all the fun moments of your whirlwind wedding weekend, and you'll be much more refreshed to enjoy your trip. As an added bonus, you can often find cheaper airline tickets on a weekday, especially a Monday or Tuesday, rather than the weekend, which is peak travel time. (This is the case even in high season.) So waiting can pay off in more ways than one. Another idea to consider is whether you want to postpone the honeymoon for a few months.

Couples do this for a variety of reasons: waiting for when they'll have more time off from work, to save up extra money (especially if they paid for their wedding themselves) or to go to their dream destination during peak season if it didn't coincide with their wedding date. If you choose to do this, one option is taking a "mini-moon" right after the wedding—perhaps to a B&B in New England, a spa in Santa Fe or a beach resort in nearby Mexico—so you'll still get to enjoy some time together as newlyweds.

Q How can I score an upgrade on my flight and hotel room?

A There's no magic formula to getting freebies, but playing up the fact that it's your honeymoon can work to your advantage. The key is connecting with hotel and airline staff without coming across like you're looking for, or expecting, a break. Inform the reservations agent that it's your honeymoon when you book your hotel room—and ask her to mark it in your guest file. You should have a better shot at getting upgraded, since resorts are rarely full except during holidays. Always sign up online for the hotel's free preferred-guests program, if they offer one, before you book—even with zero points, this can get you preferential treatment. Then call a week before your trip to reconfirm and reiterate that it's your honeymoon; the hotel will have a better

idea of occupancy and might automatically upgrade you. At the very least, they'll often treat you to some kind of special perk, like champagne and strawberries in your room. You don't have great odds of getting upgraded to first class on your flight since seats are given out based on customer status (and couples with economy-class fares generally fall to the bottom of the list). But if you have frequent-flier miles, you can put them to good use by buying a full-fare economy ticket and trading in miles when you book to upgrade to business class or first class. The number of miles required varies by airline, but you can usually score a business-class upgrade for between 10,000 and 20,000 miles per person round-trip on a domestic flight, between 15,000 and 25,000 miles per person for Mexico, Hawaii and the Caribbean, and between 30,000 and 50,000 per person for Europe. Otherwise, dressing nicely and arriving early to speak with the ticket agent can help. Casually work the fact that you're newlyweds into the conversation: "We're so excited to get to Hawaii for our honeymoon!" You can also politely ask how full the flight is and if there's any possibility of an upgrade. The gate attendant can potentially bump you up if seats are free, so it's worth trying again before you board.

Budget *Worksheet*

RECEPTION 50%*

_____ X 0.5 = _____
Your total budget   *Available $ for reception*

Site fee _____

Catering costs (tax, tip, etc.) _____

Bar and beverages _____

Wedding cake/dessert _____

Total _____

MUSIC 10%

_____ X 0.1 = _____
Your total budget   *Available $ for music*

Ceremony_____

Cocktail hour _____

Reception _____

Total _____

FLOWERS 10%

_____ X 0.1 = _____
Your total budget   *Available $ for flowers*

Ceremony-site flowers _____

Bridal bouquet _____

Flowers for wedding party _____

Reception centerpieces _____

Total _____

WEDDING ATTIRE 10%

_____ X 0.1 = _____
Your total budget   *Available $ for wedding attire*

Dress _____

Alterations _____

Headpiece/veil _____

Lingerie _____

Jewelry _____

Shoes/wrap/bag _____

Hair and makeup _____

Groom's ensemble _____

Total _____

PHOTOGRAPHY 10%

_____ X 0.1 = _____
Your total budget   *Available $ for photography*

Engagement portrait _____

Photography _____

Videography _____

Wedding-album package _____

Total _____

STATIONERY 4%

_____ X 0.04 = _____
Your total budget   *Available $ for stationery*

Announcements/save-the-dates _____

Invitations and enclosures _____

Calligraphy _____

Postage _____

Programs _____

Escort cards/place cards _____

Thank-you notes _____

Total _____

ADDITIONAL EXPENSES 6%

_____ X 0.06 = _____
Your total budget   *Available $ for additional expenses*

Wedding rings _____

Attendants' gifts _____

Wedding gifts for each other _____

Marriage license _____

Bridesmaids' luncheon _____

Welcome baskets _____

Rehearsal dinner _____

Wedding-day transportation _____

Church/synagogue/officiant fees _____

Favors _____

Total _____

*These are general estimates. If you plan to spend more (or less) on certain elements than what's suggested here, deduct (or add) percentage points from other categories. **A note about wedding planners:** If you're using a planner, don't forget to include her fee in your total calculations, but remember that her relationships with vendors may get you discounts.

Wedding Countdown

9–12 MONTHS BEFORE:

- [ ] Announce your engagement.
- [ ] Arrange for parents to get together.
- [ ] Decide on a date.
- [ ] Discuss your budget with everyone who'll be contributing to the event.
- [ ] Interview wedding planners, if using one.
- [ ] Pick the ceremony site and meet with the officiant.
- [ ] Work on the guest list to get a rough head count.
- [ ] Visit reception sites and reserve one.
- [ ] Shop for your gown.

6–9 MONTHS BEFORE:

- [ ] Choose your wedding party.
- [ ] Select a caterer.
- [ ] Enroll in a bridal-gift registry.
- [ ] Order your wedding gown.
- [ ] Shop for bridal attendants' dresses.
- [ ] Pick a photographer and/or a videographer.
- [ ] Hire a florist.
- [ ] Book the musicians and/or DJ.
- [ ] Start researching honeymoon spots.
- [ ] Mail save-the-dates, especially if you're having a destination or holiday-weekend wedding.

4–6 MONTHS BEFORE:

- [ ] Order wedding stationery and book a calligrapher, if using one.
- [ ] Shop for the cake.
- [ ] Hire wedding-day transportation.
- [ ] Book your favorite beauty pros for the big day.
- [ ] Scout accommodations for out-of-town guests.
- [ ] Complete the guest list.
- [ ] Start planning your honeymoon, and make plane and hotel reservations.
- [ ] Arrange the rehearsal dinner.

2–4 MONTHS BEFORE:

- [ ] Call the county clerk's office to find out about marriage-license requirements.
- [ ] Order the tuxedos for the groom and groomsmen.
- [ ] Meet with the caterer or banquet manager to discuss menus, service style, wine selections, etc.
- [ ] Order the wedding cake.
- [ ] Select ceremony and reception music.
- [ ] Buy thank-you gifts for the attendants.
- [ ] Choose favors and welcome baskets.
- [ ] Shop for and order your wedding bands.
- [ ] Meet with party-rental companies, if necessary.
- [ ] Book a room for your wedding night.

4–8 WEEKS BEFORE:

- [ ] Mail invitations 6 to 8 weeks ahead of the wedding date.
- [ ] Do a hair and makeup run-through (with headpiece).
- [ ] Decide on insurance-policy changes you'll need.

2–4 WEEKS BEFORE:

- [ ] Plot the seating for the reception.
- [ ] Confirm details with the photographer, florist, etc.
- [ ] Have your final dress fitting.
- [ ] Write your rehearsal-dinner toast.

1 WEEK BEFORE:

- [ ] Place the fees due on the wedding day in envelopes.
- [ ] Give the caterer a final head count.
- [ ] Appoint a reliable pal to transport the cake knife, toasting glasses or other heirlooms to and from the reception site.
- [ ] Get final beauty treatments (facial, waxing, brow-shaping, etc.) of your choice.
- [ ] Pack for the honeymoon. (Ask someone to bring your luggage to the reception if you're leaving from there.)

Registry *Checklist*

THE MUST-HAVES

dinnerware
- [ ] 8 to 12 place settings, including dinner plates, salad/dessert plates, bread-and-butter plates, bowls, teacups and saucers or mugs
- [ ] Sugar bowl and creamer
- [ ] Serving bowls and platters
- [ ] Butter dish

flatware
- [ ] 8 to 12 five-piece flatware settings
- [ ] Hostess set

crystal/glassware
- [ ] Wineglasses for red and white wine
- [ ] Highball glasses/tumblers
- [ ] Double old-fashioned glasses
- [ ] Martini glasses
- [ ] Iced-beverage glasses

kitchenware
- [ ] Soup ladle
- [ ] Steak knives
- [ ] Paring, serrated, slicing and chef's knives
- [ ] Sharpening steel
- [ ] Knife block/magnetic knife bar
- [ ] Kitchen shears
- [ ] Cutting boards
- [ ] Mixing bowls
- [ ] Grater
- [ ] Canister set
- [ ] Measuring cups and spoons
- [ ] Slotted and solid spoons
- [ ] Slotted and solid spatulas
- [ ] Wooden spoons
- [ ] Salad spinner
- [ ] Whisk
- [ ] Can/bottle opener
- [ ] Colander
- [ ] Potato masher
- [ ] Corkscrew
- [ ] Ice-cream scoop
- [ ] Salt and pepper mills
- [ ] Vegetable peeler
- [ ] Kitchen timer

cooking/baking
- [ ] Saucepans (1.5-, 2-, and 3- or 4-quart)
- [ ] Stockpot or pasta pot
- [ ] Skillet or frying pan
- [ ] Sauté pan
- [ ] Roaster and rack
- [ ] Tea kettle
- [ ] Large baking sheet
- [ ] Ceramic pie dish or metal pie pan
- [ ] Muffin pan
- [ ] Loaf pan
- [ ] Round cake pans

appliances
- [ ] Toaster oven/toaster
- [ ] Microwave oven
- [ ] Stand or hand mixer
- [ ] Blender
- [ ] Food processor
- [ ] Coffeemaker

linens/bed & bath
- [ ] Sheets and pillowcases
- [ ] Padded mattress cover
- [ ] Pillows
- [ ] Comforter, duvet cover and shams
- [ ] Bath towels and hand towels
- [ ] Washcloths and guest towels
- [ ] Bath mat/rug
- [ ] Shower curtain
- [ ] Bathroom scale
- [ ] Table linens

housekeeping
- [ ] Vacuum
- [ ] Handheld vacuum
- [ ] Iron and ironing board

FOR THE FOODIE

kitchenware
- [ ] Two-pronged fork
- [ ] Utility baking or cooking tongs
- [ ] Skimmer
- [ ] Instant-read thermometer
- [ ] Pasta machine
- [ ] Cheese knives
- [ ] Pizza cutter
- [ ] Sauce, balloon and flat whisks
- [ ] Cleaver
- [ ] Boning knife
- [ ] Rolling pin

cooking/baking
- [ ] Double boiler
- [ ] Multipurpose pot with steamer
- [ ] Casserole/Dutch oven
- [ ] Wok
- [ ] Grill pan
- [ ] French-press coffeemaker
- [ ] Pizza pan
- [ ] Bundt pan
- [ ] Tart pan
- [ ] Pastry brushes
- [ ] Flour sifter
- [ ] Springform pan

appliances
- [ ] Espresso/cappuccino machine
- [ ] Warming tray
- [ ] Ice-cream/yogurt maker
- [ ] Indoor/outdoor grill
- [ ] Bread machine
- [ ] Coffee grinder
- [ ] Juicer
- [ ] Waffle iron
- [ ] Panini press
- [ ] Mini food processor
- [ ] Rice cooker
- [ ] Pressure cooker

Big-Day Schedule

LET THIS SAMPLE BE A GUIDE FOR CREATING YOUR OWN TIMELINE

11:00 Brunch with Mom and other VIPs at hotel (or at home)

1:00–4:00 Hair and makeup (first 'maids, then Mom and me; then makeup, same order)

3:30 Photographer arrives for my getting-ready shots; photographer to groom's suite by 4 p.m.

3:45 Groomsmen arrive at groom's suite to change

4:00 Florist delivers personal flowers to me and to groom's suite

4:30 Limos arrive at hotel to take wedding party to church (limo 1: bridesmaids; limo 2: me, Mom, Dad; limo 3: all the guys)

4:45 Groomsmen begin seating guests

5:00 Ceremony begins; reverend, groom and best man at altar; groomsmen and bridesmaids enter in order: Nick, Pete, Kate, Jessie, Meghan; then flower girl, then Dad and me

6:00 Bridal party heads to reception

6:30 Cocktail hour; pictures with the bridal party and families

7:30 Reception begins

8:00 First-dance music starts (Tell bandleader: After one or two minutes, please invite our parents to join, then guests one minute after that.)

8:20 Appetizer served, wine poured; best man gives toast

8:45 Appetizer cleared; music comes back on and dancing starts again

9:10 Main course served

10:30 Cake cutting; music resumes and plays until 12 a.m.

acknowledgments

The editors of *Modern Bride* work incredibly hard every day to create the magazine on which this book is based. It is their love for what they do and their ability to find the most creative wedding ideas that bring these pages to life.

Thanks to Kara Corridan, my indefatigable executive editor, who began this project with me as soon as she joined *Modern Bride* more than three years ago. She knew it was my goal to publish *The* Modern Bride *Survival Guide,* and she has done everything she could to make this dream a reality. Thanks also to features editor Betsy Goldberg, who read every page and added her invaluable guidance and support.

Thanks to Anita Henry, my can-do managing editor, who has been by my side in every book meeting and who has worked tirelessly to handle contracts and permissions and all the nitty-gritty details that go into creating a book. Along the way she served up quite a bit of wedding advice, as well. And my gratitude also goes to her assistant, Michaela Garibaldi, who patiently worked alongside her to make sure nothing slipped through the cracks. Thanks to Lou DiLorenzo, my amazing creative director, who is relentless in his pursuit of visual perfection. When I first told him about my desire to create a book, he immediately started designing pages for a proposal. As the project became bigger (and more concrete), he handed the reins to our wonderful designer, Kerstin Michaelson, and worked with her to complete the gorgeously illustrated guide you now hold in your hands. Thanks to Wendy Mansfield for stepping in at the end to get us smoothly through those last few weeks. The power of this book is in large part due to its beautiful photos, and I have to thank Holly Watson, our photo editor, for her role in creating and cataloging these images for us. And to all the photographers whose work has appeared in the pages of *Modern Bride* and now in this book: You are the best of the best.

The ideas in this book could not have been as fully expressed without the help of lifestyle and reception editors Linda Hirst, Linda Seidman, Amber Furst and Jennifer Miskowiec. These true pros completely understand the magic of creating beautiful receptions from the save-the-date card to the chair treatments and the cake. Their inspired creativity is a hallmark of *Modern Bride* editorial content.

Thanks also to the rest of my incredible editorial and art teams: Juli Alvarez, Mary Clarke, Donna Heiderstadt, Caroline McCormick, Tania Riddell, Jamie Ahn and Amy Jaffe. Elaine Stuart went the extra mile and happily added to the advice and ideas in this book. Cristi Hansen, my unflappable assistant, deserves a separate round of applause for her dedication to *Modern Bride* and to this project. Her wonderful sense of style and bright ideas shine in everything she does. And thanks to our interns, Eimear Lynch, Marta Topran and Virginia VanZanten for the fact checking and researching.

Thanks to our exceptionally competent and efficient writer, Lisa Milbrand, a former MB editor, for working so hard to help create such a comprehensive book. You make everything hard look so easy.

My production team has put in countless hours to make this book look perfect: a big thank you to Dorothy Sullenberger, Oscar Cervera and Jennifer Peterson for their dedication and skill. Our copy editor, Joseph Mills, did a wonderful job and learned tons about weddings.

To Justin Schwartz, our editor at Wiley: You trusted me to bring you a book that every modern bride would treasure. Thanks for believing in the *Survival Guide* from the very beginning. And to our agent Linda Konner, who lets nothing get in her way; we wouldn't have had a book without your help.

I owe an enormous debt of gratitude to the *Modern Bride* Advisory Panel: Priscilla Alexander, Preston Bailey, Ron Ben-Israel, Marcy Blum, Peter Callahan, Colin Cowie, Nico De Swert, Mark Garrison, Michael George, Charlie Green, Frank and JoAnn Gregoli, Terry deRoy Gruber, Claudia Hanlin, Deanna Jones, Yifat Oren, Michelle Rago, Deborah Roth, Sasha Souza, Antony Todd, David Tutera, Sylvia Weinstock, Mindy Weiss and Jennifer Zabinski. Because of you we are able to stay on top of all the trends; you help keep the *modern* in *Modern Bride*.

Last but not least, thanks to all the real brides who brought us the ideas and real weddings that are sprinkled throughout these pages. You are the true trendsetters and problem solvers. Thanks for sharing. —*Antonia van der Meer*.

credits

COVER

Front cover, from left: Photographs by Miki Duisterhof, Anastassios Mentis, Dasha Wright, Miki Duisterhof. **Back cover, from left:** Photographs by David Prince, Charles Maraia, Miki Duisterhof, Charles Schiller.

TITLE PAGE

Page i: Photograph by Gabrielle Revere.

CONTENTS

Page vi, from left: Photographs by Dasha Wright (2), Holger Eckstein. **Page vii, from left:** Photographs by Mark Lund, Michael Weschler, Miki Duisterhof.

INTRODUCTION

Page viii: Photograph by Miki Duisterhof. Flowers by Elan Flowers, NYC.

1 CHAPTER 1: GET STARTED

Page 1: Photograph by Rick Lew. Sofa from Mitchell Gold. **Pages 3–4:** Photographs by Rick Lew. **Page 5:** Photograph by Rick Lew. Sofa from Mitchell Gold. **Page 6:** Photograph by Rick Lew. **Page 8:** Photograph by Rick Lew. **Page 9:** Photograph by Miki Duisterhof. Shot on location at Yolanda's Bridal Salon, Waltham, MA.

13 CHAPTER 2: CREATE YOUR CEREMONY

Page 13: Photograph by Michael Weschler. **Page 14:** Photograph by Sharon Schuster. **Pages 18–20:** Photographs by Faith West. **Page 21:** Photograph by Dasha Wright. **Page 23:** Photograph by Ellen McDermott.

27 CHAPTER 3: PLAN A GREAT RECEPTION

Page 27: Photograph by Dasha Wright. Event design by Karen Bussen Wedding Planning and Design. **Page 28:** Photograph by Miki Duisterhof. **Page 29:** Photograph by Dasha Wright. Escort cards by Kristina Wrenn for twentyandseven, NYC. **Page 30:** Photograph by William Geddes. Event design by Nico De Swert. **Page 31:** Photograph by Miki Duisterhof. Event design by Michelle Rago, Ltd. **Page 32, from left:** Photographs by Tom Thomson, Terry deRoy Gruber. Event produced by Marcy Blum; floral design by Preston Bailey (deRoy Gruber photo). **Page 33, from left:** Photographs by Luca Trovato, Miki Duisterhof. Event design by Michelle Rago, Ltd. (Duisterhof photo). **Page 35:** Photograph by Maring Photography. **Page 36, from left:** Photographs by Wendell Webber, Dasha Wright. Flowers by Stonekelly (Webber photo). **Page 37:** Photographs by Dasha Wright. **Pages 38–39:** Photographs by Charles Schiller. Event design by Ariella Chezar.

43 CHAPTER 4: DRESS YOUR BEST

Page 43: Photograph by Holger Eckstein. **Page 45:** Photograph by Michael Waring. **Pages 46–47:** Illustrations by Adrienne Hartman. **Page 48:** Photograph by Miki Duisterhof. **Page 49:** Illustrations by Adrienne Hartman. **Page 50:** Photograph by Rebecca Greenfield. **Page 51:** Photographs by David Turner. **Page 52:** Photograph by Miki Duisterhof. Shot on location at Yolanda's Bridal Salon, Waltham, MA. **Page 53:** Illustrations by Adrienne Hartman. **Page 54:** Photograph by Miki Duisterhof. **Page 55:** Illustration by Adrienne Hartman.

59 CHAPTER 5: GET GORGEOUS

Page 59: Photograph by Holger Eckstein. **Page 60:** Photograph by Christopher Robbins. **Page 62:** Photographs by Anna Palma. From left, hair and makeup by Nikki Wang for Sally Harlor. Hair by Lauren Lavelle for Oscar Blandi Salon; makeup by Patrycja for Stockland Martel. Hair and makeup by Nikki Wang for Sally Harlor. Hair by Lauren Lavelle for Oscar Blandi Salon; makeup by Patrycja for Stockland Martel. **Page 63:** Photograph by Anna Palma. Hair and makeup by Nikki Wang for Sally Harlor. **Page 66:** Photograph by Holger Eckstein. **Page 69:** Photograph by Alex Cao. **Page 70:** Photograph by Christopher Robbins.

75 CHAPTER 6: SELECT YOUR REGISTRY

Page 75: Photograph by Darrin Haddad. **Page 76:** Photograph by Ann Stratton. **Page 78:** Photographs by James Worrell. **Page 79, clockwise from top right:** Photographs by Darrin Haddad, James Worrell (12). **Pages 80–81:** Photographs by Darrin Haddad. **Page 82:** Photograph by Charles Maraia. **Page 85:** Photographs by Mark Thomas. **Page 86:** Photograph by Dasha Wright. **Page 87:** Photograph by Jack Miskell.

91 CHAPTER 7: CHOOSE THE CATERER

Page 91: Photograph by Dasha Wright. Food recipe by Jean-Marie Josselin, chef/owner, 808 La Jolla, La Jolla, CA, and A Pacific Café, Kauai, HI. Food styled by Alison Attenborough. Drink recipe by consulting mixologist Tony Abou Ganim, Las Vegas. **Page 92:** Photograph by Dasha Wright. Food prepared by Executive Chef Tim McLaughlin of Restaurant Associates, NYC. Event design by Karen Bussen Wedding Planning and Design. **Page 95:** Photograph by Miki Duisterhof. Food prepared by Chefs Dan Barber and Michael Anthony of Blue Hill, NYC. **Pages 96–97:** Photographs by David Lewis Taylor. **Page 98, from left:** Photographs by Dasha Wright (2), Luca Trovato, Miki Duisterhof (2), Evan Sklar. Food recipe by Rachael Ray; food styled by Roscoe Betstill (Sklar photo). **Page 100:** Photograph by Dasha Wright. **Page 101:** Photograph by Dasha Wright. Food recipe by Executive Chef Franklin Becker, Trinity in The Tribeca Grand Hotel, NYC. Food styled by Alison Attenborough. Drink recipe by Tracy Stack, Helix Lounge, Washington, D.C. **Page 102:** Photographs by Dasha Wright. Clockwise from top left: Drink recipe by Chris Russell, B. Christopher's, Burlington, NC; food styled by Toni Brogan. Drink recipe by Orla Murphy, LaScola, American Seasons, Nantucket, MA; food styled by Toni Brogan. Drink recipe by Mike Russotti, Town, NYC; food styled by Toni Brogan. Drink recipe by Jerri Banks, Taj, NYC; food styled by Toni Brogan.

107 CHAPTER 8: CREATE THE CAKE

Page 107: Photograph by David Prince. Cake by Kate Sullivan for Lovin Sullivan Cakes. **Page 108:** Photographs by David Prince. From left: Cake by Buddy Valastro for Carlo's Bakery. Cake by Collette Foley Specialty Baking. **Page 109:** Photograph by Ann Stratton. Cake by Sylvia Weinstock Cakes. **Page 110:** Photographs by David Prince. From left: Cake by Elisa Strauss for Confetti

Cakes. Cake by Cheryl Kleinman Cakes. **Page 111:** Photographs by David Prince. From left: Cake by Ron Ben-Israel Cakes. Cake by Luis Robledo-Richards for The Four Seasons. **Page 113, from left:** Photograph by Ann Stratton. Cake by Collette Foley Specialty Baking. Photograph by Dasha Wright. Cake by Buddy Valastro for Carlo's Bakery. Photograph by Ann Stratton. Cake by Ron Ben-Israel Cakes. **Page 114, from left:** Photograph by Gabrielle Revere. Cake by Kate Sullivan for Lovin Sullivan Cakes. Photograph by Charles Schiller. Cake by Brownstone Cake Company. **Page 116:** Photograph by Miki Duisterhof. Cupcakes by Cupcake Café.
Page 117: Photograph by Dasha Wright. Cake by Sylvia Weinstock Cakes.

121 CHAPTER 9: PICK YOUR FLOWERS
Page 121: Photograph by Charles Schiller. Flowers by Antheia Floral Design. **Page 122:** Photograph by Wendell Webber. Flowers by Spruce. **Pages 124–125:** Photographs by Edward Addeo. **Page 126:** Photographs by Dasha Wright. Clockwise from top left: Flowers by Magnolia Flowers & Events. Flowers by Karen Bussen Wedding Planning and Design. Flowers by Jane Packer Flowers. Flowers by Plaza Flowers. Flowers by Michelle Rago, Ltd. Flowers by Dejuan Stroud, Inc. **Page 128:** Photograph by Luca Trovato. Flowers by Michelle Rago, Ltd. **Page 129:** Photograph by Miki Duisterhof. Flowers by Jane Packer Flowers. **Page 130, clockwise from top left:** Photograph by Miki Duisterhof. Flowers by Michelle Rago, Ltd. Photographs by Dasha Wright (3). Flowers by Karen Bussen Wedding Planning and Design (3). **Pages 132–133:** Photographs by Dasha Wright. Flowers by Karen Bussen Wedding Planning and Design.

137 CHAPTER 10: SELECT YOUR STATIONERY
Page 137: Photograph by Anastassios Mentis. Invitation from Paper Source. **Page 138:** Photographs by Anastassios Mentis. From left: Invitation from Sloane Madureira Design. Invitation from Jill Smith Design. **Page 139:** Photographs by Anastassios Mentis. From left: Invitation from

Something Different by Carlson Craft. Invitation from A2 Paperie. **Page 140:** Photograph by Miki Duisterhof. Invitation from Grapevine. **Page 141, clockwise from top:** Photograph by Dasha Wright. Invitation from Red Bliss. Photograph by David Lewis Taylor. Invitation from Lehr & Black Invitationers. Accessories from Kate's Paperie. Photograph by Dasha Wright. Invitation from Grapevine. **Page 142, from left:** Photograph by Robert Mitra. Invitation from Kate Spade. Photograph by Anastassios Mentis. Invitation from Dauphine Press. **Page 143:** Photograph by Anastassios Mentis. Calligraphy by Coyle & Company Inc. **Page 146:** Photograph by Charles Maraia. Invitation from Gala Design. **Page 148:** Photograph by Geoffrey Sokol. Programs from Chelsea Paper Company. **Page 149:** Photograph by Ann Stratton. Clockwise from top left: Stationery from Papivore. Stationery from Paper Source. Stationery from Crane's. Stationery from Gala Design. Stationery from Mira Aster.

153 CHAPTER 11: MANAGE THE MUSIC
Page 153: Photograph by Dasha Wright. **Page 154:** Photograph by Nick White/Getty Images. **Page 159:** Photograph by Robert Isacson.

163 CHAPTER 12: TAKE YOUR BEST SHOTS
Page 163: Photograph by Alistair Taylor-Young. **Page 165:** Photograph by Robert Mitra. **Page 168, from left:** Photographs by Joel Marion and Tony Jacobs, Zane White. **Page 171:** Photograph by Miki Duisterhof.

175 CHAPTER 13: BE GOOD TO YOUR BRIDESMAIDS
Pages 175–176: Photographs by Coliena Rentmeester. **Page 178:** Photograph by Christine Marie. **Page 180, clockwise from top left:** Photographs by Andrew McCaul (2), David Lewis Taylor, Robert Mitra, Zane White. **Page 181:** Photograph by Andrew McCaul.

187 CHAPTER 14: GUIDE YOUR GROOMSMEN
Page 187: Photograph by Diego Merino. **Page 188:** Photograph by Stephanie

Pfriender Stylander. **Page 189, clockwise from top:** Photographs by Andrew McCaul (2), Zane White (2), David Lewis Taylor (2), Andrew McCaul. **Page 191:** Photograph by Louis DeCamps. **Page 194:** Photographs by Rebecca Greenfield.

199 CHAPTER 15: GIFT YOUR GUESTS
Page 199: Photograph by Monica Buck. **Page 200:** Photograph by Wendell Webber. **Page 202:** Photograph by Miki Duisterhof. **Page 203, from left:** Photographs by David Lewis Taylor, Dasha Wright. **Page 204:** Photograph by Dan Brooks. **Page 205:** Photograph by Alison Gootee.

209 CHAPTER 16: PLAN THE OTHER PARTIES
Page 209: Photograph by Luca Trovato. Event design by Michelle Rago, Ltd. **Page 210:** Photograph by William Geddes. Event design by Nico De Swert. **Page 211:** Photograph by Phil Kramer. **Page 212:** Photograph by Stephanie Pfriender Stylander.

217 CHAPTER 17: MAKE EVERYONE HAPPY
Page 217: Photograph by Jack Miskell. **Page 219, from top:** Photographs by Richard T. Nowitz/Corbis, George Chinsee. **Page 220:** Photograph by Mark Lund. Event design by Belle Fleur, NYC. **Page 222:** Photograph by Edward Addeo.

227 CHAPTER 18: GET MARRIED AWAY
Page 227: Photograph by Christopher Robbins. **Page 228:** Photograph by Amy Neunsinger. **Page 230:** Photograph by Christopher Robbins. **Page 232:** Photograph by Luca Trovato. **Page 233:** Photograph by Alain Brin/Blue Glass Photography.

237 CHAPTER 19: PLAN YOUR HONEYMOON
Page 237: Photograph by William Abranowicz/Art + Commerce. **Page 239, from top:** Photographs by Connie Coleman/Getty Images, Ryan McVay/Getty Images. **Page 243:** Photograph by Terry Doyle/Getty Images.

index